Titles in The West Point Military Library

BARNARD, *Military Schools and Courses of Instruction in the Science and Art of War* (1872).

BIGELOW, *The Principles of Strategy. Illustrated Mainly from American Campaigns*, 2nd ed. (1894).

BIRKHIMER, *Historical Sketch of the Organization, Administration, Matériel and Tactics of the Artillery, United States Army* (1884).

BRACKETT, *History of the United States Cavalry to 1863* (1865).

FEUQUIERES, *Memoirs Historical and Military: Containing a Distinct View of All the Considerable States of Europe* (1735-1736). 2 vols.

HALLECK, *Elements of Military Art and Science* (1846).

HAMLEY, *The Story of the Campaign of Sebastopol, Written in the Camp* (1855).

HOYT, *Practical Instructions for Military Officers* (1811).

JAMES, *A New and Enlarged Military Dictionary, in French and English* (1810). 2 vols.

JOMINI, *Summary of the Art of War* (1854).

LLOYD, *The History of the Late War in Germany, Between the King of Prussia, and the Empress of Germany and Her Allies* (1781). 3 vols.

MAC DONALD, *Rules and Regulations for the Field Exercise and Manoeuvres of the French Infantry*, 2nd ed. (1806). 2 vols.

MAHAN, *The Story of the War in South Africa, 1899-1900 (1900)*.

MAHAN, *A Complete Treatise on Field Fortification* (1836).

MALLESON, *The Battle-fields of Germany, from the Outbreak of the Thirty-Years War to the Battle of Blenheim* (1884).

MARMONT, *The Spirit of Military Institutions* (1864).

MITCHELL, *The Life of Wallenstein, Duke of Friedland* (1837).

MURRAY (ed.), *The Letters and Dispatches of John Churchill, First Duke of Marlborough, from 1702 to 1712* (1845). 5 vols.

The Officer's Manual in the Field; or, a Series of Military Plans, Representing the Principal Operations of a Campaign, 2nd ed. *(1800)*.

PRUSSIA, Kriegsministerium, *Regulations for the Prussian Cavalry* (1757).

PRUSSIA, Kriegsministerium, *Regulations for the Prussian Infantry* (1759).

SCHELIHA, *A Treatise on Coast-Defense* (1868).

SCHMIDT, *Instructions for the Training, Employment, and Leading of Cavalry* (1881).

SCOTT, *Military Dictionary* (1862).

TOUSARD, *American Artillerist's Companion, or Elements of Artillery* (1809). 3 vols.

TURNER, *Pallas Armata. Military Essays of the Ancient Grecian, Roman, and Modern Art of War* (1683).

U.S. Military Academy, West Point, *The Centennial of the United States Military Academy at West Point, New York, 1802-1902* (1904). 2 vols.

U.S. War Department, *Instruction for Field Artillery* (1861).

UPTON, *The Armies of Asia and Europe* (1878).

UPTON, *Infantry Tactics, Double and Single Rank Adapted to American Topography and Improved Fire-arms*, rev. ed. (1874).

UPTON, *The Military Policy of the United States* (1904).

VERDY DU VERNOIS, *A Tactical Study, Based on the Battle of Custozza, 24th of June, 1866* (1894).

VERDY DU VERNOIS, *With the Royal Headquarters in 1870-71* (1897).

VIELE, *Handbook for Active Service* (1861).

WAGNER, *The Campaign of Königgrätz, a Study of the Austro-Prussian Conflict in the Light of the American Civil War* (1889).

A. Vandyke, del.   W. Humphrys, sc.

ALBRECHT OF WALDSTEIN.

Duke of

Friedland, Mecklenburg & Sagan.

London, James Fraser, 215, Regent Street, 1837.

THE

LIFE OF WALLENSTEIN,

DUKE OF FRIEDLAND.

ARNOLD. And can it
Be, that the man who shook the earth is gone,
And left no footstep ?
STRANGER. There you err. His substance
Left graves enough, and woes enough, and fame
More than enough to track his memory.

BYRON.

By LIEUT.-COLONEL J. MITCHELL,

H. P.

GREENWOOD PRESS, PUBLISHERS
NEW YORK

Originally published in 1837 by James Fraser, London

First Greenwood Reprinting, 1968

Library of Congress Catalogue Card Number: 68-54800

PRINTED IN THE UNITED STATES OF AMERICA

TO

Lieut.-General Sir JAMES S. BARNES, K.C.B.

COLONEL, 2D BATTALION RIFLE BRIGADE,

AND WHO, DURING THE PENINSULAR WAR,

COMMANDED THE 3D BATTALION OF THE ROYALS,

THIS VOLUME IS INSCRIBED

BY

THE AUTHOR

TABLE OF CONTENTS.

CHAPTER IV.

CHAPTER V.

CHAPTER VI.

CHAPTER VII.

CHAPTER VIII.

PREFACE.

ANY attempt to write the Life of WALLENSTEIN, is attended with greater difficulty than might be supposed, when his striking appearance on the foreground of history is alone considered. " His character," as Schiller says, " has been so obscured by the hatred and applause of factions, as still to float unfixed and stationless in history." And though late researches have thrown considerable light on the principal events of his time,—the real causes that led to the tragedy of Eger remain, even now, enveloped in doubt, if not in darkness.

Besides this difficulty, the biographer of Wallenstein has others to contend with. The hero cannot always be kept before the reader. Wallenstein twice retires from the scene, and we know so little of his private and domestic life, that we cannot follow him into retirement. This may seem strange when Schottky of Münich has actually written a book, professing to be a history of that private life ; but though the author is a gentleman of name and learning, the book, like so many other German books, contains

nothing, as indeed the author himself allows, to justify
its title.   Wallenstein retires in early life, a disappointed soldier and an unfortunate courtier.   He
remains for ten years entirely out of sight ; and then,
without giving us the advantage, so desirable to biographers, of tracing the growth of his character, comes
before us in all the lofty originality that distinguished
him to the last.   When at the very height of dictatorial power, he again retires from public view, and
a more brilliant character occupies the foreground
during his absence : he therefore reappears, at first,
as a star of secondary magnitude only ; and he no
sooner becomes, for the second time, sole lord of the
ascendant, than the clouds which still obscure the
last part of his career, begin to close and thicken
around him.   The history of Wallenstein is therefore, rather a grouping of great events round the
principal actor, in the scenes described, than a regular
and legitimate biography.

So great, however, was the fame of the Duke of
Friedland,—so vast the influence he exercised over
his contemporaries, as well as over the events of his
time,—and so dark the mystery which shrouded the
last scenes of his life, that many attempts were made
in France, Italy and Germany, to write his history
even in the face of all the enumerated obstacles.
These attempts proved, however, very unsuccessful ;
and it remained for Schiller to bring Wallenstein forward as a popular character, by making him the hero

of three dramas, and the principal figure in the history of the Thirty years' War. The success of the dramatist ruined, however, the fair fame of the Duke of Friedland. Opinion had before been pretty well divided as to his guilt or innocence ; but Schiller, guided principally by the official statement which the Court of Vienna published after the catastrophe of Eger, took the unfavourable view of the question ; and the magic of his style, not only put his works into every hand, but made him authority with the million, on points, on which he had even expressed doubts of his own accuracy : and Wallenstein was condemned by poetry, before history had fairly tried the cause.

Doctor Förster of Berlin, librarian to the King of Prussia, was the first who undertook the defence of the once famous Duke of Friedland. Instigated by the honourable desire of rendering justice to the memory of his celebrated countryman, the learned librarian occupied himself for many years in collecting papers relative to the history of Wallenstein. In 1828 he published three volumes of letters, written by the Duke, during the most important years of his life, and addressed principally, to Field-Marshal Arnheim, his second in command. At a later period, the Doctor obtained access to the archives of the war department at Vienna, and was permitted to inspect the secret papers connected with the affair of Wallenstein, and which had for two centuries been carefully concealed from public view. The Imperial

Cabinet had always, indeed, shown itself anxious to
bury the entire transaction in oblivion ; and when
Frederick the Great asked Joseph II. " How it really
was with that story of Wallenstein ?" the Emperor
only replied, that " he could not possibly doubt the
honour and integrity of his ancestor."

To the valuable booty gained at Vienna, Förster
afterwards added all the information which could be
gathered in a careful search through the libraries and
archives of Prague, Friedland, Gitchin and Eger :
and thus provided, he published, in 1834, the Life
of Wallenstein, which the present writer has taken
as his principal authority. But Förster's book, however well executed in itself, could not serve as a
guide, or model, for an English life of the German
hero ; for it is addressed to German readers, who are
perfectly familiar with the leading events of Wallenstein's life and time. " Der Friedlander " is the
best known of all German heroes : he is constantly
before the public, not only in Schiller's History of
the Thirty years' War, a work with which every German is perfectly familiar, but he also appears before
them on the stage, in the well-known dramas of the
same author, and figures besides, in an endless variety
of tales and romances. Förster is therefore less the
biographer of Wallenstein, than a collector of documents explanatory of his history ; and the Doctor's
book, however deserving of praise, could not be taken
as a guide, or model, for an English history of a per-

son who is comparatively a stranger in our country. To be successful here, the Duke of Friedland must appear in all his power and splendour : he must come before us as the creator of mighty armies ; at once the terror and support of his sovereign : he must come as an all-powerful actor in the most important period of Christian history. It is in connection with the great events that fixed the destinies of Europe, that he must make his first impression upon us : and we must learn to take an interest in his fate, before we can take pleasure in the perusal of documents, tending to illustrate events of which we have only a partial knowledge.

Besides Förster and the other biographers of Wallenstein, the present Author has availed himself of all the aid he could derive from the most eminent writers, who have touched upon the history of the period of which he had occasion to speak. He has also collected, what information could be obtained from visiting the principal scenes mentioned in the narrative, and has searched pretty diligently, for additional materials, through the rather confused mass of modern German literature.

There could be no intention, in this volume, to give any opinion on the merits of the question at issue, between the parties engaged in the great contest for religious freedom. The Author had only to relate events as they influenced the fortunes of an individual ; but before he is charged with having

spoken too harshly of Ferdinand II. and his advisers,
it will be well to consult,—first, the instructions with
which that Emperor sent Trautmansdorff on a special message to Rome in 1619 ;—secondly, the question which he submitted to certain professors of theology, before he took the oath, and signed the obligation required by the Bohemian constitution ; and,
thirdly, the answer given by the men of learning,
and which so easily quieted the royal and imperial
conscience. Senkenberg, in the preface to volume 3,
page 48, and Erhard, page 425, give the first document. The Slavata manuscript, quoted by the above
writers, gives the second document, at page 659 of
the 5th volume.

As, in the following narrative, the Thirty years'
War has, however, been termed a contest for religious
freedom, it may be as well to justify an appellation,
often questioned by those who affirm, that the war
was carried on,—not for religious, but for worldly
objects ;—for the recovery on one side, and the maintenance on the other, of the Catholic Church property seized by the Protestant States and Princes.

There is no intention here to defend the rapacity
with which the Reformers seized upon the domains of
the Catholic Church ;—nowhere more *zealously*, indeed, than in Great Britain and Ireland, as the possessions of our leading nobility show to this day ;—
nor shall we deny the persecuting spirit too often
evinced by the early reforming churches ; the natural

consequence of their situation, perhaps, and of the oppressions to which they were exposed. But, granting the full force of what may be urged against the Protestants on these points, it must still be allowed, that they never infringed the religious Treaty of Passau : that treaty was not very favourable to their cause ; yet they adhered to it ; and refrained from all acts of violence or persecution, capable of justifying attacks on their religion or independence.

In towns and districts, as at Aix-la-Chapelle, Cologne, Strasburg,—where both parties were nearly balanced in strength and numbers, there religious animosities,—if the term is not a contradiction,— were displayed ; and feuds took place when either of the parties thought themselves strong enough to strive for exclusive supremacy, and for worldly possessions, perhaps, under the mantle of religion. But in such cases, the Catholics were as often the aggressors as the Protestants ; and Catholic power invariably decided the points at issue, in favour of Catholics.

If the Protestants did not violate the Treaty of Passau, the Catholics were less forbearing ; and from the unprovoked occupation of Münster and Osnabrück by the Spaniards in 1598,—when, at a period of profound peace, the soldiers treated a tranquil country as they would have treated a hostile town taken by assault,—down to the seizure of the churches of Brunau and Kloster-Graben, which became the signal for the general explosion ; many flagrant acts of op-

pression and persecution were committed by Catholic
powers. And when the Bohemian insurrection was
suppressed, and the Catholic arms were everywhere
triumphant, the Catholic Princes, so far from being
satisfied with reclaiming the property of their Church,
proceeded to root out the Protestant faith, from all
the subdued and recovered provinces. And so effectually was the work performed,—so completely were
the new doctrines extirpated,—that when, in the following century, the conquests of Frederick the Great,
and the tolerant disposition of Joseph II. gave religious freedom to countries in which millions had pro-
fessed the reformed faith, not a vestige of that faith
was to be found. The very seed had been torn from
the soil by the iron hand of power; for it was with
the sword of wrath, and not with the Book of God,'
that the conversion was effected.

Nor can it be said, that these persecutions were
confined to the Palatinate and to the dominions of
the House of Austria; for no sooner had the victories of Wallenstein rendered the Emperor all-powerful, than the Edict of Restitution was signed, and
the ruthless manner in which that terrible decree
was enforced, proclaimed, too surely, the fate which
awaited all Protestant countries that should fall under
Catholic dominion.

The arms of Gustavus arrested these proceedings;
and as the contest continued, the objects for which
it was carried on, also augmented. And by the time

Catholic France had taken part with Protestant Germany, and Protestant Saxony had joined the Catholic
League, the war was, as usual, maintained for spoil,
power and dominion; the ordinary objects of human
ambition.   But though these objects were added to
the original cause of strife, that cause still stood fast;
and the Protestant powers who resisted the encroach-
ments of the Emperor and the League, defended,
not only their temporal rights, and the church property formerly confiscated; they also defended the
faith which they had embraced, and fought for religious freedom, as well as for political independence.

How far the Catholic Church approved of the persecutions, exercised by Catholic princes, is a question
which belongs not to our subject.   That too many
of the clergy followed the example of Lammermann
and Quiroga is true; but the Catholic world was
divided, at the time, into moderate and ultra Catholics; and the Pope himself, Urban VIII, was at the
head of the moderate party.   The extent also, to
which a church can be held answerable for the actions
of those who acknowledge its doctrines, is a point for
churchmen to decide; and one that cannot be argued
here.   The Author's only object, in these remarks, is
to claim the full right of arraigning the conduct of
princes, without prejudice to the religion they pro-
fessed; for if we once take to settling the value of
creeds, not by the Revelation which has been vouch-

safed to us, but by the conduct of a few individual
sovereigns, the C¹   tianity even of a Constantine,
may appear to some disadvantage, when contrasted
with the polytheism of an Aurelian.

THE

LIFE OF WALLENSTEIN.

ORIGIN OF THE THIRTY YEARS' WAR.

As the history of WALLENSTEIN, is the history also
of an important period of the Thirty years' War, it
will be right to begin this account of his life, with a
brief sketch of the origin of that sanguinary struggle :
for it is only in relation to the times in which they
lived, and to the circumstances in which they were
placed, that the conduct of public men can be justly
appreciated. Wallenstein was called upon to act a
leading part in the most eventful of all times ; but
whether he acted that part for good or for evil,—
whether he acted the part of a great man, or of a
great criminal, are questions which two centuries have
still left undecided.

The Thirty years' War is the most memorable
of any recorded in history. It is a war, great from
the actions performed during its progress, as well
as from the characters which it called forth ; it is

greater still from the cause out of which it arose,
and from the results which it produced. It was this
fearful contest that first brought the different nations
of Europe into direct contact with each other, and
established them as members of one community ;
every state of which was forced to take a deep interest in the fate of its neighbour, as well as of the
commonwealth at large. The cause of religious
liberty, which was soon found to be closely identified
with national independence, successively called to
arms every people from the Tagus to the Vistula.
And the Danes, Germans, Swedes and Britons, who,
on the banks of the Rhine and the Danube, maintained the rights of the Protestant Church against
the See of Rome, defended, at the same time, the
independence of their respective countries against
the power and ambition of the House of Austria : a
house that brought all the resources of its vast possessions in Spain, Italy, Germany and the Indies,
to support, not only the spiritual absolutism of popes
and councils, but the temporal absolutism of emperors and imperial chambers also.

The very period of history in which this great
contest falls, tends to augment the interest which it
inspires. It stands alone, a separate era, dividing
modern times from the middle ages. It constitutes
the last stage on which chivalry appeared in the
splendour of high feeling and conduct : it is the last
period, during which, in opposition to the time, when
important events should be brought about by the
strength of opinion, or of wide-spread delusions, we
still see great actions performed by the force of indi-

vidual talent or character. All the manners, habits, institutions and modes of thinking, derived from an earlier age, gradually lose themselves, or become modified, during the war : those that survive, re-appear at its close in a more polished form, perhaps, but too often without their antique nerve and value. Even man himself, who entered on the terrible struggle the slave of false opinion, issues from the fiery ordeal, free in belief, and released from the shackles of the Church of Rome ; but, already bearing in triumph the very arms, destined to form the chains that despotic power was alike preparing for the victors and the vanquished.

Religious freedom and national independence, had been secured by Protestant Europe ; but civil liberty was lost to both parties in the strife. The very strength sovereigns had acquired in resisting foreign foes, rendered them independent of the institutions which, in all countries, had still sheltered the rights of the subject against the will of the ruler. In the early part of the seventeenth century, we see these ill-defined rights and privileges, as nobly contended for, as bravely maintained. During the long struggle for religious liberty they disappear entirely from the continent of Europe, and take their last stand on the more congenial soil of Britain. The Protestant princes and rulers of the period, less politic than their Catholic contemporaries, fell into a great error when they supposed that men, allowed to think freely on the most important points on which hu-man thoughts can be engaged, would long refrain from speculating on the civil rights to which they might deem themselves entitled ; or, that having once entered on the inquiry, they would limit their demands for power by their ability to make a proper use of freedom. In this error were already contained the seeds of the great political convulsions witnessed during our own days.

Deep and indelible is the debt, which religion and civilisation owe to early Roman Pontiffs and to the Church of Rome. They strove, long and nobly, to forward the cause of human improvement ; and it is difficult to say what other power could have exercised so beneficial an influence, over the fierce and fiery nations, who established themselves on the ruins of the Roman Empire, after rooting out all that remained of ancient art and ancient knowledge. Nor were their efforts confined within these territorial limits : monks and missionaries, disregarding personal danger, penetrated into the forests of Germany and into the distant regions of the North, and, unappalled by the deaths of torture to which so many holy men had fallen victims, preached to heathens and barbarians the mild doctrines of Christianity, which only sprung up in Europe, watered by the blood of saints and martyrs. Even the efforts of the Church, to interpose its spiritual power in the direction of temporal affairs, and to control the conduct of kings and princes, were beneficial in an age when the clergy alone possessed whatever learning and knowledge was extant ; and the uniformity of belief which rendered all the western churches dependent on the authority of the Popes, an authority so greatly enlightened, when contrasted with the general darkness of the times, became a principal cause of the progress and prosperity of the Catholic world.

And vast was the power, and boundless the influence, which the Church acquired by this superior knowledge and conduct. But as its influence extended, so it began to deviate from the principles of the Founder of Christianity; and in striving after worldly greatness, the cause of religion was forgotten. With the extension of knowledge, the nations strove to free themselves from clerical thraldom, as the boy, advancing to manhood, gradually shakes off the control of the tutor, who had ably guided his infancy. But, unfortunately, neither the Popes nor the clergy were willing to yield an authority that the spirit of the age was every day outgrowing, and of which an improper use was too frequently made. The Church, along with its power, had amassed wealth also. The income of some of the monastic establishments was immense; and the pride and arrogance, of priests and prelates, shocked the chivalrous feelings of princes and nobles. The dissolute and debauched lives, led by so many of the clergy, injured not only the entire order, but the cause of religion itself; so that, in the fourteenth century, a call for the reform of the Church was already heard. The great schism, also, which, in that and the following century, divided the Church, only rendered this call louder and more general.

John Wycliff, an Englishman, born at Richmond in Yorkshire, and one of those men of whom even a proud country may be proud, was the first, in the midst of darkness, to raise the torch destined to shed

the light of truth over so many benighted nations.
The writings of this learned and pious man, the first
and most highly gifted of all the reformers, spread
with such rapidity over Christian Europe, that twelve
hundred volumes of his works were burned at Prague
alone, after the condemnation of John Huss, his follower and disciple.

Huss, who trode in the footsteps of Wycliff, perished at the stake. It was in vain that he appealed to
the Emperor, for the fulfilment of the imperial safe-
conduct, on the faith of which he had come to Constance, in order to appear before the council there
assembled. Sigismund blushed for very shame, indeed, yet allowed the murder to proceed. But
though the ashes of Huss were thrown into the
Rhine, to prevent them from being worn as relics
by his disciples, the truth which he had so eloquently
preached still survived. The noble and heroic manner in which he, and Jerome of Prague, met their
fiery deaths, was not forgotten ; and the Bohemian
Hussites avenged, in more than a hundred battles,
gained over the German and Imperial troops, the
treachery which had been practised on their unfortunate master. But the dreadful cruelties they
committed while fighting under the fierce and unrelenting Ziska,—he " of the chalice," as he styled himself, and who, in the art of war, was the scholar of our
Henry V.—rather strengthened, than weakened the
cause of their enemies. And fifteen years of almost
uninterrupted triumph, and, in some respects, ultimate success also, proved, that the time for granting to
men full freedom of thought, together with the free-

dom of action, which, to a certain extent, must ever accompany it, had not yet arrived. This was no cause, however, for delaying the reform in ecclesiastical discipline, which had long been called for by all enlightened Catholics. Even St Bernard had already expressed a wish for such a reformation ; and in the Councils of Constance and Pisa, a similar wish had been repeated. Cardinal Julian, in his Epistle to Eugenius IV, foretells, with prophetic spirit, the inevitable consequence of delaying such a measure. Speaking of the " disorders of the clergy," this great divine says, " they excite the hatred of the people against the whole ecclesiastical order ; and should they not be corrected, it is to be feared lest the laity, like the Hussites, should rise against the clergy, as they loudly threaten us." Again, " the rancour they" (the laity) " have imbibed against us becomes more manifest ; and when they shall no longer have any hopes of our amendment, then will they fall upon us. They will soon think it an agreeable sacrifice to God to rob and abuse ecclesiastics, as abandoned to extreme disorders, and hateful to God and man. Men will cast the blame of these abuses on the Court of Rome, which will be considered as the cause of them, from having neglected to apply the necessary remedy."

True it is, that the Catholics, on their side, spoke only of a reform in church discipline, and not in faith ; but it was impossible not to foresee, as Cardinal Julian clearly foresaw, that the two questions would be mixed up together. Men were every day acquiring additional knowledge, and it was not to be supposed that they would quietly witness the mere suppression of gross and long-maintained abuses, without inquiring into the origin of that power by which they had been tolerated. The art of printing had been invented, and gave a new, and hitherto unknown, impulse to learning. The authors of Greece and Rome became more generally known ; and the clear, simple, and beautiful manner, as free from false glitter and ornament, as from scholastic subtleties, in which they bring the most important truths home to the understanding, tended, far more than any particular system of ancient philosophy, to develope the reasoning faculties, and to give the spirit of investigation a just direction. The number of universities was augmenting : seven were founded in Germany alone, during the first half of the sixteenth century. The number of students who already frequented these seats of learning appears almost incredible, when contrasted with the small increase that has since taken place,—an increase that bears no proportion to the vast augmentation in population, and in the general spread of wealth and civilisation ; causes that would seem to render learning and knowledge more indispensable than ever. But along with all its so-called barbarism, there was a nerve, vigour and freshness, a free and youthful breathing, about the sixteenth century, which are altogether wanting in these times ; and which our frequent failures to explain the manners, habits and actions of that early age, shew that we do not always understand, and cannot altogether appreciate.

The Church of Rome had never, in its pleni-

tude of power, been able to root out, or entirely to
obliterate, the doctrines of Wycliff and Huss. The
wild and fanatic Taborites had indeed been exter-
minated, after the defeat at Erzeb, on the 30th of
May 1434 ; but the Calixtenists, Utraquists, and the
more moderate of the Hussites, made good their
cause, and obtained, in 1435, by the so-called com-
pacts of Brenaun, entire freedom of religion, together with a full share of the civil privileges enjoyed
by their Catholic fellow-subjects. They maintained
these rights through a succession of civil and religious wars, that devastated Bohemia and the neighbouring countries till the year 1512, when the peace
of Prague put, for a period, a stop to the sanguinary
contests, the most barbarous and inhuman, perhaps,
of any recorded in the annals of a Christian people.
Resistance to the papal power had thus, in one shape
or the other, been carried on from the time of Wycliff;
and every pile at which a victim to truth was consumed, had become a beacon of light, that helped to dis-
pel the very darkness it was intended to perpetuate.

The Church of Rome had wealth and power : it
therefore had the envious and grasping for its natural
enemies. The Church of Rome had faults and failings ; it had committed many errors ; had, in its
pride of strength, been guilty of mighty and manifold
crimes, in order to uphold its supremacy : it had
therefore manly and honourable adversaries also.
To these was of course to be added the loud, noisy
and ignorant crowd, always eager for whatever change
or disturbance, holds out a prospect of individual
profit. The time for more general resistance had

thus arrived, and thousands were ready to array themselves under the banner of opposition, the moment it should be raised by strong and skilful hands. The task was reserved for Martin Luther, a friar of the order of St Augustin, and professor of theology in the newly founded university of Wittenberg. And it is a curious circumstance, that from the first university, founded without papal sanction, were to go forth the thunders destined to smite the papal power. Luther was endowed by nature with a clear, penetrating understanding ; a strong, comprehensive, but coarse mind ; a deep and fervent zeal for religion. Though inferior, as a scholar, to many of his less celebrated contemporaries, he possessed, nevertheless, a considerable share of learning. But the qualities that were of the greatest advantage to him as a reformer, were his direct, manly and vehement style of eloquence, his dauntless courage and boundless energy ;—a courage that quailed before no danger, and an energy that rose superior to every difficulty. This noble strength of character was clearly depicted in every feature of his face, we might almost say, in the very outlines of his strong, robust and square-built figure. As a scholar and a man of refined genius, he was much below his follower and associate Melanchthon ; as a chief of reformers, he far surpassed all who had before, or who have since trodden in the same path.

A single spark is sufficient to fire the mine that is fully prepared for explosion ; and so it was with the commencement of the revolution that led to the great reformation of the Church. The sale of indulgences was an abuse of old standing, to which the Popes had often resorted, in order to replenish their treasury. Leo X, a Pontiff fond of pleasure and splendour, and a liberal patron of the arts, happening, about the year 1516, to be in want of money, empowered Albrecht, Elector of Mayence, and Bishop of Magdeburg, a prelate, who, in many respects, resembled his superior, to authorise a sale of indulgences; half the profits of which were to be remitted to Rome. Among other agents employed by the bishop on this occasion, was one John Tezel, a Dominican friar of dissolute and debauched habits, but already acquainted with the nature of the trade, and distinguished by a noisy sort of eloquence ; vile and blasphemous in reality, but unfortunately too well calculated to act on the hopes and fears of the ignorant and unthinking ; a class to which nearly all the lower orders of the period belonged. Chance brought this man, during the course of his trading tour, to Jutterbock, near Wittenberg. The papal bull authorising the sale of indulgences had, at least, the decency to require from the purchasers repentance and amendment. Tezel was far more liberal : he sold unconditional pardon for all sins, past and future ; and as his terms were as moderate, as his promises were brilliant, he carried on a most lucrative traffic.

An abuse so gross and scandalous, practised in his immediate presence, and almost under his own eyes, excited the indignation of Luther. He preached against the right of indulgences ; and the novelty of the theme, together with the power and eloquence of the orator, attracted immediate notice. The approbation and encouragement he experienced aug-

mented his zeal; and, in accordance with the custom
of the period, he soon afterwards published his ninety-
five celebrated theses against the right of indulgences.
Doctrines that affected so many, and such high interests, were not allowed to pass unchallenged.   The
champions of papal power attacked Luther with a
fierceness of zeal, that tended to injure their own
cause; for not only was the reformer their superior
in skill and learning, but he stood upon vantage
ground, and met all their appeals to schoolmen and
papal decrees, by direct appeals to the Word of God
itself.   Every day augmented the number of his adherents.   His own views also enlarged as the contro-
versy proceeded; and from having at first attacked
only the practice of granting indulgences, professing
at the same time the utmost submission to the papal
See, he came at last to question the authority of the
Pope altogether.   Leo X. occupied with plans for the
aggrandisement of his family, and disliking theological controversies, tried at first to allay the storm
by gentle means; but the indiscreet zeal of the
clergy forced him to resort to more violent measures.
Luther having refused to recant his errors, was ex-
communicated as an obstinate heretic, and delivered
over to Satan.

The great reformer was not daunted by a blow
which he had long anticipated.   He examined the
papal bull very minutely; and being convinced that
Leo had been guilty of injustice and impiety, he declared the Pope to be the antichrist of Scripture,
and called upon all Christian princes to throw off
the yoke of Rome.   Not satisfied with this public

appeal, he proceeded, in great pomp, accompanied by the professors and students at Wittenberg, to burn the Pontiff's bull, and the volume of the canon law, an example immediately followed in many parts of Germany. In Switzerland, Ulrich Zuingli was at the same time forwarding the cause of the Reformation. Like Luther, he had begun by simply attacking the doctrine of indulgences, but was, like the German reformer, carried far beyond the mark which had been the first object of his attainment. Zuingli was killed in an action, fought between the people of Zurich and the Catholics of Schwitz, Luzern, Uri and Zug, on the 11th October 1531. Calvin became, after him, the head of the Swiss reformers. He was the first who dishonoured his calling, by bringing an adversary to the stake: an act of which many think that his church long afterwards bore the impress.

In 1522, Luther published his German translation of the New Testament. It was everywhere read with the greatest avidity ; and in 1524, Nuremberg, Frankfort, Hamburg, and many others of the free towns of Germany, the real cradles of European freedom, openly embraced the cause of the Reformation. And the Protestant Confession of Faith, known by the name of the Confession of Augsburg, presented to Charles V. while presiding at the diet held there in 1530, was already signed by three Electoral Princes, twenty Dukes and Princes of the Empire, twenty-four Counts and Barons, and by the deputies of thirty-five imperial free towns. Before sixty years had elapsed, from the breaking out of this great revolution, all the countries now professing the Protestant religion had fallen off from the Church of Rome ; and the new doctrine had, besides, made numerous converts in France, Austria, Hungary and the Netherlands. In France, the Hugenots long maintained a gallant struggle for religious freedom. In Austria and the Netherlands, address and persecution succeeded in putting them down at an earlier period. The fate of the Bohemian Hussites, Utraquists and Calixtenists, we shall have further occasion to touch upon in the course of this narrative. In Spain, Portugal and Italy, the Reformation made comparatively little progress. The natives of those countries want the clear and comprehensive mental power, for which the children of the North are more particularly distinguished : they also want the energy and constancy of character requisite for bringing great and hazardous enterprizes to a successful termination ; and with weak men, the force of imagination, on which the rites of the Church of Rome are well calculated to act with effect, too easily overcomes the force of truth. The rapid spread of the Reformation over so many countries in so short a period, and the singular check that arrested its further progress within the boundaries which it had reached in the first instance, is one of those extraordinary phenomena that no writer has yet explained on philosophical principles.

Charles V. was neither a bigot nor a persecutor, and was even suspected of leaning towards the new doctrine ; but the sinews of his power lay in Catholic countries, and the views of political aggrandizement,

which influenced all the actions of his reign, induced
him to take part against the Protestants. The grasping spirit in which the domains of the Catholic Church
had been seized by Protestant princes told strongly
against their cause. In many parts of Germany, the
ignorant peasantry, excited to rebellion by fanatics
and designing agitators, were guilty of crimes that
greatly injured the Reformation, which these mis-
guided men pretended to forward. The madness,
cruelty and licentiousness of the Anabaptists, under
Stork and Muncer, made even Luther threaten to re-
tract all he had written ; while the horrible extravagances committed by John Bockhold, a tailor of
Leyden, who, for nearly three years, exercised absolute sway at Munster in Westphalia, helped also to
cast discredit on the new doctrines, which these ferocious maniacs pleaded in justification of their conduct. The reformers were thus accused of discard-
ing, without any true guide, the Catholic rule of faith,
and of throwing open the door to that belief in private inspiration, from false claims or fanatical preten-
sions to which, so many atrocities had arisen.

Urged on by these causes, Charles took arms against
the Protestants, and, in 1547, vanquished the princes
of the Smalcaldick league, in the decisive battle of
Mühlberg. This victory would have given him the
means of crushing, at once, both the civil and religious
liberties of Germany, had not the unexpected defection of his former friend and ally, Maurice of Saxony, deprived him, when at the very height of power,
of all the fruits of his previous triumphs. The success
of Maurice obtained for the Protestants, by the treaty

of Passau, the free exercise of their religion ; a boon
which was afterwards confirmed at a general diet of
the Empire, held at Augsburg, in 1555.   This first
settlement of the religious dissensions in Germany,
and first acknowledgment of the Protestant states,
is generally termed the " Religious pacification of
Augsburg." The many points in dispute between
the contending parties which this diet left unsettled,
particularly as regarded the appropriation of the Catholic Church property seized by Protestant princes,
proved, in a great measure, the cause of the troubles
we shall have to relate.

While Luther was forwarding the Reformation in
Germany, the House of Austria, destined to become
its most determined foe, was acquiring vast accessions
of territory, if not of immediate power.   Lewis II.
King of Hungary and Bohemia, had fallen, with the
flower of the Hungarian nobility, in the unfortunate
battle of Mohacz, fought, in 1526, against the Turks,
under Soleyman the Magnificent.   His extensive
dominions devolved, partly by treaty, partly by election, on Ferdinand of Austria, the same who, in
1557, succeeded to his brother Charles V. on the
imperial throne.

The peace of Augsburg remained unbroken, during this prince's reign, and the mildness, wisdom
and toleration evinced by his son, who, in 1564, succeeded him in the imperial dignity, under the title
of Maximilian II. went far to appease the religious
animosities that still ran high in the empire.   But
the task, which he did not live to fulfil, was above
the power of Rudolph, his feeble son, who ascended

the throne in 1575. Owing to the wise measures
which Maximilian had pursued, the early part of
this reign was comparatively tranquil ; and for a time
Rudolph was allowed to indulge in his favourite occupation, the study of alchemy, and to seek for the
philosopher's stone in peace. The calm that pre-
cedes the tempest seemed necessary, in order to
strengthen the nations for the terrible struggle that
was approaching.

But though the general peace of the Empire was
hardly disturbed during the early part of Rudolph's
reign, yet was the hostile feeling existing between
the two parties constantly augmenting. The Catholics were accused of tyrannising, wherever they
had power, over the Protestants ; and of striving, by
fair and unfair means, to recover the property which
had belonged to their church. The other party,
again, were charged with, abusing the toleration
which they enjoyed in Catholic countries, insulting
the rites of the Church of Rome, and with preaching
up doctrines inconsistent with peace, loyalty, and
good order. There was probably cause enough for
these recriminations ; but the Catholics acted, where
the others only preached. And though the forbearance of the latter may have resulted from insufficient power, we should not be justified in ascribing
it to such a cause : we are bound to acquit where
we want the means to condemn : and we nowhere
find the Protestants the active persecutors the Catholics so frequently proved themselves. The latter,
in addition to other acts of violence, surprised the

Protestant town of Padersborn, expelled its wealthiest citizens, and confiscated their property; while the chief magistrate, Loborius Wishart, was drawn and quartered because he refused to change his religion *. A few years afterwards Donauwerth, another Protestant free town, was forcibly occupied, oppressed in every way, and kept for many years under Catholic dominion; shewing how ready the Catholics were to commit acts of aggression at the expense of their Protestant brethren. The spirits were thus embittered, and the evident necessity for self-defence, together with the disputes that arose respecting the succession to the Duchy of Cleves, led to the formation of the Evangelical Union on one side, and of the Catholic League on the other. Frederick IV. Elector of the Palatinate, was head of the Union, and Maximilian of Bavaria chief of the League. The circumstance is mentioned here, only in order to indicate the terms by which the respective parties were long distinguished; for not only did the Elector of Saxony, the most powerful of the Protestant princes, join the Catholics, but the Union disbanded their forces as soon as the time for action arrived.

The feebleness of Rudolph encouraged his more ambitious brother Mathias to rise against him. The rebel first deprived the Emperor of Hungary, Austria, and Moravia. Two years afterwards he obtained the reversion of the crown of Bohemia; leaving the unhappy Rudolph nothing but the vain title of King, as useless to him as that of Emperor.

* Erhart, Echo aus den Zeiten des 30 Jährigen Krieges, p. 241.

German historians term this contest the " Fraternal War."

Notwithstanding this unnatural rebellion, Mathias succeeded his brother on the imperial throne in 1612. Under the wise and tolerant administration of Maximilian II. the number of Protestants had greatly increased in the hereditary states of the House of Austria. They had also obtained, from that enlightened monarch, many additional privileges.— Rudolph had subsequently oppressed and persecuted them ; and, it was only in the hour of need, that he granted to the people of Bohemia the celebrated charter, known by the name of the Letter of Majesty, a charter which confirmed all their ancient privileges, and gave them entire freedom of religion. Mathias acted at first with more duplicity : he flattered the Protestants, confirmed, and even augmented their privileges, whenever he acquired power, and thus secured their support during the contest for the crowns; so that the cause of the Reformation was continuing to acquire strength by the dissension of its enemies. And how fully the Bohemians, who were mostly Protestants, already felt that strength, may be judged of, from the ceremony that took place when Mathias was first crowned King. The elected Sovereign having sworn at the altar, with his hand on the Bible, to maintain the charter granted by Rudolph, the Lord Marshal of the Empire turned round to the deputies of states, and to the assembled people, and asked, " Is it your will and pleasure that his Majesty's Grace shall be crowned ?" " It is our will," replied the multitude, with loud acclamations ; and then only was the ceremony permitted to proceed.

The Emperor Mathias having no children, was anxious to secure for his cousin, Ferdinand of Grätz, already chosen as his successor in the imperial dignity, the succession to all the dominions of the German branch of the Austrian Family.   For this purpose he again strove to conciliate the Protestants, whom, in the hour of victory, he had oppressed, and in 1617 he actually succeeded in causing Ferdinand to be elected future King of Bohemia.   But, as this prince was known to be a determined enemy of the Reformation, the people of that country refused to crown or to acknowledge him, till he should sign a reverse, freeing them from their allegiance as subjects, in the event of his infringing any of those rights which the coronation oath would call upon him to maintain. Ferdinand complied, and was crowned : how he kept faith and word we shall see presently.

Ferdinand of Grätz, Archduke of Carniola and Styria, thus chosen King of Bohemia, had been educated at Ingolstadt, under the tuition of the Jesuits. Unfortunately for himself and the world, he entered too readily into the views and policy ascribed to that celebrated order ; for, by all accounts, he wanted not the qualities that, under more auspicious leading, might have made his reign a blessing to humanity. No sovereign was ever called to the throne at a more eventful crisis ; no one more fortunately placed for bestowing happiness on the extensive countries entrusted to his rule.   He might have been a messenger of peace ; and became the harbinger of war and de-

solation. His name, which might have been respond-
ed to by the blessings of millions, is mentioned only
with abhorrence. He might have closed the temple
of Janus ; by one wild and fanatic effort he flung it
open. He never lived to see it closed ; and his reign
appears, on the page of history, as only one frightful mark of blood and flame.

If we are to believe many respectable writers, this
prince, the author of a thirty years' war, was of a mild
and moderate disposition, assiduous in business, fond
of field sports, pomp and music. In manners and
deportment he was polite and courteous ; he was also
well informed, and master of the Latin, Spanish and
Italian languages. His devotion was extreme : he
often scourged himself, prayed frequently, attended
mass twice a-day, read the lives of the Saints, the
Fathers of the Church, and the Bible ; and was, by
the account of Lammerman, his confessor, the very
pattern of a perfect prince. " I will rather," said
Ferdinand, on assuming the government of his hereditary dominions, in 1596, " be cut to pieces, or beg
my bread outside of the gates of my palace, than suffer heresy to exist any longer in my country." " It
is because I love the heretics that I wish to convert
them from the paths of evil ; and I would lay my
head upon the block to-morrow, if, by so doing, I
could make them renounce their errors." Having
first made a pilgrimage to Loretto, for the purpose
of surrendering his dominions to the Virgin, he next
proceeded to Rome, in order to seek counsel from
Pope Clement VIII. and, as it is generally said, to
obtain absolution from the oath which he had taken

on assuming the government of Styria and Carniola. He had no sooner returned from his pious voyage, than he set about extirpating what he termed heresy from both his principalities. All Protestants were ordered to renounce their religion, or to depart the country forthwith, leaving, however, one-tenth of their property behind them. All the evangelical schools and churches were pulled down, or closed. On the 8th of August, 10,000 Bibles and religious books were burned by the hands of the executioner; and Ferdinand laid the foundation of a Capuchin convent, on the very spot where this strange *auto da fé* had been held. The Catholic clergy, forgetting that their duty called upon them to appear as the messengers of peace only, headed the soldiers in pressing the execution of the Archduke's decrees; and scaffolds were everywhere erected for all who delayed obedience. Vain was the intercession of magistrates and authorities; vain the representation of the deputies of the provinces; as vain all appeals to 'former oaths and charters; death and confiscation of property awaited all who attempted to resist.

The feebleness of the Emperor Rudolph rendered application to him for redress altogether hopeless; and his brother Mathias, forgetful of the promises he had made to the Protestants, issued a decree, annulling the privileges conferred by the " ill-advised Maximilian," on the grounds that the Church alone had the power to bestow such rights. He further added, that " lords and princes were not bound to abide by the charters and promises which their predecessors might have granted."

While Ferdinand of Grätz was thus carrying persecution and sorrow into every town, hamlet, castle and district of his dominions, Maximilian, the young Elector of Bavaria, was acting a similar, but more moderate part in the country he had been called upon to govern.

This prince, who possessed both talents and ability, had been educated at Ingolstadt along with his relative Ferdinand ; and been brought up, like him, in strict accordance with the views of the Jesuits.   The holy fathers at first interdicted the young prince from reading even the classical writers of Greece and Rome.   The followers of Loyola termed the immortal writers of antiquity " heathen dotards, and relaters of old women's tales :" and it was cunningly said ; for where those writers are read, cultivated and understood, there light will ultimately prevail, however deep the previous darkness may have been.   Fortunately for the young prince, some man of better judgment interfered, and this strange interdict was recalled by order of his father, the reigning Elector of Bavaria.   Maximilian's ability and assiduity are universally praised; but how soon his natural good sense and good feeling were corrupted by erring zeal and false devotion, may be judged from the following extract of a letter addressed to his mother.   On the 21st of August 1589, the young prince writes thus : " I yesterday heard, with great pleasure, that the King of France had been assassinated.   Should the account be confirmed, I shall have still greater cause to rejoice."   This hopeful scholar of the Jesuits was then sixteen years of age.   Similarity of character already established, at Ingolstadt, a bond of friendship between Maximilian and Ferdinand, which was never shaken or impaired during the severest trials of their reigns.

The Bohemians, who, as we have before seen, had elected Ferdinand of Grätz for their future king, are not, properly speaking, a German people, though forming part of the German Confederation. They are the descendants of a Slavonic tribe, called the Czechi, who, about the sixth century, settled in the country ; after subduing, or, what with the Slaves was pretty nearly synonimous, exterminating its previous occupants. When Charlemagne and his successors drove the other Slavonians, who had penetrated into Germany, back beyond the Vistula, the Czechi maintained their ground in Bohemia, where they still continue, retaining, even to this day, the name, language, and something of the Slavonic appearance of their ancestors. At the period of which we are writing, they were said to retain much also of that fiery impetuosity of character, which distinguished the early Slavonic invaders of Germany, and which made them too often rush into difficulties and dangers, without considering what means they possessed to extricate themselves from the former, or to overcome the latter.

Fancy sometimes loves to trace a resemblance between the natural appearance of a country and the history and character of its inhabitants. If this theory be not altogether an idle one, it may derive a certain degree of confirmation from the history of the Bohemians, and from the appearance of their country. Bohemia stands isolated in the midst of

Germany : it is on every side divided from the adjoining countries by high mountains of volcanic origin ; and is inhabited by a people, strangers also among those that surround them. Volumes of flame must once have issued from the craters of those forest-crowned hills : torrents of glowing lava must have descended into the valleys below ; while clouds of burning ashes were carried far and wide over neighbouring and affrighted regions. But the volcanoes are extinct : nature has cast a rich mantle of verdure over all the scenes of former desolation ; and it is only by the skill of the geologist that we now discover where the elements once raged in their might. In like manner have the wild passions of men raged and been allayed in that wild country. The savage hordes of ruthless Slavonians, who descended from the mountains of Bohemia, were long the terror of all surrounding nations ; but it is only in the pages of history that we now discover the marks of their fury. No traces remain of the flames lighted at the pyres of Huss and Jerome of Prague : nothing is left of the fierce, fanatic zeal that instigated the followers of Zisca to the commission of so many crimes. The religious fervour and enthusiasm that made an entire nation rise, as one man, against the tyranny of Ferdinand, have sunk within their just and silent limits. A wise and paternal government has atoned for early wrongs by the mildness of its sway : for two centuries, peace has smiled upon the land ; and, in Bohemia, every thing is

" as tranquil and as still,
As the mist slumbering on the hill."

We must, however, return to times of strife. In
the charter which the Emperor Rudolph had granted
to the people of Bohemia, and which both Mathias
and Ferdinand had so solemnly sworn to maintain,
it was distinctly specified, " that the Protestants
should have the full right to build new schools and
churches ; not only in the towns, but in the country
also." The citizens of Prague had made undisputed
use of this privilege ; but when the evangelical congregations of Brunau and Klostergraben were about
to consecrate their new churches, the Catholic clergy
seized them both, by express order, as they stated,
of the Emperor, and pulled down the one, and shut
up the other.

The injured congregations immediately presented
a complaint, in form, to the Lords of the Council,
the Emperor's representatives at Prague ; but these
authorities, instead of granting redress, caused the
deputies to be thrown into prison. The Protestant
members of the states then assembled in the capital,
took part with their brethren in belief, and addressed
a strong, but respectful, remonstrance to the Emperor against such a breach of privilege, requesting,
at the same time, that the wrong committed might
be redressed.

The Jesuits were all-powerful at Vienna, and to
their influence, and to that of Ferdinand, is ascribed
the severe and haughty answer which the Emperor
Mathias returned to this remonstrance. On the
22d of May 1618, the deputies of the Protestant
states were called before the Council at Prague, in
order that the imperial reply might be communicated

to them. It was to the following effect : " His
Imperial Majesty had, for good and sufficient reasons, deemed it right to command that the church
of Brunau should be closed, and the one of Klostergraben demolished. His Imperial Majesty further
thought that the states had abused the charter, and
that the deputies had rendered themselves liable to
be punished as rebels and traitors." The deputies
were not surprised by an answer, the purport of
which was already well known, as the Protestant
clergy had proclaimed it from their pulpits, and had
every where exerted themselves, to rouse the indignation of the people, against so flagrant an encroach-
ment on their religious liberties. The deputation,
therefore, only solicited a copy of the imperial letter,
together with permission to return, and deliver their
explanation, on the following day. Both requests
were granted of course.

While minds were still in the state of excitement
which this announcement, however fully anticipated,
could hardly fail to produce, a meeting of the Protestant noblemen, then in Prague, was held at the
house of Count Thurn. It was here resolved to inform the Lords of the Council, that, " after the signature of the Great Charter by the Emperor, no
order or decree, tending to endanger the liberties
of the Protestant religion, could be received or
obeyed." The most distinguished men of the party
were selected, for the purpose of conveying to the
Emperor's representatives this decisive resolution.
The persons on whom devolved the dangerous and
precarious duty, were Counts Henry Mathias of

Thurn, Joachim, Andreas and Alboni of Schlisk; the Lords William of Lobkowitz, Wenzel of Raupowna, Koln of Fels, and Paul of Reiczan. The people had, in the meantime, assembled in great crowds in the market-place. They were here addressed by the leaders of the Protestant party, who first read to them the charter of Bohemian liberty, and then the imperial mandate. The consequence was, that the multitude, always so easily excited, either for good or for evil, immediately insisted upon storming the castle; and it was with difficulty that the deputies of the states succeeded in appeasing the tumult : the first roar of the surge that foretold the storm.

When, on the following morning, the 23d of May, the Protestant noblemen proceeded to the castle, they were in full armour, and were followed by vast multitudes of armed persons, all calling aloud for vengeance. Among the Lords of the Council, William of Slavata, and Jaraslaw of Martinez, had rendered themselves particularly obnoxious, as well by their pride and harshness, as by the false reports, injurious to the liberties of the country, which they were said to have forwarded to Vienna. In full reliance, however, on their inviolability, as representatives of the Emperor, they attended the council to receive the deputies, who, on their side, had probably no intention of proceeding to acts of violence. But in the outer hall of the palace, it was agreed, at the suggestion of Count Thurn, to send away Slavata and Martinez, in the first instance, and to employ even force, if fair means should fail.

On entering the chamber of audience, the discussion was nevertheless carried on for a time with moderation and calmness, though a number of armed persons had forced themselves into the presence, along with the deputies. Count Adam of Sternberg presided at the council ; near him were Slavata, Martinez, and Diephold of Lobkowitz : William Fabricius acted as secretary. Paul of Reiczan, who had been chosen speaker of the states, specified, in their name, the grievances of which the Protestants had to complain ; declaring also, that they were not disposed to obey the unconstitutional mandates that had been communicated to them, and against which they were secured by the Emperor's own signature, as well as by the oath he had taken, even on the Holy Scripture itself. He further added, that they, the Lords of the Council, were the real disturbers of the public peace, having violated the charter, and thus forced the Protestants to seek redress in the present manner.

Count Sternberg, who, from age, character and conduct, was generally respected, succeeded for a moment, in calming the uproar that followed on the conclusion of this speech. He obtained a short hearing for what he had to say in defence of the council, which only went to shew, that they were agents possessing no power of their own, and acting merely by order of the Emperor and King. On the other side, the Lord Kolon of Fels replied, that every respect was entertained for the count himself, whose good disposition was well known. " But with you," he said, turning to Slavata and Martinez, " we shall never agree, for you are traitors to the liberties of the country." Martinez returned taunt for taunt, but was speedily interrupted by the fiery and impetuous Wenzel of Raupowna, who called aloud, " Wherefore all this delay ? Let them be thrown out of the window, according to good old Bohemian fashion."

To excited multitudes, the counsels of folly are never more acceptable than when recommending acts of cowardly violence. The ill-omened words were no sooner uttered, than they were loudly cheered by the thoughtless crowd, more excusable than their leaders, whom such ignorant applause encouraged and instigated. Sternberg and Lobkowitz were hurried into an adjoining apartment by friends, who protected them from injury. But Martinez was instantly seized : a window, some fifty feet above the level of the castle moat, into which it looked, was thrown open, and the unhappy Lord Commissioner, notwithstanding his supplications, was fairly hurled out of it, while in the very act of repeating a Latin prayer. Another and another followed : it was in vain that Slavata entreated to have a confessor, or to be allowed time to pray. The waves of the ocean are not more deaf to the voice of mercy, than are the ears of an enraged multitude : he was thrown out without an instant's respite. The secretary Fabricius had concealed himself under a table ; he was discovered and dragged forth. No harm had been intended to him ; but madness ruled the hour. " The fox's tail must follow the head," was re-echoed

through the hall, and the unhappy secretary was immediately sent after his superiors.

The escape of these victims of popùlar fury seems
almost miraculous.   It was, in a great measure,
owing to the circumstance of a mound of rubbish
having, in consequence of some repairs, been collected exactly beneath the fatal window.   Martinez
fell on this mound, and received little injury : Slavata rolled off it, struck against the iron bars of the
castle vaults, and was severely cut about the head.
Fabricius was so little hurt, that, with courtly politeness, he is said to have begged Martinez's pardon for
falling above his excellency.   All three happened to
be in full state costume, and it is probable that the
flowing silk mantles which they wore, helped to break
their fall.   The few musket shots fired after them,
the first shots of the Thirty years' War, were fortunately so ill aimed, as to prove altogether harmless.
Fabricius escaped immediately, and was already on
the road to Vienna, to report what had happened,
before he was missed.   Martinez hurried to the aid
of the bruised and bleeding Slavata, and both, by the
aid of some of their domestics, got into the house of
the Countess of Lobkowitz.   They were instantly
claimed by Count Thurn and his followers ; but the
countess, with great firmness and dexterity, avoided
compliance.   Martinez soon effected his escape ; and
Slavata obtained his parole, which he took the earliest
opportunity of breaking.

No sooner had this act of senseless violence been
committed, an act which injured the noblest cause
that ever put arms into the hands of men, than the

leaders saw the abyss into which they were hurrying their unhappy country, and strove, apparently with honest repentance, to arrest the progress of the evil. An humble apology and justification was immediately sent to Vienna. The states declared, in this document, that it was their full intention to live and die the faithful and obedient subjects of the Emperor, and that their only object was to maintain his power and their own charter.

Not, however, relying altogether on the imperial clemency, they took precautionary measures also. They elected a council of thirty, composed of the most distinguished men of their body, to administer the civil and military affairs of the country. The Archbishop of Prague, the Abbot of Brunau, and many of the Catholic clergy, were banished the kingdom. The Jesuits were instantly expelled ; and the severe decree issued against them, applies to the entire order the most opprobrious epithets. Measures of defence were not wanting. Count Thurn was placed at the head of the army : alliances were entered into with the neighbouring countries of Silecia and Lusatia ; and applications for aid and support were addressed to all the Protestant states of Germany. Thus one champion already stood, armed in the arena : evil were the auspices under which the lists had been entered : fearful the odds to be encountered, but just and noble the cause that was to be defended. No blow had yet been struck : on the head of the assailant was therefore to rest the blood that might be shed in the strife.

Before proceeding to narrate events, in which all

the nations of Europe took, directly or indirectly, some share, it will be right, briefly to view the situations in which the different powers were placed at the moment, when the great struggle for religious freedom broke out in Germany.

Spain, mistress of Portugal, Naples, Milan, Sicily, Rousillion and the Netherlands, possessing, besides, boundless empires in the new world, was still looked upon as the most powerful nation of Europe. But internal misgovernment, and corruption in every department of the state, more than counterbalanced these great advantages ; and Spain was weak in the midst of vast possessions, and poor with the mines of Mexico and Peru at her command. Philip III. unable to subdue the revolted people of Holland, had concluded with them a twelve years' truce, which was on the eve of expiring. The war that followed, secured to the Dutch their independence. These seafaring and commercial republicans had already, by wise economy, acquired the reputation of being better paymasters than the lords of the Indies.

The German Empire was a federation of free towns, and of temporal and spiritual princes, all independent of each other, but avowing subjection to the decrees of the general diets, and to certain antiquated, and ill-defined laws, over the execution of which the Emperor was supposed to preside. But as the imperial dignity was unaccompanied by power, the decrees of the diet, and the laws of the empire, generally remained dead letters, unless when the strong were authorised to execute them at the expense of the feeble.

France had lost, during the corrupt and turbulent
regency of Maria of Medicis, much of the strength
and influence acquired under Henry the Great.   An
act of assassination, placed the reins of government
in the hands of Louis XIII, a weak prince, ill calculated to rule a country everywhere split into parties, and torn by contending factions.   But his weakness became beneficial to the nation; it gave Richelieu
the power, which enabled that celebrated minister to
lay the foundation of the future greatness of France.
Under the guidance of this wily churchman, the most
Christian King oppressed and subdued the Protestants of his own country, at the same time that he
supported those of Germany against the House of
Austria.

Italy could hardly be said to have any independence.   As the papal states were surrounded by
the dominions of the House of Austria, the Roman
Pontiffs were little more than vassals at the will of the
Emperor and the King of Spain. Venice, though still
in possession of Dalmatia, Candia and the Morea,
was no longer the power which had so bravely resisted the league of Cambray; nor did the Signoria
take any direct part in the Thirty years' War. The
other Italian states were too feeble to deserve notice.
As a nation, the Swiss also, had disappeared from the
great stage of political contention. The defeats of
Marignan and Biccoca, had tamed their insolence
and pride : they now shrank within their hills, and
only sold, as they still continue to sell, the blood of
their sons for foreign pay.

Great Britain had, for the first time, seen the

crowns of the three kingdoms placed on the head of the same prince. But the advantages of this fortunate union, the source of so much future greatness and glory, were not at first perceived ; and England, under the reign of Elizabeth, was more powerful, and exercised more influence abroad, than Great Britain under the first kings of the House of Stuart. As a nation, Britain took no direct part in the Thirty years' War, but thousands of her sons supported in arms, the honour of their country. Several foreign states and princes, acquired greater fame during the contest, than any which the most patriotic writer, can possibly claim for Great Britain or its rulers ; but no laurels, gathered in the field, shone brighter or more nobly, than those gained by the British soldiers, who followed the fortunes of Gustavus Adolphus. Schiller, speaking of the arrival in Germany of a British force, under the Marquis of Hamilton, says, " the landing of these troops is all that fame relates of the British during the Thirty years' War." A more impartial inspection of the rolls of fame, would probably have induced the great historian to alter his opinion.

In the north, Gustavus Vasa had freed Sweden from the yoke of Denmark, and had placed his own family on the throne : it was occupied, at the period of which we are writing, by his grandson, Gustavus Adolphus. Christian IV. reigned in Denmark. Both these countries were alike poor, but governed by wise princes, and inhabited by bold and warlike subjects. They both took, with different fortunes indeed, a prominent part in the great struggle for religious freedom. Though now outgrown by other nations, the Scandinavians remained great, as long as courage and manly conduct, were sufficient to counterbalance the power of well-regulated numbers.

Poland, always a prey to contending factions, had little internal strength or exterior influence. It carried on an unsuccessful war against Sweden, in support of the claims of its own sovereign, King Sigismund, to the throne of that country.

Russia had not emerged from barbarism; and Turkey was still looked upon by all its neighbours, as the most formidable military state in Europe.

But though most of the European nations had already, in the seventeenth century, assumed a good deal of their present shape and form, they were still ignorant of the practical art, or science of government, which has been so greatly perfected of late years. The theory of legislation was, at least, as well understood two hundred years ago, as it is now; but the art, so to strengthen the hands of government, as to enable kings and princes to collect and wield the power and resources of their respective dominions, was an art or science, totally unknown; and one that subjects were not, perhaps, willing that their rulers should acquire. For mere acts of capricious violence, tyranny or oppression, there were always means at hand; but for great and permanent objects, whether for good or evil,—for national defence or external aggression, strength, proportionate to the territorial resources of the parties engaged, was constantly wanting. The rulers of nations had not yet obtained so firm a hold of the reins of government, as they have since acquired.   There was no perfect and unbroken chain of authority, proceeding, by regular links, from the cabinet of the sovereign, down to the most distant provincial functionary, and carrying the sparks of command, lightning-like, through all the departments of the state.

In times, when the machinery of government is imperfect, without being barbarous, when the general principles of justice are well understood, while their application is uncertain ; individual strength of character naturally shines out, more conspicuously, than in tax-paying and well-regulated police-days, like the present.   In the seventeenth century, the wild passions of men, had, no doubt, more scope, and led more openly to deeds of evil, than they do now ; but they were far better balanced, by the kindness, generosity and high feeling, that suffering virtue was sure to call forth, than they have ever been since ; whether in the so-called philosophical age of the next century, or in our own more refined, and artificial times.   Men stood more upon their own ground ; and manly character was brought out, in bolder traits, than it is at present ; the outlines, whether good or bad, were more marked and decided.   With more of violence than we now find, there was more of greatness ; less of admired sameness and vaunted mediocrity.   And it is this stage of civilisation, that renders the men of that century so strikingly interesting.   The age was not one of ignorance, or barbarism.   On the contrary, it was an age when much brilliant light was already abroad : a light rendered more brilliant and vivid, perhaps, by the very darkness against which it was set off, and which still formed the background of the picture.

Literature, architecture, painting, and the fine arts in general, had attained a height, which has not been much surpassed. The moral sciences also were well understood ; but the physical sciences were comparatively in their infancy, though, all the great and leading inventions, on which those sciences have since been advanced, had already been made. Tycho de Brahe, honoured and protected in Germany by the Emperor Rudolph, had been persecuted in his own country, on account of superior knowledge ; and his scholar, Keppler, the greatest astronomer of his time, was still valued, more for his supposed skill in astrology, than for his astronomical discoveries. A good deal of splendour and magnificence was displayed by princes and men of rank, and by none more than Wallenstein himself ; but the elegances of life, and what we would now, perhaps, call the art of living, were little known. But, though affluence was confined to few, the excess of poverty, now so frequently seen even in the most prosperous countries of Europe, was of rare occurrence : and if there was less luxury, there was also less misery. Compared to our own, the seventeenth century presents us with a romantic and spirit-stirring state of society ; not always secure and comfortable, perhaps, but robust, healthy and picturesque, and well calculated to call forth talent, genius and courage.

During the period, indeed, of which we have to speak, we shall constantly see more effected by individual character, than by the weight of physical force : we shall even find talent and valour, taking fairly the lead of imperial decrees and royal ordinances.   Private adventurers maintain, in the field, the cause of princes, abandoned by their subjects and relations.   The landless, but chivalrous, Bernhard of Weimar, carries on a war of conquest against the greatest sovereigns of Catholic Germany : the heroism of Gustavus outweighs, at the head of only thirteen thousand men, the strength and resources of Spain, Austria and Italy : and the mere name of Wallenstein, calls a formidable army into life, at the very moment when his imperial master, the absolute ruler of kingdoms and principalities, had not a disposable soldier at command.

CHAPTER I.

ALBRECHT EUSEBIUS WENZESLAUS of Waldstein, known in history under the name of Wallenstein, was born at Hermanic in Bohemia, on the 15th of September 1583. He was the third and youngest son of John Waldstein of Hermanic, and of Margaret of Smirricky, a lady of ancient and noble family, who brought to her husband nearly all the moderate fortune he possessed. As both parents were Protestants, the young Albrecht received the first rudiments of religious instruction in the same faith.

It is related of Wallenstein, that he already evinced, as a boy, the fierce, haughty and self-willed disposition, which afterwards distinguished him as a man. We are told that he was averse to study, of ungovernable temper, and fond only of military games, in which he always assumed the command over his companions. It is also said, that, being one day sharply rebuked by an uncle, for speaking more in the tone of a prince than of a gentleman's son, he replied, with great fire and quickness, " If I am not a prince, I may yet live to become one." There is nothing either very impossible or improbable in these statements ; but similar traits might, with equal truth, be related of many boys who never evinced any talents, and never rose, in after life, above mediocrity. We are not yet sufficiently acquainted with the route by which human character arrives at maturity, and know too little, what degree of impression it receives from exterior circumstances and situation, to tell, by the manners and apparent aptitude of the boy, what the man will ultimately prove. Rivers formed by numerous springs and rills, none of which can, singly, indicate the nature and magnitude of the future stream, are emblematical, perhaps, of human character. Many that promise fairly at the outset, collect whatever is rank and gross in the swamps and poisoned grounds which they traverse, and infest, as they roll along, whole districts with noxious exhalations : while others, rising from dark and turbid sources, are purified in their progress ; flow in fertilising beauty through the lands, and carry with them only the golden portions of the soil over which they hold their clear and sparkling course. It is even so with character and talent : they are formed and developed by circumstances that rarely begin to exercise much influence at a very early period of life. But the world, in its love of the wonderful, will have it otherwise : and we have seen the certificate given to Napoleon Bonaparte at the college of Brienne, a certificate which was evidently intended to represent him as a young man of inferior ability, possessing only a moderate knowledge of mathematics, metamorphosed into an early proof of the high genius, which, on the strength of subsequent events, was so generally ascribed to the triumphant commander.

The family of Walstein are, as the name implies, of German origin ; but they appear to have been long settled in Bohemia ; and ever since the brave Lord Waldstein of Dux, joined King Ottakar's army, in the thirteenth century, at the head of his four and twenty sons, all mail-clad men, they seem to have acted a prominent part in the history of that country. But though noble and numerous, they appear to have been poor ; and, as the father of our Albrecht was the youngest of six brothers, the hero of the present memoir could look forward only to very slender expectations.

The early years of the boy were dark and unpromising. Owing to his stubborn disposition and aversion to study, he was treated with great harshness by his father : a circumstance to which much of his subsequent severity has been ascribed. Before he was twelve years of age, he lost both parents : the greatest loss, perhaps, youth can sustain, however sternly parental authority, may, at times, be exercised. The orphan was first taken under the protection of a maternal uncle, the Lord Slavata of Chulm ; and as this nobleman was a Protestant, young Albrecht continued to be educated in the faith of his fathers. We next find him under the care of another maternal uncle, a Lord Kavka of Ricam, a zealous friend of the Jesuits, who placed the young man at the college of Nobles, which the society of Jesus had established at Olmütz. The followers of Loyola soon discovered the talents of their pupil, and failed not to take immediate steps to insure his conversion to the Roman Church. The task was assigned to a Father

Pachta, and found easy enough of execution; for Wallenstein not only embraced the Catholic religion, in order to be released from Latin and other serious studies, but conceived for his indulgent tutor a friendship which made him, ever afterwards, speak of the good Jesuit as the real founder of his fortune.

All the biographers of Wallenstein have asserted that he studied at the university of Altorf, near Nuremberg, and was there distinguished for extravagances, and punished for misconduct. And, strange to say, the acts of the university are still preserved, shewing that a " Baro a Waldstein," who signs himself Albrecht of Waldstein, was punished there at the period specified. The same veracious writers also inform us, that Wallenstein, after leaving the university, became page to Charles, Count of Burgau, son of Ferdinand, Duke of Tyrol; and embraced the Catholic religion while serving in that capacity at the court of Inspruck. He had one day, as the tale goes, fallen asleep near an open window, in the third storey of the castle. Frightened by a dream he threw himself over the parapet, but escaped unhurt, a circumstance that was looked upon as a miracle, and universally ascribed to the direct interposition of the Virgin. So signal a mark of favour, called, of course, for some grateful return, and Wallenstein could do nothing less than become a Catholic, and bend the knee before the shrine of his heavenly patroness.

This strange event, say historians, produced a very marked effect on the disposition of young Wallenstein. " He came to himself," as they express it,

" and learned to reflect. He acknowledged the existence of some great, unknown and all-ruling power that watched over him ; believed himself reserved for extraordinary achievements ; and it became, from that moment, the study of his life, to penetrate into futurity, and to discover the high destiny that awaited him." Unfortunately for these speculations, there is not a word of truth in the statement on which they rest. Forster proves, on good authority, that Wallenstein never studied at Altorf, and that he never was in the service of the Prince of Burgau. On the contrary, he appears to have remained a considerable time at Olmütz, and only to have left the academy when, by the exertion of his friend, Father Pachta, an arrangement was made, which enabled him to join a wealthy young nobleman, the Lord Liek of Riesentein, who was setting out on his travels.

In company with this gentleman, Wallenstein visited a great part of France, Spain, Germany, England, Holland and Italy. Peter Verdungo, the mathematician and astrologer, afterwards known as the friend of Keppler, accompanied the travellers during part of their tour, in the character of tutor, perhaps ; and it is more than probable that he was the first who initiated Wallenstein into the mysterious and speculative science of astrology. Of the particulars of the journey we know nothing ; but all writers allow that Wallenstein was an acute and observant traveller. He made himself acquainted with the manners and languages of the countries he visited ; studied the nature of their military institutions ; examined into the causes of their external and in-

ternal strength, and already inspected fortresses with
professional accuracy.   In Spain he wore the mantle
of Castile,—he dressed like a Frenchman in France,
and acted the Briton in England.   He entered into
the customs of all countries, his genius assumed every
form, and he was, if we believe his biographers, the
very Alcibiades of his time.

Italy was the country in which he made the long-
est stay.   This was not owing to any great prede-
liction for the people, or their manners, as Count
Prierato has asserted; for Wallenstein seldom, in his
letters, mentions the Italians, without some term of
ridicule or reproach ; but in order to pursue the study
of astrology, to which he had seriously devoted himself.   He appears to have remained some time at
Padua, under the tuition of Professor Argoli.

It has been thought strange that a person of Wallenstein's enlightened understanding, should have
been so firm a believer in astrology.   But, to say
nothing of the endless contradictions and anomalies,
discoverable in the human mind, astrology was the
weakness of the age, and occupied the attention of
many men of high talents and station.   Keppler
himself was an astrologer, and was employed as such
by the Emperors Rudolph, Mathias and Ferdinand.
These sovereigns not only had their nativities cast
by him, but they consulted him on important state
affairs : and the great astronomer acquired more
celebrity by the singular accuracy with which he
foretold the death of the Emperor Mathias, than for
having discovered the independent motion of the
heavenly bodies.   Nor can we wonder that, in an age,

when science had not yet made the progress it has done
since, men should have sought to penetrate the mystery that surrounds our narrow sphere ; sought alliance with beings of superior nature, and tried to discover their future destiny in the stars. In feeble minds
this would be only weakness, but in men of loftier
character and intellect, it was a high and creditable
aspiration. There is something noble and elevating
in the thought, that our fate may be linked with the
course of those brilliant orbs, placed so far above all
our little world's control and influence. To believe
that we are so closely connected with the machinery
of the universe ; that the part assigned to us in its
mighty working is of so exalted a character, as to
make the very stars trace our destiny on the dial-
plate of heaven, is to entertain a lofty idea of the
greatness and dignity of human nature. There is
a grandeur in the conception that belongs not to
ordinary men, and, abstracted from ignorant superstition, which takes fear and credulity for belief, it
is one that can hardly fix itself in any but minds
of great and imaginative power. The progress of
science has, of course, dispelled these illusions : we
now know that, in size and strength, we are mere
atoms, imperceptible in the vastness of creation ;
but at the period of which we are writing, this
knowledge was not so universal : men of character
and talent stood also upon higher ground ; astrology was in general vogue ; and it is not so very surprising, therefore, that Wallenstein should, at times,
have consulted the stars. But, though the fact itself is undeniable, we have nowhere the slightest

evidence to show that he was ever guided by their decrees ; or, if he really did take advice from the planets, it must be allowed that they proved, for many years at least, good and faithful counsellors.

By the aid of his art, Professor Argoli had discovered that great martial fame, and a brilliant destiny, awaited his pupil. Young Wallenstein's ambition did not perhaps require such excitement ; but the prophecy seems to have fired his imagination ; and already fancying himself equal to Cæsar and Alexander, he left Padua and joined the imperial army, then contending against the Turks in Hungary. In what capacity he first served is not known, but it must have been in some very humble rank ; for it was only after he had been present in several campaigns, that, at the siege of Gran, he was promoted to the command of a company of infantry.

Whether this tardy preferment arose from his want of money, or from the circumstance of the army in which he served, being commanded by the celebrated George Basta, it is not easy to say. In those times money formed, in all the armies of Europe, as it now forms in the British, a far surer ladder to promotion than professional merit ; and Wallenstein was poor. The practice of selling military rank, though always discreditable, was less so at the period of which we are speaking, than it is at present. In early times, officers only bought the right of commanding the men, whom their own money had levied. The soldiers hired themselves to those in whom they confided : it was a voluntary engagement entered into between the parties. At present, the nation sells the right of commanding the troops it has raised for the service of the state, and is satisfied with receiving, from the purchaser, a sum of money as a sufficient proof that he is capable of exercising the authority attached to his rank. Honour, bravery and talent go for nothing in these ignoble bargains, by which a country barters for gold, nearly absolute power over the lives and fortunes of its sons. And as to George Basta, if we judge of him by his system of tactics, which was then exactly what Saldern's is now, and which, when the object of such a system is considered, must be looked upon as second only, in feebleness and insufficiency, to the one followed in our own time, he was not a likely person to appreciate talent, or to encourage and call forth genius. Wallenstein's want of preferment is not therefore surprising.

The tacticians, having held their ground but indifferently against the Turks, peace was concluded in 1606, when our hero returned to Bohemia, and entered upon the legacy bequeathed him by his father. As it is the custom, if not the absolute law of the country, for parents to divide their property equally between all their children, and as Wallenstein had three sisters, besides his brothers already mentioned, the fortune that fell to his share, must have been extremely moderate. Without money or patrons, his prospects were naturally unpromising ; and we find his brother-in-law, Count Zerotin, the friend and companion in arms of Henry IV, exerting himself to obtain for the young soldier, an appointment as chamberlain to the Archduke Mathias, in order,

as the writer very frankly avows, " that his kinsman
may have a ladder by which to ascend to fortune."
Zerotin, whose love of truth is well known, and
whose letters are preserved, speaks in high terms of
Wallenstein's talents, says that " he is extremely reserved, and entertains the most ardent predilection
for the profession of arms."

The result of this negotiation does not appear.
Certain it is that, if Wallenstein obtained the situation, he did not retain it long, and there is even reason to believe that he displeased or offended the
Archduke in some way or other.   He was either one
of those men who cannot find themselves in subordinate situations, or who, with the best intentions,
are never popular in such situations ; who cannot
submit gracefully to superior control, or who, with
the most perfect disposition and willingness to obey,
carry along with them a look and manner of natural
superiority, from which ordinary men so constantly
shrink back with dislike.   Wallenstein was ever afterwards considered a most decided enemy of courtiers
and court functionaries.

It may be said with some truth, that women appreciate talent sooner, and value men of genius more
highly than men do.   They are also free from the
painful and uneasy feeling under which so many of
our own sex labour, when they find themselves in immediate contact with persons of superior intellect.
Men bow readily enough, and shamefully enough to
wealth and power ; but there is always the mental
reservation, that they are bowing to the possessions
and not to the possessor, who may still be looked

upon as individually their inferior ; a reservation that
falls away when they are called upon to do homage
to genius and talent : considering how unwillingly
this homage is paid, it may perhaps be taken as a
proof that the gifts of the mind are, after all, more
envied even than those of fortune.

When perfectly unbiassed, women seldom err in
their judgment of men ; but the cleverest of the sex
are so constantly led into error, by the influence of
wealth, rank, fashion, distinction and notoriety, as
well as by the persuasion of others, that their opinion
is rarely of much value.   When, however, they are
allowed to love men of genius, the probability is that
their attachments will prove generous, ardent and
sincere ; and Wallenstein was destined to owe his first
step on fortune's ladder, to female favour and discern-
ment.   He had failed in his attempt to rise at court ;
in the field of war he had been equally unsuccessful :
another career was now to be tried ; and love, though
not exactly "love divine," smiled upon the young
aspiring soldier.   By the advice of friends, he paid
his addresses to a wealthy widow, the Lady Lu-
cretia Nikessin of Landek.   The fair object of his
pursuit was not only advanced in years ; she was actually engaged to another person, a gentleman of far
higher rank than Wallenstein ; but our hero acted
his part so well, and was so ably seconded by the exertions of the Archbishop of Prague,—and well for
them who have such assistance,—that he gained the
lady's heart and hand, and what was probably more
to the purpose, her very large fortune also.   How
the parties lived together we do not know ; certain

it is, that the lady was extremely jealous, as all ladies
who marry husbands younger than themselves, should
lay their account to be.   This continued affection,
speaks however in Wallenstein's favour : it shews
that, if he married a lady for money, he was yet
too much a man of honour and feeling, to use her
afterwards with the coarse and vulgar rudeness, so
generally resorted to on similar occasions.   Such, indeed, was his wife's attachment to him, that it nearly
occasioned his death ; for the good lady doubting the
power of her own charms, and anxious to preserve
her husband's affections, administered to him a love-
draught, that brought on a dangerous illness, from
which he only recovered after long and severe suffering.   It was well for Wallenstein that the lady
herself did not long survive this extraordinary expe-
riment, or she would certainly, as Count Prierato assures us, have killed him in the end by " drugs and
magical incantations."

The Italian biographer takes occasion, in mention-
ing this circumstance, to read the sex a grave and
severe lesson on their conduct in general, and on
practices of this nature in particular.   We shall not,
for two reasons, repeat what he says.   In the first
place, ladies have now obtained a better hold on the
affection of men, than any which could be acquired
by the dangerous and long-forgotten arts here mentioned : their sway over all who deserve to be ruled
is sufficiently certain ; and the coarse, the rude and
illiterate, are alone placed, by insensibility, beyond
the power of female control.   These cannot be subdued by draughts and incantations, and are in truth,

much better lost than gained.   In the second place,
the very best lecture on female conduct and manners, delivered in the seventeenth century, would
appear very simple and superficial in the nineteenth.   Women have now risen to a higher and
more influential station in society, than the one they
held at the period of which we are writing.   In exterior deportment, a more dignified and respectful
kind of politeness was evinced towards them ; far
greater deference was observed in conversation ; a
reserved stateliness of behaviour marked all intercourse between the sexes.   No prince or sovereign,
pretending to the slightest degree of politeness, ever
spoke to a lady, except hat in hand.   The free and
easy manners of our time, which, when not founded
on the highest polish and mental cultivation, or on
great goodness and singleness of heart, are generally very bad manners, were completely unknown.
Women were more looked up to ; far greater respect
and attention were shewn them.   On all occasions of
state and ceremony, at jousts, masks, banquets and
festivals, they reigned supreme : their favours were
worn at balls, and in battle fields ; but their actual
station was comparatively humble ; and the deference, reserve and submission, with which we find
ladies of the highest rank, writing to their husbands,
would astonish the least presuming wife of the present time.

The augmented sway which women have acquired
in society, has been productive of great benefit ; because they naturally possess more kindness, taste,
feeling and delicacy, as well as more quickness of

perception than men can claim, and they have
brought all these qualities along with them into the
bustling intercourse of life.   It is therefore a matter of regret, to see them counteracting the good
they have themselves effected, by encouraging a tone
of fashion tending only to nourish and extend the
very selfishness on which it is founded ; and which
cannot fail to destroy all female influence resting
solely on the better feelings of the heart.

How long, and how deeply, Wallenstein lamented
the death of his wife, to whose extensive domains
he succeeded, we have no means of ascertaining,
and from the year 1607 to 1617, that is, from his
twenty-third to his thirty-third year, we completely
lose sight of him ; a circumstance sufficiently curious
when the ardent, restless and ambitious character of
the man is considered, and one that tends to confirm
the belief that he had, in some way or other, rendered himself obnoxious to the Archduke, afterwards Emperor Mathias.   During this long interval
he resided quietly on his estates in Moravia, and
took no share in the Fraternal War, though strongly
solicited by both parties.   Neither of the brothers
were very deserving of support; and it is probable, that
he did not consider either of them possessed of sufficient strength of character to help him on to the
greatness, he is said to have always had in view.   It
was only in 1617, when Ferdinand of Grätz had some
dispute with the Venetians, that he left his retreat.
He then raised, at his own expense, a corps of 200
horsemen, and hurried to the aid of his future sovereign.

It is from this expedition, that Wallenstein's brilliant career is to be dated. The operations of the Friuli campaign, consisted in throwing supplies into the fortress of Granitza, which had for some time been blockaded by the enemy. Wallenstein performed the service without, as it appears, striking a blow, a proof that it could hardly have been attended with much difficulty ; but it brought him into notice, which was his great object, and could hardly fail to do so ; for it was not only the principal action of the campaign, and it matters not how little a principal action is, but it was achieved by one whose magnificence and generosity already formed the theme of universal applause.   No troops in the army were so liberally paid, and so magnificently appointed, as those of Wallenstein ; no commander had ever been known to reward merit in so munificent a manner.   He lived in the most splendid style ; his table and his purse seemed not to be private property, but open to all who were willing to partake of the hospitality of the one, or who required the aid of the other.   The fame of such an officer, failed not to attract the attention of Ferdinand : he invited Wallenstein to Vienna, and introduced him at court, where all former offences were soon forgotten.   The Emperor raised the new favourite of fortune to the rank of Count, gave him a chamberlain's key, and named him commander of the Moravian militia, a post that appears to have been of great trust and importance.

When a gallant young soldier of fortune, destitute alike of wealth and patrons, possessing only genius and talents, Wallenstein had served, unre-

warded and unnoticed, in several campaigns, under
the great tactician George Basta. He then contended against the Turks, the most formidable soldiers of the period, men against whom honour was to
be acquired ; but he remained in the background.
No sooner, however, had the wealthy nobleman made
his appearance at the head of a gallant band of well-
appointed horsemen, than the voice of fame was loud
in his praise. He no sooner takes the field against
the worthless mercenaries of Venice, troops constantly kept in a state of mutiny and insufficiency,
by the ignorant fears of their despicable government,
than he is overwhelmed with rewards. As fortune
is a lady, we are bound to speak of her in measured
terms, though it must be confessed that she sometimes behaves in a manner very discreditable to her
sex : Wallenstein's unsupported merit could not obtain a single smile for him ; but his wealth, instantly
called the goddess herself to his arms.

It was at this promising period of his life, that
our hero married his second wife, Isabella Catherine,
Countess of Harrach, daughter of Count Harrach,
the imperial minister ; a lady who not only brought
him a great accession of fortune, but of influence
also. Count Prierato knew her personally, and
assures us that she was a lady of great merit and
virtue : " *Dama veramente modesta, e di una gran-
dissima purita ;*" but as so excellent a courtier says
nothing of her beauty, there was probably not much
to record. Of the peculiar style and manner of
Wallenstein's courtship, we know nothing, a circumstance to be regretted ; for in all we do know of him,

he is so unlike what is generally termed a lady's man,
that it would be as interesting, as instructive perhaps,
to see him making love, or only talking familiarly
with the countess and his intimate friends : the absence of information respecting his domestic life forms
the great blank in his biography.   We only know,
that his splendid style of living, which had attracted
so much attention during the Friuli campaign, was
continued during his stay at court ; where his liberality and magnificence, obtained for him as usual,
both friends and enemies.   Soon after his marriage
he repaired to Olmütz, and assumed the command
of the provincial militia, which had been placed under
his orders.

At a period when the power of sovereigns was in
most countries, very precarious, depending as often
on the willingness of the subjects to obey, as on
the means of enforcing obedience, which the laws
did not always very clearly prescribe, the command
of the armed force of a province, was evidently a
situation of great trust, and shews how high Wallenstein already stood in favour.   For the present, we
must leave him in his new dignity, and bring up the
events that first bore him aloft to the pinnacle almost
of human greatness, to dash him afterwards against
the rocks of treachery and ingratitude : as the waves
of ocean bear highest on their breast, the bark destined to destruction, at the moment when about to
hurl it against the sunken reef, which defies alike the
skill and courage of the mariner.

The act of violence, committed on the Imperial
Commissioners at Prague, soon led to open hostilities.

Negotiations were indeed attempted before recourse was had to arms; but all endeavours to bring about an amicable arrangement failed, owing, as is generally believed, to the influence of Ferdinand and of the Jesuits.   Lammermann frankly avows, in a letter, that " if war takes place it will furnish a desirable opportunity for depriving the Bohemians of all their privileges."   And Ferdinand, writing to the King of Spain, declares, " that princes must lose all influence and authority if they are to be dependant for power and money on the good will of provincial deputies *."   The Emperor Mathias, old and infirm, seemed indeed anxious for peace, but he was probably overruled ; and, as the Bohemians, though submissive enough in words, would not disarm, two Austrian armies, under Dampier and Bucquoi, entered the country.   The Catholics and Protestants having however joined their forces, and resigned, for a time, their religious animosities, to complain of general grievances, the imperial troops were repulsed. Count Mansfeld, the celebrated Condottieri leader, also brought 4000 men to the aid of the states. With this force he took Pilsen, the second town in the kingdom, and the last which adhered to the Austrian cause : the entire country was thus in possession of the insurgents.

From the first breaking out of the war, the Bohemians had vainly endeavoured to gain Wallenstein over to their cause ; but he refused, with haughty disdain, and not only declared his resolution of ad-

* Raumer, Geschicht von, Europa, vol. iii.

hering to the Emperor, but used every exertion to maintain the Moravians in their allegiance : and when the states of the province agreed, notwithstanding his efforts, to meet the Bohemian deputies at Brun, he attempted to intercept them, and to crush rebellion in the bud. In this attempt he failed, and the states in return passed a decree depriving him of his command ; and though he opposed his imperial commission to their mandate, he was forced to yield, and evacuate Olmütz, on the approach of a body of troops which Count Thurn sent against the town.   In doing so, however, he carried the public treasure along with him, and delivered to the Emperor 100,000 crowns on his arrival at Vienna.   The Moravians indeed, forced the Emperor to restore part of the money, by detaining the Cardinal of Dietrich-stein as a hostage for its repayment : but part of it was nevertheless given to Wallenstein for the purpose of raising a regiment of cuirassiers.

At a time, when most men were familiar with the use of arms, such a force was soon embodied ; and in June following, he was already present with his corps at the battle of Teyne, fought between Count Mansfeld and General Bocquoi.   Mansfeld's mercenaries had made a gallant stand against the Imperialists, and when forced to give way, had retired, according to the custom of the old German and Slavonic nations, within an inclosure formed of cars and waggons.   Making good use of these defences, which were not so feeble as might at first be supposed, they resisted, with great obstinacy ; till at last Wallenstein broke through, at the head of his men, and decided, not only the fate of the action, but of the Emperor, who was, at that moment, sorely pressed in the very palace of his capital.

Ferdinand of Grätz, already, as we have seen, elected King of Hungary, Bohemia, and of the Romans, had, by the death of the Emperor Mathias, succeeded, on the 20th March 1618, to all the German dominions of the House of Austria. It was a splendid heritage, no doubt; but it had to be gathered beneath the fiercest storm, that ever, perhaps, threatened a kingly crown. The Bohemians, proud of their first success, refused the plausible terms which Ferdinand offered. Count Thurn, at the head of an insurgent army, advanced into Moravia, captured Brün, and brought the entire country over to his side. The Protestants of Upper Austria, encouraged by the success of their brethren in belief, rose in arms, and joined the Bohemian forces on their advance towards Vienna. The Protestants of Lower Austria began to raise troops with a view to follow the same example, and Bethlem Gabor, Prince of Transylvania, was in full march to assist the invaders, with an army of 50,000 men. The storm no longer threatened at a distance, but gathered round the very seat of empire. Thurn, at the head of his Bohemians, encamped at the Danube bridge, and the sound of hostile guns already shook the halls of the imperial palace.

Vienna was destitute of troops : the citizens were not to be depended upon : no aid of any kind was near. Ferdinand seemed lost ; and the most zealous Protestants already hoped to see this dan-

gerous enemy of their faith, consigned to a convent
instead of being raised to a throne. Many advised
him to fly; but he easily perceived, that to leave the
town, was to abandon it to the enemy, and to resign
the cause. He braved the danger, and his courage
saved him. Twelve Austrian deputies had already
forced their way into the palace, and demanded,
rather than solicited, his signature to the conditions
required by the insurgents. One of the noblemen
went so far as to seize hold of the button of the
Emperor's coat, fiercely exclaiming, " Nandel," a
familiar abbreviation of Ferdinand, " do'st hesitate
to subscribe ?" Ferdinand wavered, submission appeared indeed unavoidable ; when the sound of trumpets was unexpectedly heard in the castle yard. A
party of Dampier's cuirassiers had arrived to defend
the sovereign ; fame augmented the number ; deputy
after deputy left the castle and retired to the camp ;
the court party recovered courage, the Catholic students and citizens flew to arms, and breathing time,
at least, was gained. But the insurgents still held
their ground ; Bethlem Gabor was still advancing ;
destruction appeared certain if the hostile armies
united ; and what was to prevent their junction ?

At this critical moment, news arrived that Wallenstein and Bocquoi had defeated Count Mansfeld at
Teyne, and were in full march towards Prague. The
Bohemians instantly broke up their camp, and hurried away to the defence of their own country.

It is curious to consider how closely linked together, are all the threads of human history; and
how often world-changing events are brought about

by the most trifling causes. What would have been
the fate of the Catholic religion had Ferdinand
yielded to the demands of the Austrian and Bohemian insurgents ? What would have been the fate of
Europe had the Protestants gained the ascendancy
in Germany, and overthrown the main bulwark of
the Roman Church ? Might not the tide of the
Reformation have swept across the Alps, and borne
down the feebleness of Italian resistance ? Would
not the closely contested battle have been renewed
in France with an augmented chance of success ?
And would not the new doctrine have again found
its way into Spain, where it had been repressed only
by the force of temporal power ? What prevented
the great probability, at least, of so mighty a revolution ? A charge of cavalry in the plains of Teyne ;
and the gain of a battle which was little better than
a skirmish, when compared to a hundred actions
fought, without results, during the thirty years of
strife that followed.

The Austrian capital thus saved, and the roads
open, Ferdinand was enabled to set out for Frankfort,
where, notwithstanding the efforts of the Bohemians
and of several other Protestant states, he carried his
election to the imperial throne.

The acquisition of this high dignity was of vast
importance to Ferdinand. It gave him great moral
force at a time when that force was of all others
the most essential. Once established in public opinion as a sovereign, deserving of confidence and support, and one whose rights were unjustly invaded by
his subjects, he could hardly fail to secure champions

among sovereigns equally jealous of their privileges, and who, in defending his rights, defended the general cause of princes also. And time it was that he should obtain such aid, for his own power was rapidly falling away. At the very moment when he received at Frankfort, the news of his elevation to the imperial throne, he learned that the Bohemians had, on the 19th August, formally renounced their allegiance, a step which they followed up by offering the sovereignty of the country to Frederick V, Elector of the Palatinate, a young prince of pleasing manners and address. John George, Elector of Saxony, had also been proposed ; but he was objected to as being " a drunkard, a friend to Austria, and led by others, though rude, coarse and vulgar in his manners." It might with truth have been added, that this prince, who, from the situation of his country, acted so important a part in the great events of the period, was nevertheless the most selfish and ignoble sovereign of his time.

Frederick, after some hesitation, accepted the proffered dignity, and historians generally assert, that he was influenced in his decision, by the ambition of his wife, the unfortunate and high-minded Elizabeth of England, daughter of James I. This Princess, whose beauty gained for her husband's cause, more hearts than would, if bravely led, have defended three empires, is said to have overcome the doubts of the wavering elector, as much by her haughty taunts, as by her charms. " Thou hast married the daughter of a King," she said, " and fearest to accept a kingly crown ! I would rather eat black bread at thy royal

board, than feast at thy electoral table." The tale
may be true, and certainly tells well; but there exists
a letter from Elizabeth to her husband, who it appears had consulted her, in which she expresses, with
the utmost deference and humility, her perfect readiness to acquiesce in whatever resolution he may
adopt *.

While the Bohemians were thus depriving Ferdinand of one kingdom, their ally, Bethlem Gabor, was
overrunning another. This restless pretender to the
Crown of Hungary, advanced within sight of Vienna,
and occupied the very ground where Count Thurn's
army had just before been encamped. It was in vain
that General Bocquoi attempted to impede the progress of the Hungarian and Transylvanian swarms;
he was defeated and forced to give way before them;
and it was entirely owing to Wallenstein that the
Austrians were enabled to effect their retreat into
the large islands that intervened between Vienna and
the left bank of the river. He defended the approaches to the bridge, and broke it down, after a
severe struggle, when the last of the troops had passed.
Bethlem Gabor finding his allies gone, the country
exhausted, the bad weather approaching, and having
no means of forcing the passage of the Danube, soon
struck his tents and retired. Ferdinand relieved
from this adversary, was at last enabled to direct his
efforts against the Bohemians; and the opportunity
was not neglected.

The Emperor, on his way to Frankfort, had gained

* Senkenberg, p. 370.

over to his cause Maximilian of Bavaria, once the
companion of his studies at Ingolstadt, now head
of the League, and the ablest and most powerful of
the Catholic princes. France, forgetful of the wise
policy of Henry IV, had brought about an arrangement between the princes of the Union and the
League, by which the former promised to afford Frederick no assistance, except for the defence of his
hereditary dominions. This shameful convention,
concluded at Ulm, excited the indignation of Protestant Europe, and enabled Ferdinand to turn the arms
of all Catholic Germany against the newly elected
King of Bohemia, who was but indifferently prepared
for defence.

This ill-fated prince, accompanied by his wife, and
a gay and gallant band of knights and nobles, made
his entry into Prague on the 1st of November.
He was received with all the noisy and joyous enthusiasm that marks the reception of new kings, or,
as the fashion may be, of new constitutions, from
which the unreflecting, everywhere the most numerous, usually anticipate vast and immediate benefits,
never yet conferred by mere changes of laws or
rulers. Frederick's affability, his pleasing manners
and natural kindness of disposition, rendered him, at
first, extremely popular ; and the constant succession
of shows, festivals and carousals that followed on his
coronation, helped to blind the many to the rapidly
approaching danger. But symptoms of dissatisfac-
tion soon began to appear. The young King was
discovered to be fonder of banquets than of business ;
the stern remnants of the old Hussite party were

shocked at the levities of the court ; the Lutherans
were displeased at Frederick's Calvinistical zeal ; the
Catholics still more so. Instigated by the fanaticism
of his chaplain Scultetus, he ordered the principal
church at Prague to be deprived of its pictures, orna-
ments and relics ; an act which gave great and just
offence ; and it was the speedy intervention of more
judicious friends alone, that prevented the statue of
Saint Nepomuck, the revered patron of Bohemia,
from being precipitated into the river Moldau.

The imperial confessor Lammermann, the Luthe-
ran minister Hoenegg, principal chaplain to the
Elector of Saxony, and this Scultetus, may all have
been convinced of the justness of their own views.
But, it is to the spiritual pride, resulting from this
overbearing conviction,—a pride that acknowledges
neither truth, honesty nor virtue beyond the sphere
of its own belief, which condemns every deviation
from that belief, and seeks to establish, even by force,
absolute conformity, and rejoices when successful in
the achievement of such unchristian victories,—that
the countless evils of the thirty years' wars must be
ascribed. These three influential men proved, as
many others have proved, how easy it is to be carried away by false zeal, and to violate the first precepts
of Christianity, even within the rules of the principal
Christian confessions.

In addition to the complaints which the Bohemians
began to make about internal grievances, came the
anxiety resulting from the non-arrival of external aid.
King James of England declined to interfere in
their affairs ; Christian IV. of Denmark, Frederick's

brother-in-law, remained tranquil ; Holland was hard
pressed by the Spaniards ; and the Elector of Saxony
openly took part with the Emperor and invaded
Lusatia, at the same time that a Spanish army, under
Spinola, was advancing against the Palatinate. The
Bohemians were therefore left to their own resources,
and even these were impaired by the want of unani-
mity in their councils. Both Thurn and Mansfeld
had aspired to the command of the army, and served
unwillingly under Hohenloe and Anhalt; and though
the latter was a man of high talent, and one of the
ablest soldiers, perhaps, of the age, he obtained,
as a foreigner and a stranger, but little power and
influence. At the commencement of the revolution,
the insurgents had boasted a good deal about the
victories formerly gained by their Hussite ancestors;
but they forgot, on this occasion, to bring into the
field, the prompt, instant and implicit obedience
which the " Captain in the hope of God," as the
unrelenting Zisca styled himself, exacted from all his
followers : for without obedience there is no victory,
and even valour itself is vain.

No sooner had the dishonourable convention of
Ulm disarmed the Protestant Union, and given Maximilian free hands, than he appeared in Upper Austria, at the head of an army, which rendered resistance unavailing. The revolted peasantry were
defeated, and the states of the province forced to
submit, unconditionally, to the will of the Emperor.
The victor being joined by the imperial troops, under
Wallenstein and Bocquoi, advanced immediately into
the very heart of Bohemia. All the insurgent par-

ties, dispersed in Lower Austria and Moravia, gave way before the invaders : the towns that resisted were carried by storm : others, terrified by the severities exercised on the vanquished, opened their gates and implored mercy : nothing arrested the progress of Maximilian.

The gallant Prince Christian of Anhalt, at the head of an ill-disciplined, and half-mutinous army, could only retreat.   But even this was effected with skill : he gained a march upon the allies, and took up an advantageous position, on, what is called, the White Mountain, near Prague.   Here he intended to fortify himself, but no one would work ; and when, on the 8th November 1620, the enemy arrived, not a single redoubt was finished.   Even at the eleventh hour, there was hope had there been discipline.   The passage of a narrow bridge, leading over a swampy rivulet, had broken the advancing columns, and the attempt to turn the obstacle separated the Bavarians from the Austrians.   Anhalt saw the favourable opening, and instantly proposed to fall, with the whole army, on the unsupported Bavarians ; but his advice was overruled : and it proved the last chance.   Maximilian having reunited and reformed his divisions, immediately advanced to the attack.   The combined army of the Emperor and the League amounted to nearly 30,000 men : the Bohemians had about 25,000 present : a number more than equal to have struck a fair blow for victory, if duty had been bravely done.   The reverse, however, was the case.   The young Prince of Anhalt, at the head of the cavalry, among whom were a number of English and Scottish cavaliers, made indeed a gallant and successful charge upon the right wing of the Austrians, and fell, as the latter expressed it, " like thunder and lightning on their cavalry." But the prince was wounded and taken ; and the advantage was not followed up. Some Moravian troops, under Count Schlick, also fought bravely ; but all the other corps fled the moment they were attacked : the Hungarian auxiliaries did not even wait the approach of the foe. It was a perfect rout ; and in less than an hour from the commencement of the action, the whole of the Bohemian army was completely dispersed and driven from the field.

Frederick, though not exactly banqueting, as historians have asserted, was not present in the battle. It was Sunday, and the ill-fated prince had been very quietly listening to a sermon, not perhaps of the shortest, delivered by the learned Scultetus, and was only about to proceed to dinner, with the Queen and a party of ladies, when news was brought him that the armies were engaged. He immediately set out for the scene of action ; but had not proceeded far, when the Prince of Anhalt, arriving without his hat, informed him that the day was completely lost. The unfortunate King solicited from Maximilian, a cessation of arms for four and twenty hours ; eight only were granted. Frederick availed himself of this short respite, and left the town during the night, accompanied only by the Queen, and a few intimate friends. So precipitate was his departure, that he left his crown and most important state papers behind him. He nowhere attempted to make a stand, but retired immediately into Holland, thus forfeiting his electoral hat and kingly crown at the same time. Prague surrendered next day, and the states of the kingdom submitted without condition.

Frederick's pusillanimous flight was a virtual abandonment of a cause, that, in itself, was far from being hopeless. Prague was fortified, and could have been defended. Mansfeld's army was at Pilsen, and had taken no share in the action ; the winter was approaching, and the Imperialists could hardly have kept the field long after the exertions of the summer campaign ; the Bohemians had been more frightened than hurt, and might easily have been rallied ; and Bethlem Gabor was again preparing to invade Austria. Courage and energy might have saved every thing : but the want of these king-making qualities lost every thing : and Frederick could hardly say, that honour had been saved. It is understood that the unfortunate King dreaded the inconstancy of the people, and was afraid that his loving subjects would deliver him up, in order to make their peace with the Emperor. This was certainly not entertaining a very favourable opinion of those who had, only a year before, so enthusiastically received him. But allowing the suspicion to have existed, it should not have been taken into account, when fame and empire were at stake. Such brilliant prizes must be played for, sword in hand, and in first line : the aspirant for diadems, must throw away the scabbard, must keep bright honour alone in view, and set his life as nothing on the cast ; for history, though too lenient, perhaps, to the crimes of a Sylla, and the failings of a Cæsar, will never acquit the man who, having sent thousands to battle in his cause, dreads himself to stand the " hazard of the die." Zisca " of the Chalice " would not have been at sermon while his troops were fighting : Cromwell would not, like Charles Edward, have kept aloof, with the reserve, while the bravest of the clans were cut down, without support, on Culloden moor ; and had this " sagest of usurpers " been called upon, by the senates and chambers of his own creation, to abdicate imperial power, he would, in scorn and pity, have told them " to begone, as he had found other tools wherewith to do his work."

Wallenstein was not present at the battle of Prague. He had been detached, and was occupied with the capture of Tanen, at the moment when the decisive action took place. The entire kingdom having, in imitation of the capital, yielded to the victors, he was sent into Moravia, to receive the submission of that province also : but before we accompany him, we must relate events, in which he took no part indeed, but which greatly influenced his fortunes.

The victory gained under the walls of Prague, not only placed Ferdinand in possession of all his dominions, but placed him in that possession with far greater powers than any of his predecessors had ever enjoyed. The war was at an end : the sword might have been sheathed, had it not been kept drawn to aid the vengeful work of inquisitors and executioners, to whom the unhappy kingdom was remorselessly given over. Three months elapsed before any steps were taken against those who had joined the insurgents. Many who had fled in the first instance, were deceived by this moderation, and returned to their homes. It is due to the honour of Count Tilly to say, that he more than warned the suspected *, though unfortunately the many trusted rather to the Emperor's clemency, than to the general's warning. On the same day, and at the same hour, eight and forty of the principal actors in the late events were arrested at Prague. The Elector Frederick, and the Prince of Anhalt, were proscribed, and put under ban; and nine and twenty others, mostly men of high rank, were publicly cited to appear, and failing to do so, they were to be outlawed and their property confiscated. Of the prisoners, seven and twenty were condemned to death, others to perpetual imprisonment, some to minor punishments, and all to the total loss of property. Not a single act of pardon, — not a single remission of punishment was granted. Prince Charles of Lichtenstein, the Emperor's representative, a convert from the Protestant faith, and who laboured under the heavy accusation of having been an active plunderer at the capture of the town, did not send to Vienna a single one of the many petitions for mercy which had been presented to him †.

The noble bearing of the condemned, merits the highest praise ; on the Sunday previous to their execution, they requested to be included in the prayers of the Protestant congregations ; they solicited for-

* Habernfeld De Bello Bohem. p. 61.
† Erhard, Echo aus den zeiten des 30. Jahrigen Kriges, p. 203.

giveness from all men, and passed the last of their
nights assembled in acts of devotion. On the morning of the 1st of June, they were singly conducted to
the place of execution. The scaffold was surrounded
by soldiers, and the constant rolling of the muffled
drums, proved, that victorious power dreaded to the
last the voices of these destined victims of oppression.
At the moment when the scene of blood was about
to commence, a rainbow appeared in the sky, and
continued to shine in all its radiance, for upwards
of an hour. The condemned received it as a sign,
that the mercy which had been refused below, would
be granted on high ; and met their fate with the
serenity and resignation that became Christians and
patriots.

The venerable Count Schlick, nearly eighty years
of age, led the march of death. Unsupported, holding a prayer book in his hands, he advanced with a
firm step, between the files of soldiers. Arrived on
the scaffold he bared his neck with the aid of his
servant ; then kneeling down, his hands clasped on
his breast, and with eyes raised to heaven, received
the blow of the executioner, which, at a single stroke,
severed his head from his body. His right hand
was next struck off : it was kept with the head to
be publicly exposed : the body was delivered over
to his friends by masked attendants. Three and
twenty men of noble families suffered successively in
this manner. Jessinius, the chancellor of the university, suffered in a manner more horrible still, for
his tongue was torn out by the executioner before he
was beheaded. Three of the condemned, being of

plebeian rank, were hanged ; and one unhappy man
of the name of Debis, was, with unheard-of barbarity,
nailed by the tongue to the gibbet, where death only
relieved him, next day, from his sufferings.   The
number of the lower orders who were put to death
in the provinces, is said to have been immense.

These executions were soon afterwards followed
by a proclamation, calling upon all persons who had,
directly or indirectly, taken part in the rebellion, to
appear before specified tribunals, and render an account of their conduct : thus, on pain of death, to
become their own accusers.   And such was the terror
inspired by the severities exercised, that no less than
seven hundred and twenty-eight individuals of rank
and property, actually appeared and denounced themselves.   After having been detained a short time in
prison, they were informed, that though they had
forfeited honour, life and property, by their treason,
his Imperial Majesty was nevertheless pleased to spare
their lives and restore their honour ; only reserving
to himself, the right of disposing of their property.
Some lost the entire, some half, and others minor
portions of their wealth.   In less than two years, six
hundred and twenty-two estates, belonging to Protestant nobles, were confiscated for the benefit of the
Crown.

One act of severity rapidly followed another. Ferdinand, with his own hands, cut in two the Bohemian Magna Charta, and burned the seal. Relieved
from the obligations which it imposed, all Protestant
ministers were banished the kingdom, and sent helpless, with their families, to seek shelter in foreign

countries, of which few even knew the language. The pastorless flocks were next subjected to every kind of oppression, for the purpose of making them embrace the Catholic religion. Public and private libraries were ransacked, and all works deemed heretical, including the new translations of the Bible, were seized and burned. Protestants were removed from all public institutions ; they were prohibited from acting as guardians to the young ; were deprived of the rights of citizens ; could not be received as apprentices ; were precluded from the privilege of making wills and testaments ; and all marriages, between persons professing different religions, were interdicted.

On the 9th of December 1624, all Protestant schoolmasters were, on pain of death, ordered to leave the country within eight days ; till at last it was decreed, that whoever had not, by Easter 1626, embraced the Catholic faith, was to quit the kingdom. Prayers, petitions and appeals, remained, as before, without effect ; and 30,000 families, 500 of whom belonged to the patrician and equestrian orders, emigrated from Bohemia alone : many of these were totally destitute, and all, from the difficulty of finding purchasers for their property, in greatly reduced circumstances. " The Muses," says Galleti, in speaking of these scenes, " accompanied the learned in their flight ; and all that remained of old Bohemian valour and gallantry, forsook the land when its chivalry departed."

Commissioners, attended by military parties, traversed the country to enforce obedience to the imperial decree. In many places, despair led to resistance and insurrections, and these again, to punishments of fearful severity. Soldiers were placed at free quarters; children were taken from their parents; wives from their husbands; and death or blows followed resistance. Towns and villages were laid in ashes, sometimes by the troops, sometimes by the maddened inhabitants themselves; and the savage and unrelenting ferocity, displayed by the Spanish colonel, Don Martin de Huerta, has never, perhaps, been equalled, except by the exterminators of the Peruvians, and the oppressors of the Flemings. Neither feeble age, nor helpless infancy,—neither youth, beauty, valour nor merit, found mercy before this man of blood, who, on one occasion, caused no less than 1600 persons to be massacred in the streets of Prachshatilz alone *.

In the Palatinate, which the Emperor bestowed upon Maximilian, the Spaniards and Bavarians carried on their reformation on similar principles; while Ferdinand spared his Austrian subjects as little as he spared his Bohemians; and the French Ambassadors write, that they can hardly describe the cruelties exercised even in the capital. The knowledge that deeds so dreadful have been committed by men, humbles at once and confounds the judgment; for we are bound to confess, that we cannot look so far into the heart, as to discover the sources of dark and deadly fanaticism. The cause of many crimes may be revealed to us, but the source whence arises the spirit of religious persecution, remains impenetrable. That barbarous nations should deem offerings of blood ac-

* Erhard, page 224.

ceptable to the divinities of wrath, whom their wild imaginations conjure up, is easily understood ; but that men who called themselves Christians, to whom the doctrines of Christianity had at least been revealed, should ever have thought that the slaughter and oppression of thousands, though even of erring thousands, could be acceptable to a God of love and benevolence, exceeds altogether the bounds of human understanding.

We must now return to Wallenstein, who, as we have seen, had immediately after the victory of Prague been dispatched into Moravia. As no resistance was offered, he soon entered Olmütz, and not only repossessed himself of his own estates, which had been confiscated during the rebellion, but already began that system of buying up confiscated domains, which in the course of a few years made him master of such boundless wealth. Nobler pursuits interfered, however, for a time, with this mean traffic. Bethlem Gabor, not intimidated by the defeat of his allies, had again invaded the Austrian states. Bocquoi and Dampier, the two most renowned imperial generals of the period, fell, in vain attempts to arrest the progress of the Turkish and Transylvanian hordes. Wallenstein was more fortunate : he first defeated the Prince himself at Shanutz, and on the 18th October 1621, completely routed another body of the army at Kremser. This second blow was so severe, that Gabor renounced all claim to the crown of Hungary, and concluded a peace with the Emperor. But, as he never looked upon such a peace as more than a cessation of arms, he always renewed the war whenever he thought his means equal to the contest : and in 1623, he once more took the field, at the head of a numerous army.

The Italians, who were never able to defend their own country, had at this time, acquired some reputation for military science : a reputation, not founded upon actions, indeed, but principally on George Basta's Treatise on Tactics, and some other works, of nearly similar merit.   On the strength of this fame for excellent soldiership, a number of Italian officers were employed in the imperial service ; and the country had often to pay dearly for the proofs of their skill : on this occasion it nearly cost a whole army.   The Marquis Caraffa di Montenegro, a scientific Neapolitan, was placed at the head of the troops destined to oppose unscientific Turks and Transylvanians.   According to rule, victory should not have been doubtful : but victory is painted with wings, and the science that shall bind them, has not yet been discovered.   At all events, Caraffa knew it not ; for, like many other vastly scientific men, he was not only defeated, but so completely inclosed by the enemy, that, nothing but the arrival of Wallenstein, who raised the blockade, saved the army from absolute destruction.

It is stated, that Prince Charles of Lichtenstein accused Wallenstein of having endangered the safety of Caraffa's army by the tardiness of his march ; and it is added, that the accused found it advisable to secure the good opinion of the Aulic Council by a present of 12,000 ducats.   The story is not very likely to be true ; for, by the honours bestowed upon him, it is evident Wallenstein was at this time, in

high favour with the Emperor ; though his extreme
liberality, at the expense of the countries occupied
by his troops, already began to attract notice ; and
we find Ferdinand writing to him about certain
" *disordini* " that existed in a regiment of cavalry,
the men and officers of which, had exacted from
some districts no less than 170,000 florins, in a single
month : a sum so large, that we venture to repeat it
only, on royal and imperial authority.

In reward of the many brilliant services which he
had performed, Wallenstein was, towards the end of
the year 1623, created Count Palatine and Duke of
Friedland ; with the right of striking coin and granting patents of nobility. The domains forming the
duchy had been confiscated, and Wallenstein had
purchased them for 150,000 florins, a sum, which we
may easily suppose him to have had at command But
where he obtained the 7,290,228 florins with which
he afterwards purchased more than sixty other confiscated estates, we cannot well understand. As the
acquisition of such property was not deemed very creditable, nor the tenure looked upon as very secure,
Wallenstein bought the domains at less than a third
of their real value ; a circumstance that accounts for
his being wealthy, but not to the extent of the sum
in question, and still less to the extent of the much
larger sums he afterwards had at his disposal. He
inherited a considerable fortune from his first wife,
and had received a large portion with the Countess
of Harrach : he had also, as we know, handed to the
Emperor a pretty long account, for the arms, pay
and appointments of the regiments he had raised.

†

But all this could hardly amount to a sum that would now be more than a million sterling ; for, though a good manager, and always preaching economy to his agents, he was magnificent in his expenses ; and his Bohemian and Moravian estates had been confiscated during the rebellion, and had no doubt suffered by the war. This extraordinary command of money, still remains an enigma in Wallenstein's history.

But, by whatever means he obtained the sums necessary for the purchase of these domains, it is but justice to say, that having once acquired so many splendid estates and principalities, he used every exertion to improve them ; and to render those happy, whom fortune had placed under his rule. Though still termed " colonel of certain troops of infantry and cavalry," over whom he continued to hold active command, we find him constantly employed, during the two years that followed the last Hungarian campaign, in performing the duties of a good prince and landlord. We use the word " prince " in translation of the German word " Fürst," though it is difficult to say, what was the extent of sovereign power which the rulers of such principalities had a right to exercise.

From this period of his life, to within a few days of his death, Wallenstein's own letters throw a great deal of light on his occupations and pursuits. At one time he directs a good French tailor to be sent to Gitchin, which he intends to make his future residence. Here the number of his noble pages is already to be augmented ; and liveries for fifty servants are to be prepared. Then, again, he

issues strict orders for the establishment of schools ;
preaches up the necessity of education ; lectures
about the conduct of the clergy, and all but commands the citizens of Leipa, to send their children to
an academy which he had founded for their benefit
and advantage.   He is a practical farmer also ; gives
long detailed orders about draining and planting, and
improving the breed of cattle ; of horses he is very
fond, has a splendid stud, is learned on the treatment
of colts ; and in a letter to his agent says, " You
know that I value a single foal more than two farms."

The new ruler is stern enough too, at times ; the
expelled Lord of Friedland having excited some of
his former vassals to revolt, Wallenstein instantly
orders a price of 5000 crowns to be put on the head
of the intruder, and threatens, with instant death, all
who shall presume to join him.   This proves, however, but a passing storm, and is noticed only in one
or two letters, and he returns immediately to his
plans for ameliorating the condition of his vassals, and
improving the principalities.   He makes roads, builds
palaces, brings artizans, architects and instructors
from foreign countries ; invites men of letters and
of learning to his court.   Keppler was in his service ;
and a situation was offered to Grotius : he encourages
and establishes manufactories, and gives even, what
would now be termed a constitution, to his subjects.
This charter still exists ; it conferred very extensive
privileges on the inhabitants of certain towns and districts, and reflects, when the times are considered,
the very highest credit on the head and heart of its
author.

It is in this constant striving to elevate and benefit his subordinates, to import the arts into his country, and to raise up monuments of splendour and magnificence, amidst the wilds of Bohemia, that the lofty genius of this man is to be discovered. Born to a throne, he would probably have been a great and benevolent monarch : born in an humble station, and raised by his talents to all but regal sway, it is difficult perhaps, to say what he really became. But whatever fortune, virtue or ambition made him, nature had certainly endowed him with rare and noble qualities. To a lofty and aspiring disposition, he added a singular ability for the details of business, whether civil or military. It was not, however, from partiality that he entered into the minutiæ of ordinary affairs ; but for the purpose of instructing others to aid in the execution of his own views. His genius was of a high caste, and naturally above details ; he seemed formed for the conception of vast and magnificent plans, and saw farther into European politics than any public character that had gone before him ; but this did not blind him to the just proportion and construction of ambition's ladder.

It is idle indeed to say, often as the assertion is made, that men of first-rate talents cannot enter into minute details of business. The reverse is the case : they enter into such details with a facility that is astonishing to those who can comprehend details only ; nor can we suppose a really great man, ignorant of the working of the very machinery which he employs to effect his elevation. Cæsar not only commanded armies, but instructed his soldiers how to use

their arms. Many men have, no doubt, been raised
to greatness on the mere tide of events, which they
could neither guide nor direct, and the moving cause
of which they did not even understand; but they were
only fortunate men, whom the world, in its adoration
of greatness, called able men.

While Wallenstein was thus occupied with the internal administration of his newly acquired principalities, Tilly was reaping laurels in the fields of war.
No sooner had the Bohemian insurrection been suppressed, than the Emperor turned his arms against
the hereditary dominions of the expelled King; and
Tilly entered the Palatinate from one side, while a
Spanish army entered it from the other. Left almost
without protection, by the troops of the Protestant
Union, which dissolved itself on the first approach of
danger, the electorate would have been overrun without opposition, had not an outlawed adventurer, without home, family or country, undertaken its defence.
This was Count Ernest of Mansfeld, the natural son
of an Austrian general of that name. With no other
fortune but his sword, possessing no resources but
those with which courage supplied him, this extraordinary man undertook the defence of a country, abandoned by its sovereign, and the support of a prince
forsaken by his relations. So successfully did Mansfeld maintain the contest for a time, that he brought
two other champions, the Markgraf of Baden-Dur-
lach, and Prince Christian of Brunswick, to the aid
of the cause.

Without stores, fortresses, money or resources,
these adventurers were, of course, obliged to make

the countries which they traversed, support their ro-
ving and undisciplined bands : they lived by plunder,
rather than by regular contributions, and came over
the affrighted lands, more like flocks of devouring
harpies, than banded soldiers and defenders.   But
such irregular armies, however boldly led, could not
long resist the united forces of the Emperor and the
League.   The adventurers were successively defeated
by Tilly, in the battles of Wimphen, Darmstadt and
Höchst.   Of the Markgraf of Baden we hear nothing
more after his defeat :   The other two fought their
way through the Spanish forces, and reached Holland, where they disbanded their troops ; but had not
long to remain inactive, before the events of the war
again called them into the field.

CHAPTER II.

THE conquest of the Palatinate, and the expulsion
from Germany, of Mansfeld and the Duke of Brunswick, terminated the second act of the Thirty years'
War.   It was again in Ferdinand's power to sheathe
the sword : he stood alone in the arena ; but he stood
armed, and his conduct and formidable attitude soon
forced the remnants of the opposite party to adopt
measures of security.   Not only had the Palatinate
been conferred on Maximilian of Bavaria, contrary to
the laws of the empire, and in total disregard of the
representations made by all Protestant Germany, but
Tilly remained at the head of a victorious army on
the frontiers of Lower Saxony ; and, on pretence
of following the Duke of Brunswick, made several
plundering inroads on the territory of the Circle.
Alarmed by the presence of so dangerous a neighbour, as well as by the acts of oppression exercised
wherever the power of the Emperor and the League
extended, the states began to arm.   They called
upon England for assistance, and entered into an
alliance with Christian IV. of Denmark, who, as
Duke of Holstein, was already one of their members,
and who was declared commander-in-chief of the
combined forces.   Mansfeld and the Duke of Brunswick, aided by English subsidies, again made their

appearance ; so that an army of 60,000 men was actually brought together. The states declared this force to be solely intended for the protection of their rights and independence. A different language, however, was held at Vienna : it was there said that the army was far too numerous for such a purpose, and had been raised to reconquer the Palatinate, and to circumscribe the power of the Emperor. There may have been truth in both statements ; for it was easy to see that the liberty of Protestant Germany could not long be maintained, unless the power of the Emperor and the Catholics were confined within narrower bounds.

Ferdinand having vainly tried, by threats and remonstrances, to induce the King of Denmark and the states of the Circle to disband their forces, ordered Tilly to enter the country : Upper Germany had been entirely subdued : Lower Germany was now to become the theatre of war. The imperial general advanced along the banks of the Weser, and overran Calenberg, but made no great progress ; for Christian was an able commander, and the Danes proved themselves, on every occasion, brave and determined soldiers. Tilly applied for reinforcements ; but the Emperor had none to send. Ferdinand had, from the commencement, carried on the war, principally with the forces of Maximilian and the Catholic League, and even Tilly, who commanded their army, was a Bavarian general. This entire dependence on the good will of others, was not altogether pleasing to the Emperor, whose views of conquest gradually expanded with success; but the long-continued contest had so completely exhausted his resources, that he found it impossible to remedy the evil. The few troops at his disposal, were employed in watching the movements of Bethlem Gabor, and preserving tranquillity in the newly reconquered provinces; and he was too poor to augment their number.

It was under these circumstances, that Wallenstein came forward with a proposal, which placed the lofty and aspiring nature of his genius in full view. And the same man, who only a few years before, had been an humble candidate for some subordinate situation about court, now undertook, what kings could not effect, and offered to raise and equip at his own expense, an army of 50,000 men. Many laughed at the proposal, as altogether chimerical; while others thought there might be danger in confiding so much power, to an individual of Wallenstein's haughty and peculiar disposition. Even the Emperor hesitated, and wished to limit the strength of the army to half the number; but Wallenstein cut the matter short, by declaring that " twenty thousand men would die of hunger, whereas fifty thousand would enable him to raise contributions at pleasure;" and as the troops were wanted, the conditions were soon agreed upon. The new commander was allowed to nominate his own officers, and was, besides, empowered to reward himself and his followers, out of the property that might be confiscated in the conquered countries. On this occasion, he is first styled General : in his commission he is called " Colonel General, and Field Captain," and is promised a salary of 6000 florins per month.

No sooner had districts, for assembling the troops, been assigned, than adventurers, allured by the fame of Wallenstein's liberality, flocked, from far and near, to his standard.   Light horsemen came from Poland, Croats from Hungary, and heavy-armed Cuirassiers from Belgium and the Netherlands.   The new commander made no distinction of religion or country : all who were promising soldiers, were gladly received ; so that by the end of a month, he had already 20,000 men under arms.   Leaving Eger on the 3d of September 1625, he soon afterwards appeared, at the head of 30,000 men, on the frontiers of Lower Saxony.   This army, if we believe the report of an officer who saw it, and gave an account of its appearance to the Duke of Wolfenbüttle, bore at first no inconsiderable resemblance to Sir John Falstaff's celebrated corps.   The men are described as being mostly in rags, greatly dissatisfied for want of pay, the cavalry wretchedly mounted, and almost destitute of arms.   They must have made good use of their time and opportunities, for we soon afterwards find them distinguished for all the splendour that characterised the soldiers of the time.

The Duke of Wolfenbüttle's agent says, that " all the regiments had been raised at the expense of the officers who had received no money from the Emperor."   But as Ferdinand allowed 600,000 florins levy money for every regiment of infantry,—about 3000 men,—we may easily form an idea of the immense sums that Wallenstein, and others, would ultimately have to claim for embodying and supporting such numerous armies.   How these matters were settled we do not exactly understand. The troops always lived at free quarters, and raised vast sums in the countries through which they passed ; and yet we find enormous accounts rendered to the government for the support of the men, as well as for supplies of arms, clothing and ammunition. That the Emperor could not be deceived on these points is evident ; because complaints were constantly made of the sums levied by the troops, and he was too careful of his own money, to allow double payments, even where one payment was made at the expense of others.

If Wallenstein's soldiers were not at first overwell equipped, it is evident that he knew how to render them useful : for at Göttingen he already defeated the corps sent against him by the Duke of Brunswick-Lünenburg, and then placed himself in communication with Count Tilly. He took good care, however, to keep at a distance from that general, as he had no intention to share, with any one, the glory he might acquire in the field. No sooner, indeed, had he entered Saxony, than differences, respecting rank and precedence, arose between the two commanders. The Emperor would not decide the question ; and only recommended a continued good understanding, which, as far as correspondence went, seems always to have existed between them ; but fortunately for their enemies, the two armies never joined.

The King of Denmark finding himself threatened by such formidable adversaries, made advances towards a negotiation for peace. The allied generals readily met these proposals ; but the attempt only tended to shew the dictatorial and domineering tone which Wallenstein already thought himself entitled to assume. As the Danish and Saxon forces were still unbroken, the King and the states considered themselves strong enough to demand, that " the imperial troops should immediately be withdrawn from the territory of the Circle : that the Emperor should pay the expenses of the war, and give full security for the maintenance of the civil and religious liberty of the Protestant states."

To these demands, which were positive enough, Wallenstein replied immediately, and to the following effect : " It is for the Emperor and not for the Saxons to give laws. They, the latter, and not the Emperor, must be the first to disband their troops. The King of Denmark and his army must leave Germany. The disbanded Saxon soldiers are not to be given to the outlawed Mansfeld, nor to the Duke of Brunswick ; and the former must, without delay, quit the territory of the empire. Neither the King of Denmark nor the Circle of Lower Saxony are, for the future, to undertake any thing, directly or indirectly, against the Emperor and his faithful states : nor shall the Circle be allowed to levy troops, unless by the express permission of the court of Vienna. The King of Denmark and the states of the Circle are to defray all expenses of the war ; and when security for the fulfilment of these conditions is given, then, and not till then, will the imperial troops be disbanded *."

With views so opposite, supported, on both sides, by unbroken forces, no friendly arrangement could

---

* Kevenhüller, vol. x. p. 888.

be expected. The war continued : the country was ravaged in every direction ; towns and castles were taken and retaken ; but no very decisive action was fought. The armies of the period were too dependent upon casual and accidental supplies, to pursue regular and systematic plans of operation. They were frequently obliged to disperse, when they should have united, and compelled to march in directions, exactly opposite to those in which success could best have been achieved.

Wallenstein evidently strove to remedy this dependence on uncertain supplies ; for during the whole course of these campaigns, he is constantly urging his agent in Bohemia, a gentleman of the name of Taxis, who is termed " Landhauptman," or captain of the district, to forward stores and provision for the troops. Sometimes the general orders corn to be sent down the Elbe, sometimes flour : at other times boots and shoes are to be made, " and carefully tied together, pair and pair, in order to prevent mistakes in the distribution." Cloth and linen are to be bought ; arms, matches and powder are to be got ready. His own vassals always to have the preference in making and supplying the articles, which are to be paid for in ready money. He desires to have no profit himself on the business ; but directs the accounts to be well and regularly kept, so that he may call upon the Emperor for payment.

Wallenstein appears, from these letters, to have been, not only commander-in-chief, but adjutant, quartermaster, and commissary-general also. The agent Taxis, is often reminded to be careful of money ;

but when Wallenstein is himself in debt, he constantly urges for prompt payment to his creditors;
being always in dread of losing his credit. A debt
due to the house of De Witt at Hamburgh, presses for
a long time upon his mind, and he complains of it in
at least twenty letters. While in the field, he also
desires coin to be struck, which is evidently to give
him a name for wealth and liberality. " Coin away
as fast as you can," he writes to Taxis; " I only
want credit and no profit by the coin ; but must have
the 30,000 ducats ready before the end of the year."
He is also very particular about the die, and does not
know what could have put " Dominus protector
meus " into Taxis's head, as his, Wallenstein's motto
is, " Invita invidia."

The ducats were coined out of " gold chains and
other effects," furnished by the banking house of De
Witt ; but the question is still, where did the wealth
come from ? Independently of his largesses and enormous expenses, Wallenstein occasionally advances
money to the imperial treasury, and pays, at this
time, two hundred thousand crowns for the Duchy
of Sagan, which he had purchased in addition to his
other domains. Over this principality the Emperor
offered to make him lord superior ; but he preferred
holding it by feudal tenure. To refute Schiller's
assertion, that the Duke of Friedland levied sixty
thousand millions of crowns in Germany, during the
seven years of his first command, would only be a
waste of words. No sum of this kind could be raised
in the country, rich as it certainly was ; and though
we have evidence to show that vast sums were ex-

torted by the troops, it is not clear that Wallenstein
ever received any part of the unworthy spoil; for we
constantly find him drawing money from his principalities, and never remitting any.   On two occasions
he even refuses, with apparent disdain, to accept portions of certain contributions which his second in
command had set aside for him; and orders the
money to be very openly employed in forwarding
some naval armament then in progress; " as the
world," he says, " would speak ill of him were he
suspected of applying such sums to his own use."
Wallenstein was as much above his contemporaries
as above the princes and marshals, who, in our own
time, " played such fantastic tricks before high
heaven," as to make even Fortune blush for the rapacity of the ignoble minions she had raised to thrones,
power and command.

   The letters which he writes during these campaigns throw no new light upon any point of history;
but they furnish curious proofs of his clear and ever
active mind.   The subjects that occupy his attention
seem endless; and from the most important to the
most trifling, they are all treated with order and dis-
tinctness.   These letters, so various in their contents,
are, of course, addressed to various persons.   One
letter, after giving instructions about silk-worms and
mulberry trees, which he had imported from Italy,
in order to establish silk manufactories,—concludes
with directions for building additional powder-mills,
" to keep the army well supplied with ammunition."   Sometimes they are about public, sometimes
about private affairs: parks, palaces and plantations;

buildings, decorations and improvements of all kind, occupy his attention even in the field ; and the works which he commands to be made, are upon a scale of imperial magnificence.   A vast number of the letters relate to military matters and the movements of troops : many are about politics and alliances.   Taxis sometimes receives instruction to give money to certain distressed persons, and during a year of scarcity, Wallenstein orders the poor of his principalities to be furnished with bread at a reduced price.

No less than five and twenty of these letters are occasionally despatched in one day, many of them written with his own hand.   The orders and directions which they contain are invariably distinct, and can never be misunderstood by those to whom they are addressed : nor does he ever use the ambiguous expressions that admit of being construed according to after circumstances.   His style is concise ; and as good, perhaps, as was consistent with the hard and intractable German of the period.   In the seventeenth century, the German language had evinced nothing but the rude elements of that power which it has since displayed.   To the philologer, its strength might, even then, have been apparent, but its pliancy and grandeur, could hardly have been imagined : its infancy was that of the gnarled oak only, promising the force, indeed, but not the beauty of the majestic tree which is now developing its far-spreading boughs before us ; and displaying a luxuriance of foliage which the foresters have, as yet, shown themselves but indifferently qualified to shape and form.

When full allowance is made for the treasures of

German literature, and these treasures are great, it must still be confessed, that the richness of the language has, strange as it may appear, greatly injured that literature.   It has given a facility of composition, of which men have availed themselves who had, in fact, nothing to communicate ; and it has enabled ordinary writers to overload poor and meagre sentiments, with an exuberance of well-rounded, full-sounding sentences, that too often impose upon the reader, and obtain for the mere obscurity resulting from an absence of clear and well-defined ideas, a reputation for depth and power, which learning and talent are alone supposed capable of appreciating.

Wallenstein's handwriting is large and plain ; and his letters, written in the German character, would still pass for good specimens of calligraphy : he somewhere, indeed, expresses great contempt for persons who are too fine to write intelligibly.   The many Latin phrases and quotations which he uses, show that he was not so very inapt a scholar as his biographers assert : his orthography is, however, careless, and he never punctuates.

It is rather singular, that among all the letters of Wallenstein which have been handed down to us, there is not one addressed to his Duchess.   Whenever he mentions her in writing to others, it is always with affection ; and the legacies bequeathed to her by his will, and by codicils at different times affixed to it, are, in his usual style, splendid and munificent.   This testament is, in all respects, in full keeping with his character ; and there is much more of real character evinced in testaments than might at

first be supposed. How often do we see these unhappy documents displaying the pride, fear, ha.. .d,
envy or servility it had been the object, perhaps, of
a long life to conceal, and exhibit, after death, all
the poor and ignoble feelings which had lingered to
the end in the dark recesses of the heart, and which
the grave should, in mercy, have buried along with
the last remnants of feeble mortality.

On what terms Wallenstein lived with his wife, we
have no means of knowing ; but it is evident tha' he
always behaved to her with kindness and atte.ition.
On one occasion, it appears that a criminal was pardoned at her intercession ; and, from the Duchess's
letters, it is equally evident that she was greatly
attached to him. She writes to him, indeed, as all
the ladies of the seventeenth century seem to have
written to their husbands, with a degree of distant
and respectful submission, that would now appear a
little extraordinary ; but there is nevertheless, much
feminine gentleness and tenderness concealed beneath the formal reserve which the manners of the
period commanded ; and it is clear, that the good
Duchess would have written with great affection, if
she had dared. We have little to say of this lady in
our work ; but we record her attachment to her lord,
because the love of a truly virtuous woman must
always redound to the honour of the man who long
remains its object.

What were the reasons that prevented the imperial generals from uniting, in order, at once, to crush
the King of Denmark by the superiority of their
combined forces, we have no means of knowing,

unless we ascribe it to jealousy between them, or to
the difficulty of finding, on one line of march, supplies for such numerous armies. Certain it is, that
they kept at a distance from each other ; for on the
opening of the next campaign, we find Tilly occupied on the banks of the Weser, and Wallenstein on
the banks of the Elbe.

The Duke of Friedland, to command the passage
of the river, had secured the bridge of Dessau, and
fort'~ed it by strong redoubts, erected on the right
bank. Count Mansfeld attacked this post, without
success, on the first and eleventh of April, and again
advanced to renew the assault on the twenty-fifth.
Wallenstein, aware of his approach, caused the bridge
to be hung over with sails, passed the river unobserved with his whole army, sallied from the works and
totally routed the Condottieri, who are said to have
lost 9000 men in the action. The indefatigable
Mansfeld fled, unpursued, into the sands of Brandenburg, where he soon recovered from the effects
of his overthrow ; for in the month of June, he re-
appeared in the field, at the head of 20,000 men.
This sudden augmentation of force, is ascribed, by
German writers, to reinforcements received from
England ; and, on the second of April, Wallenstein
writes to the Emperor, saying, that " 6000 British
soldiers, intended for Mansfeld's army, were reported
to have landed at Hamburgh." There is, nevertheless, great reason to doubt these statements ; for all
the British auxiliaries, of which we know any thing,
were serving, at this time, under the immediate orders

of the King, or under the command of Colonel Morgan, on the banks of the Weser.

Be this, however, as it may, Mansfeld began operations in June, and directed his march through Silesia, for the purpose of joining Bethlem Gabor in Hungary ; whence the combined armies were to advance upon the Austrian capital. It was a bold plan ; and was no sooner known at Vienna, than orders were despatched to Wallenstein, commanding him to hasten after the Condottieri, and to protect the Emperor's hereditary dominions from attack. Remonstrances and representations were vain ; the general was forced to obey, and sustained, as he had foreseen, great losses in his rapid march across the Carpathian mountains, where few supplies could be found, and where none could follow.

Mansfeld, though closely pursued, and contending against a thousand difficulties, forced his way into Hungary, where Bethlem Gabor, in the expectation that a favourable diversion would be made from Lower Saxony, and that considerable subsidies would be sent from England, had again taken the field, supported by the troops of the neighbouring Turkish Pachas. But Mansfeld, instead of bringing English subsidies along with him, brought Wallenstein's army in his train, and solicited money instead of supplying it ; and the Transylvanians, unable to effect any thing under such adverse circumstances, hastened, as usual, to conclude a truce, till a more favourable opportunity for renewing the war should present itself. Mansfeld, thus forsaken by his ally, resigned his troops to Prince Ernest of Weimar, who

led them back into Silesia.   He, himself, set out for
Venice, in hopes of obtaining aid from the Republic,
but died on his way, at Wrakowitz in Dalmatia ;
having only, by a few weeks, survived his pupil,
and comrade in arms, Prince Christian of Brunswick.
The actions of these men had been attended with
too much cruelty, and depended too much upon deeds
of rapine and oppression, to be looked upon as great
or laudable, however extraordinary they must ever
appear.

Wallenstein having placed his diminished army in
winter quarters along the banks of the Danube, proceeded to Vienna, to make preparations for the en-
suing campaign, and, as it would seem, to make friends
also ; for complaints, if not actual charges, had been
preferred against him.   The loss sustained by the
army in its march over the Carpathian mountains,
furnished the ostensible grounds for these complaints :
the devastation of some domains belonging to Prince
Lichtenstein and Count Dietrichstein, was however
believed to be the real cause.

It was easy for Wallenstein to clear himself of all
blame respecting the march into Hungary, as the expedition had been undertaken contrary to his advice,
and against his strongly urged representation.   How
he settled with Counts and Princes we do not know ;
but he equipped and reformed his army in a manner
which was striking when compared to the dilatory
mode of proceeding then in use.   The contrast is so
admirably drawn by Schiller, in a speech which he
puts into the mouth of Count Isolan, one of Wallen-

stein's generals, that we transcribe the passage from
Mr Moir's excellent translation of the great drama :

> " I never shall forget—seven years ago,
> When to Vienna I was sent, to obtain
> Remounts of horses for our cavalry,
> How, from one antechamber to another,
> They turned me round and round, and left me standing
> Beneath the threshold, ay, for hours together.
> At last a capuchin was sent to me ;
> I thought, God wot, it must be for my sins.
> Not so—but this, sir, was the man with whom
> I was to drive a bargain for my horses.
> I was compelled to go with nothing done ;
> And in three days the Duke procured for me
> What in Vienna thirty failed to gain."

During Wallenstein's absence in Hungary, Tilly
had completely defeated the King of Denmark at
Luther-am-Baremberg. Terror immediately seized
upon the Protestants. The states of Mecklenburg
forced their Dukes to renounce the Danish alliance,
and submit to the Emperor ; from whom, as their
lord superior, they at once discovered that they had
nothing to dread. The states of Holstein followed
the same example, and the Elector of Brandenburg
persisted in remaining neutral, though totally destitute of the means requisite for maintaining that
neutrality. The Elector applied, indeed, to the provincial states for money to raise the troops necessary
for the protection of the country ; but they declared
" that troops were no longer wanted : the country
had," they said, " been most shamefully plundered
by Mansfeld's bands, and by Danish soldiers, who
without leave had traversed it in every direction ;

and as these marauders were now happily gone, nothing more was to be dreaded ; least of all from the
Emperor, with whom they had always been on good
terms."

In one place, the love of peace was pleaded, as
an excuse for submission ; in another, the deference
due to the Emperor, the natural head of the empire:
one set of men pretended, that the expense of maintaining armies, exceeded the benefit derived from
the protection which they afforded ; some asserted
that resistance was vain ; and many declared that
peaceful states and peaceful subjects had nothing to
dread from any quarter. " Let us behave with justice
to all men," said these profound philosophers, " and
all men will behave with justice to us." This brilliant reasoning, which was, of course, nothing but a
cloak for cowardice and avarice, the consequences of
which we shall see presently, is deserving of particular notice, owing to the striking resemblance it bears
to the logic so often heard in our own country. In
reading the decisions of the German Protestant
states, or parliaments, of the seventeenth century, we
may, at times, fancy ourselves reading speeches delivered in the British Senate during our own time :
a proof that absolute wisdom belongs to no particular
age, or country.

Wallenstein opened the campaign of 1627, at the
head of a refreshed and well-equipped army of 40,000
men. His first effort was directed against Silesia ;
and the Danish troops, few in number, and ill commanded, gave way at his approach. To prevent the
fugitives from infringing on the neutrality of Bran-

denburg, he occupied the whole electorate. Mecklenburg and Pomerania soon shared the same fate. Remonstrances and assurances of perfect neutrality, were treated with absolute scorn ; and Wallenstein declared, in his usual haughty style, that " the time had arrived for dispensing altogether with electors ; and that Germany ought to be governed like France and Spain, by a single and absolute sovereign." In his rapid march towards the frontiers of Holstein, he acted fully up to the principle he had laid down, and naturally exercised despotic power, as the representative of the absolute monarch of whom he spoke. Too proud to share with another the honours of victory, he caused Tilly to be sent across the Elbe, to watch the frontiers of Holland. He himself followed up the Danes, defeated their armies in a series of actions near Heiligenhausen, overran the whole peninsula of Jutland before the end of the campaign, and forced the unhappy King to seek shelter, with the wrecks of his army, in the islands beyond the Belt.

The sea at last arrested Wallenstein's progress ; and his biographers assert, that, indignant at finding himself checked, he ordered red-hot shot to be fired into the rebellious element which had thus set bound to his conquests. The repetition of these puerile tales proves how the character of this celebrated person has been misrepresented ; for the writers who could ascribe such conduct to the Duke of Friedland, were evidently incapable of appreciating the mind and genius of the man whose life they attempted to describe.

Brilliant as the campaign of 1627 proved in its

general result, few very striking feats of arms were
performed during its progress. Three of these we
are bound, however, to mention : two, because they
were performed by our own countrymen, who have
been so unjustly treated, in Schiller's great history
of the Thirty years' War ; and the third, because it
stands alone of its kind in military annals.

Along with some other field-works, which the King
of Denmark had thrown up near Boizenburg, was a
bridgehead on the left bank of the Elbe. When the
Danes fell back before Tilly's army, these works were
all either carried by the Imperialists, or abandoned
by their defenders. The bridgehead alone, garri-
soned by four companies of Scottish infantry, under
the command of Major Dunbar, made resistance.
And so effectually did the brave defenders perform
their duty, that they forced the imperial general to
raise the siege, though he had actually broken ground
before a mere redoubt, and attempted three regular
assaults in the course of four days. "The Scots," says
an eye-witness, "fought with the butt ends of their
muskets ; and when their ammunition was expended,
they threw sand into the eyes of the assailants, and
wanting better missiles, made even good use of stones."
These gallant men were not yet encumbered with
bayonets, to impress on their minds the necessity of
yielding, the moment the object contended for was
no longer to be obtained by firing.

At the period of which we are speaking, most of
the seats of the Holstein nobility retained the appearance, and something also of the strength, of the old
baronial castles of the middle ages. But though the

owners had refused to pay for the support of troops, on the plea that they were the natural protectors of the country ; one only of these strongholds made the least resistance, and that was defended, not by Holstein nobles, but by Scottish soldiers. The castle of Breitenburg, belonging to the ancient family of Ranzau, was occupied by Major Dunbar with his four companies : it was surrounded only by an old, ill-flanked wall, and by a ditch which had long been more than half filled up : but gallant men find bulwarks of strength where the feeble see only untenable ruins. To give the unhappy peasantry as much time for flight as possible, the Major, at first, spread his troops over as great an extent of country as he could cover : when closely pressed, he withdrew within the castle, where a six days' cannonade followed. The defences of the place were completely levelled ; but the courage of the defenders remained unshaken. On the seventh day the assault was given ; and to the defenders an assault in those days was a different affair altogether from what it is now : such attacks were then made by heavy-armed infantry, who wore breastplates and skull-caps of proof, and were armed, not with useless bayonets, but with swords, halberts and partisans. The defenders were equally well prepared ; and knowing that certain death was the consequence of defeat, they never stood an assault without making a most determined resistance ; even in the breach itself.

In modern times, if the assailants pass through the storm of fiery missiles hurled upon them from every direction ; if they ascend the breach and pass over

the defences, always, when there is time and skill,
raised behind the ruins, then every thing is settled ;
the defenders fly for shelter and implore mercy : no
manly contest takes place between modern infantry ;
every thing is effected by distant firing. Since the
introduction of bayonets, the Turks alone have defended their towns and fortresses hand to hand, in
gallant and manly style ; and the terrible price paid
for the capture of Ockzacow and Ismailow, the only
places thus taken from them, seems to have cooled
the ardour of their enemies for the renewal of such
contests.

On the occasion of which we are speaking, the
fiercest of Wallenstein's Walloon bands made the
onset against the castle ; they were driven back with
great loss ; a second attack was foiled in like manner by the dauntless courage of the defenders ; a
third, made with fresh troops and redoubled fury,
found the Scots, exhausted by toil, wounds and fa-
tigue, unable to resist the shock. The victors, exasperated by the loss which they had sustained, gave
no quarter : every person found in the castle was put
to death ; and the body of Dunbar, its gallant de-
fender, who had fallen in front rank, was mangled
in the most barbarous manner. But the unworthy
treatment of a dead body, lessened not the fame
which a brave soldier had so nobly purchased with
his life ; and the resolute defence of the feeble castle
of Breitenburg against a whole army, will ever prove
how much one gallant spirit may effect in war. The
name of Major Dunbar is still remembered with
honour in the country where he fell ; and it should

not be forgotten in the land of his birth, which may
be justly proud of his conduct. Independently of
the pleasure there is at all times, in recording the
actions of the brave, it is the duty of an English
writer, who speaks of the Thirty years' War, and
above all of Wallenstein, to collect and place in the
most conspicuous view, as many of the noble deeds
of arms performed by his countrymen, as can be
brought within the compass of his subject : we must
strive to find, in their military glory, some compen-
sation for the foul blot we shall see British hands in-
flicting on the name and fame of our country.

The singular manner in which Wolfenbüttle was
taken, has now to be related.

Tilly had caused this place, which was of some
strength, and was defended by a numerous garrison
under Count Solmes, to be invested at the very commencement of the campaign. The bravery of the defenders foiled all the attacks, and the siege was twice
raised. At last Pappenheim appeared before the
town. The approach of the bad season, and the
want of a sufficient battering train, soon convinced
him that the place was not to be taken by regular
siege. But the truly great man, and such was Pappenheim, is seldom at a loss. Obstacles only tend to
call forth his energy and augment his exertions ; his
genius supplies him with resources, which the ordinary observer no longer perceives, the moment they
are to be sought for beyond the rules of professional
science ; and Pappenheim, finding himself unable
to reduce Wolfenbüttle by the strength of fire, determined to reduce it by the strength of water. For

this purpose, he erected a stop-water across the river Ocker, close below the town; and though Count Solmes used every effort by sallies, and by a heavy fire of artillery, to destroy the work, it proved completely successful. At the expiration of fourteen days, the water had risen to such a height, as completely to fill the streets and the lower stories of the houses, so that all communication, as well between the different parts of the town, as between the town and the works, had to be carried on in boats, and the brave governor was forced to yield to an adversary, whose genius could make even the elements contribute to the execution of his designs *.

And now it was that the princes and states of Lower Germany began to feel the consequences of their pusillanimous conduct; and the very provinces which had just before refused to raise troops for their own protection, were obliged to submit without a murmur, to every species of insult and exaction. Wallenstein's army, augmented to a hundred thousand men, occupied the whole country; and the lordly leader following, on a far greater scale, the principle on which Mansfeld had acted, made the war maintain the war, and trampled alike on the rights of sovereigns and of subjects. And terrible was the penalty now paid for the short-sighted policy which avarice and cowardice had suggested, and which cunning had vainly tried to disguise beneath affected philanthropy, and a generous love of peace. Provided with imperial authority, and at the head of a force that

* Zur Geschichte Christian des IV. von Mauvillion.

could no longer be resisted, Wallenstein made the empire serve as a vast storehouse, and wealthy treasury for the benefit of the imperial army. He forbade even sovereigns and electors to raise supplies in their own countries, and was justly termed " the princes' scourge, and soldiers' idol."

The system of living by contributions had completely demoralised the troops. Honour and discipline were entirely gone ; and it was only beneath the eye of the stern and unrelenting commander, that any thing like order continued to be observed. Dissipation and profligacy reigned in all ranks : bands of dissolute persons accompanied every regiment, and helped to extinguish the last sparks of morality in the breast of the soldier. The generals levied arbitrary taxes ; the inferior officers followed the example of their superiors ; and the privates, soon ceasing to obey those whom they ceased to respect, plundered in every direction ; while blows, insults, or death awaited all who dared to resist. The celebrated Montecucoli demanded from the single province of New-Markt 30,000 florins a-month for the support of the twelve companies of his regiment, besides 1200 florins for his own table, 600 for the table of every lieutenant-colonel, and 5000 florins over and above for exigencies ; and as the authorities were able to raise only 25,000 florins, the rest was levied by main force. Other officers proceeded in a similar manner, each according to his rank and power.

The sums extorted, in this manner, prove that Germany must have been a wealthy country in the seventeenth century ; for the money pressed out of some districts, by the imperial troops, far exceeds any thing which the same quarters could now be made to furnish. Complaints against the author of such evils were, of course, not wanting; but the man complained of, had rendered the Emperor all-powerful in Germany: from the Adriatic to the Baltic, Ferdinand reigned absolute, as no monarch had reigned since the days of the Othos. This supremacy was due to Wallenstein alone; and what could the voice of the humble and oppressed effect against such an offender? Or when did the voice of suffering nations, arrest the progress of power and ambition?

During the winter that followed on the campaign of 1627, Wallenstein repaired to Prague, to claim from the Emperor, who was residing in the Bohemian capital, additional rewards for the important services so lately rendered. The boon solicited was nothing less than the Duchy of Mecklenburg, which was to be taken from its legitimate princes, on the ground of their having joined the King of Denmark, and bestowed on the successful general. There were not wanting persons in the imperial council who opposed this grant. It was unjust, they said, to deprive the Dukes of Mecklenburg of their hereditary dominions, on account of a fault, already repented of, and, to a certain extent, even atoned for: and it might also be dangerous, to bestow such power on a person of Wallenstein's aspiring disposition. Others maintained, that the services which he had rendered could not be too highly rewarded; and that it would, besides, be an act of piety to rescue so fine a province as Mecklenburg from heretical hands, and bring it back, by means of a Catholic prince, into the bosom of the Catholic Church.

This last argument, supported by an account of three millions of florins, which Wallenstein claimed as arrears due for the support of the army, determined Ferdinand. By letters-patent, dated Prague, 1st February 1628, the Dukes of Mecklenburg are declared to have forfeited their dominions ; " because they had entered into an alliance with the King of Denmark ; cast all good advice to the winds ; conspired against the empire ; and helped to bring even Turks and infidels upon its soil." The states and the people are freed from their former allegiance, and the Duchy, with all the rights thereto belonging, " transferred to the Duke of Friedland, his heirs and successors ; who are to hold it in pledge for the repayment of certain war expenses," which were never expected to be offered or accepted. Though Wallenstein entered immediately into possession of this splendid acquisition, and strove to gain the good will of his new subjects by relieving them, as much as possible, from the burdens consequent on the support of troops, it was not till the year following, that he was actually created Duke of Mecklenburg, and began to assume the title.

We have seen, that even in the field, and when weighed down by the heavy load of business which necessarily presses upon the commander of an army engaged in active operations, he never lost sight of the administration of his own principalities. From the camp he was constantly sending directions about the improvement of his domains, and when at home,

in the midst of such pursuits, he is as constantly
sending orders to the army, on the most important
points of military duty and discipline.

The letters written at this period are the most
curious of those handed down to us. They are mostly
addressed to Colonel Arnheim, who had been left in
command of the army, and who seems to have possessed Wallenstein's entire confidence ; and the manner in which he illustrates the trust that should be
placed in officers holding high military situations, is
too striking to be passed over. In a letter to Arnheim, dated 2d July 1628, is the following passage :
" Count Piccolomini informs me that a Swedish
admiral has come to Stralsund, on purpose to speak
with you, but that you decline meeting him, on the
ground of having no authority from me to hold such
a conference. Your present situation shows how perfect is the confidence I repose in you ; and those to
whom we intrust the command of armies, may surely
be allowed to hold conversation with an adversary."

Before the acquisition of Mecklenburg is distinctly
mentioned, he desires Arnheim not to permit a single
man of Tilly's army to be quartered in the Duchies ;
adding, in strict " *secretezza*," " that they,"—the
Duke of Bavaria and Tilly,—" have designs upon
the country." He then recommends that information for charges against the Dukes of Mecklenburg
may be collected, as reports of " strange practices
have come to his ears ;" and, at a later period, desires
that both princes may be frightened, or, if necessary,
forced out of the country.

No sooner had the King of Poland notified to him

the truce concluded with Sweden, on the 9th of October 1627, than he foresees the storm which, from that quarter, was destined to burst upon the empire. He immediately directs Arnheim to " keep a sharp look-out." " We shall certainly," he says, " have the Swedes landing on the coast of Pomerania or Mecklenburg." In a second letter, written on the same day, are these ominous words : " Gustavus Adolphus is a dangerous guest, who cannot be too closely watched." Wallenstein here shews himself no bad prophet, or judge of character ; and from this moment he never loses sight of the King of Sweden. He is willing, indeed, to enter into an alliance with him, and gives a friendly reception to some advances, which had come from Oxenstiern ; but foretells, from the first, that they will lead to nothing. " The King of Sweden will only play with us ; he means us no good," are Wallenstein's usual words.

Most men are certainly endowed, at times, with prophetic feeling ; or they are open to receive, from the shadows of coming events, impressions that indicate the figure, form, or nature of approaching changes. Such at least appears to have been the case with Wallenstein : he never, from first to last, mentions the King of Sweden except with evident marks of dislike and mistrust : even when trying to gain him over by the most flattering proposals, some dark foreboding tells him that the star of Friedland is doomed to wane before the star of Gustavus. Yet were the offers made to the Scandinavian monarch well calculated to tempt a young, ambitious sovereign, eager for fame and extended rule. He was invited to join in the

war against Denmark, and conquer Norway, which,
together with some other provinces, not specified,
were to form his share of the spoil. It is highly
to the honour of the King of Sweden that he ultimately rejected these proposals ; for he had good
cause to complain of the Danes, and had, on his first
accession to the throne, been forced to purchase, at
great sacrifices, a most disadvantageous peace from
Christian IV.

Another, and more extraordinary project occupies, about this time, the ever active mind of the
Duke of Friedland. Reports had reached Prague
that the Danes, irritated by the losses sustained during the war, as well as by the burdens which it continued to impose upon them, were dissatisfied with
their King, and anxious to place another Prince on
the throne. Wallenstein instantly sends orders for
Arnheim to encourage the disaffected ; and to use
every effort to secure the crown for Ferdinand. Letter after letter is dispatched on this business. In
one he says, " I yesterday spoke to the Emperor
about it; and you may depend upon being well rewarded for your exertions : you are, I assure you, in high
favour." In another, he says, *en passant,* " At court
they would willingly have given me this crown ; but
I should not be able to maintain myself on the
throne; and am well satisfied with what I have."
Not even the prospect of a crown could blind Wallenstein ; and where is the other man of whom so
much can be said ?

In continuing the negotiation, he promises, " on
his word of honour," that the Danes shall retain all

their rights and privileges, provided they choose Ferdinand for their King ; adding, by way of threat, however, that " they must of course become our vassals, if we subdue them by force of arms." This, like the Swedish negotiation, ended in nothing ; but if undertaken with the view of deceiving Wallenstein for the purpose of making him relinquish his military preparations, it failed completely. A Count Swarzenberg, a diplomatic agent of the court of Vienna, appears to have been the principal mover of the intrigue. He afterwards, when in some official situation about the army, incurred the displeasure of Wallenstein, who, in a very peremptory manner, made the Emperor recall him, leaving his Imperial Majesty no choice, but to dispense with the services of his successful general or of his unsuccessful diplomatist.

Hitherto the ocean had alone arrested the progress of Wallenstein : a fleet was now to be formed, which should enable him to give laws beyond the Belts, and perhaps beyond the Baltic also. Every seaport in Mecklenburg and Pomerania is ordered to be taken possession of and fortified. Ships are collected from all quarters ; some are to be armed, others are to serve as transports. During Wallenstein's stay in Bohemia, he is constantly pressing this subject upon Arnheim's attention. " Whatever is now done," he says, " must be done by sea." Napoleon himself was not more anxious for " ships, colonies and commerce," than Wallenstein was at this time for ships, arsenals and seaports. He soon afterwards assumes the title of " Admiral on the Ocean and the Baltic ;" and having obtained from Spain the promise of twenty-five ships of war, together with a supply of money, he says in a letter, that he " soon hopes to seek out the Danes in their very islands." But he still dreads the Swedes; and desires Arnheim to obtain for him a more perfect horoscope of Gustavus Adolphus than the one which had, it seems, been already furnished. Wallenstein gives good astrological reasons for requiring the additional information which he specifies; but we are nowhere told what the royal nativity ultimately indicated; nor is the subject ever again alluded to; a proof perhaps, that Wallenstein only amused himself with astrology; for whatever idea seriously occupies his mind, is always followed up with great spirit, and may be as constantly traced through a long and rapid succession of letters.

Thus, we find him at this period, projecting the destruction of the Danish and Swedish fleets: he proposes to have them burned; and the plan occupies his attention for a long time. And though he is, at the moment, so poor, that he cannot, by his own account, command 1000 florins, and actually sells an estate to Colonel Hebron, merely to raise a little ready money, he nevertheless offers 35,000 crowns for the performance of this extraordinary service. Arnheim is desired to spare neither trouble nor expense in effecting the desirable object: and a Scotchman, whose name is not mentioned, actually obtains, more ingeniously perhaps than honestly, the sum of 5000 crowns for some purpose connected with the undertaking. It appears that the man died before any thing was attempted.

Nor was Wallenstein, though absent, inattentive

to the discipline of the army.   He sends frequent
and severe orders on the subject ; and desires that all
delinquents, of whatever rank ; may be punished in
the most exemplary manner, even with death when
the law ordains it. These orders seem to have fallen
with peculiar force upon the Italians, who only speak
of him as *il tiranno ;* and some of their countrymen,
Count Montecucoli, Caraffa, and the Marquis di
Boisy, are particularly mentioned among the delinquents.

CHAPTER III.

THE siege of Stralsund, which was resolved upon early
in 1628, constitutes one of the most memorable
operations of the war. Not merely because it furnishes an additional proof of what may be effected by
skill, courage and resolution, against vastly superior
forces, but because its result influenced, in an eminent degree, some of the most important events that
followed. When Wallenstein ordered the seaports
along the coast of Pomerania to be occupied, Stralsund, claiming its privilege as an imperial and Han-
seatic free town, refused to admit his troops. Arnheim, who, as regular gradations were not much
attended to at the period, had been promoted, at
one step, from Colonel to Field-Marshal *, pressed
and threatened ; but in vain : the citizens remained
firm, and began to improve the fortifications of the
place. Wallenstein easily saw the importance of
Stralsund, and desired Arnheim not to yield the
point.   " These rascals of Stralsund," he writes,
" will prevent us from making peace in Germany,

---

* In the 17th century the rank of Field-Marshal corresponded,
however, rather to the French rank of *Marshal-de-camp*, than to the
Field-Marshal Commander-in-Chief of our own time : a Lieutenant-
General was superior to a Field-Marshal.

and leading the army against the Turks, a measure
to which the Pope and the Emperor have already
consented.   There are, I know, many persons who
desire to draw the war *a la longa*, but, by the help
of God, I have counteracted their schemes." This
Turkish war was another favourite plan of his; but
he sees no means, except the complete occupation of
the coast, that can prevent the Swedes from invading
the Empire, while the army is engaged against the
infidels.

Stralsund, strong from position, and having a fine
harbour, is situated on the Baltic, opposite the isle
of Rugen.   It is built in form of a triangle; one side
of which is washed by the sea, while the others are,
to a certain extent, defended by lagoons or salt
marshes, that can be passed only on three causeways
leading to gates of the town.   The fortifications consisted, at the time, of an inner wall, flanked by bastions, and of a double line of exterior redoubts.   The
garrison was, at first, composed of only 150 soldiers,
but there were 2000 citizens capable of bearing arms.
After a good deal of negotiation, which only cost the
people of Stralsund some large sums of money, paid
away in presents to the imperial officers, Arnheim
invested the place on the 7th of May with 8000 men.
The senate and the wealthier classes immediately took
the alarm, and proposed to purchase pardon by instantly surrendering the town.   Not so the citizens
and lower orders: composed in a great measure of
sailors and seafaring persons, endowed with the daring
and energy that men so generally acquire by a long
familiarity with the ocean and its dangers, they

would hear of no submission whatever. On the contrary, they claimed a share in the executive administration; and having carried this point, they passed a resolution that the walls should be defended to the last extremity. It soon became necessary to act up to this bold resolve; for danger, in its wildest form, was rapidly approaching.

Arnheim, in the hopes of coming to an amicable arrangement with the senate, had carried on his first operations very slowly; but he no sooner found himself deceived in his expectations, than, on the 16th May, he assaulted the outworks, and made himself master of two redoubts. Another attack followed on the 23d, in which all the outworks were taken: and the town itself would, as tradition and grave historians alike assure us, have been carried two days afterwards, but for the presence of mind displayed by a citizen's wife.

It was Sunday; and the people of Stralsund, knowing that Arnheim was a Protestant, and believing him therefore, too good a Christian to break the Lord's day, had all repaired to church, without leaving a single centinel on the ramparts. By some happy chance, however, a lady was on the alert: she perceived that the enemy, instead of being engaged in acts of devotion, were actually advancing to the assault: seizing a drum that by good fortune was at hand, she beat to arms: the citizens rushed to the walls, and the attack was repulsed after a fierce and determined contest. Now, the sex have, avowedly, great merit,—greater merit, perhaps, than they generally get credit for: but in this particular instance,

we rather suspect that a compliment has been need-
lessly paid them, at the expense of the good citizens
of Stralsund. We can well conceive that a lady would
beat a drum, if necessary ; but we can hardly understand how the defenders of a besieged town should,
on the mere belief that the assailants were too pious
to fight on Sunday, abandon the ramparts without
leaving either watch or ward. Knowing how military
history has been written, in our own time, we must
not be surprised to find such tales occasionally handed
down to us from the seventeenth century.

Alarmed by these fierce and repeated assaults, the
inhabitants of Stralsund again resorted to negotiations ; but the arrival of three companies of Scottish,
and one company of German infantry, which the
King of Denmark sent to their aid, as quickly re-
vived their courage : a company of infantry counted
at the period, from 150 to 300 men. Wallenstein,
who was at the moment on his way to join the army,
also desires Arnheim to negotiate, but to conclude
nothing. " I want to put the people of Stralsund off
their guard," he says, " but shall not forgive them ;
I shall yet pay them home for all the trouble they
have given us." Hostilities were soon renewed, and
well it was for the besieged that they trusted more
to arms than to fine words and fair promises ; and
well it is for nations and communities that follow the
same rule. This intended treachery on the part of
Wallenstein, is the only low and unworthy act or intention that can be fairly brought home to him. It
was soon destined to meet with just retribution.

The town of Stralsund, unable to obtain assistance

from the Duke of Pomerania, the lord superior of
the province, who, however willing, had no means
of furnishing relief, placed itself under the protection of Sweden : and Gustavus Adolphus, fully sen-
sible of the importance of the place, immediately dispatched the celebrated David Leslie, at the head of
600 men, to aid in its defence. Count Brahe, with
1000 more, soon followed ; so that when Wallenstein reached the army on the 27th of June, he found
himself opposed by a garrison of experienced soldiers,
who had already retaken all the outworks which
Arnheim had captured in the first instance.

The lordly commander-in-chief announced his arrival before the town, by a general assault upon all the
outworks. The most important of these fell into the
hands of the Imperialists ; and the inner line itself,
would have been carried, but for the gallantry of
Colonel Munro, and the Scottish troops, who there
repulsed the assailants with great loss. The approaches were, however, brought so near the ramparts ; and so heavy a fire was opened upon the place,
that deputies, sent to solicit terms, soon made their
appearance in the imperial camp. Wallenstein,
though he only consented to suspend hostilities for
a quarter of an hour, received the parties in a very
frank and friendly manner, and on their representing
the dreadful state to which the bombardment had
reduced the town, asked them " Who had occasioned
the mischief ?"

The senate were, as usual, willing enough to submit ; Wallenstein had assembled nearly 20,000 men
round the place, and had declared that he would

take Stralsund " were it fastened with chains to heaven ;" and he was not a man to threaten in vain. As
the courage of the citizens also began to cool, an
armistice was, contrary to the opinion of foreign officers, agreed upon, in order that terms of submission
might be drawn up.

Difficulties having for some days retarded the progress of the negotiation, a Danish fleet appeared off
the harbour ; the defenders again took courage, and
sent out to say that they would enter into no terms,
unless the foreign troops consented to withdraw of
their own accord. " You see what the knaves now
tell me," was all that Wallenstein wrote on the mar-
gin of the letter which he sent to Arnheim, who happened to be absent at the moment. The attack was
of course renewed ; but the opportunity was lost.
Rain began to fall in such torrents that the trenches
were entirely filled, and the flat moor ground, on
which the army was encamped, became completely
inundated and untenable. The proud spirit of Friedland, unused to yield, still persevered ; but sickness
attacked the troops, and the Danes having landed at
Jasmund, he was obliged to march against them with
the best part of his forces ; and in fact to raise the
siege. From Gustrow he writes to Arnheim, " so to
manage matters that we may retire with credit ;" and
desires him to give out that the enterprise was abandoned, " solely with a view to oblige the Duke of
Pomerania."

The Danes having effected their object, in causing
the siege of Stralsund to be raised, withdrew their
troops from Jasmund, and landed them again at

Wolgast. Here, however, Wallenstein surprised, and defeated them with great loss, and would probably have destroyed their whole army, had not the castle held out, and secured the embarkation of the fugitives, who only reached their ships under the protection of its guns. This victory afforded, to his wounded spirit, some balm for the failure sustained in the late siege.

From Pomerania, Wallenstein went to Holstein, where he took Krempe, but was unable to reduce Glückstadt, which the Danes constantly relieved by means of their ships. The Spaniards not having sent the fleet they had promised, and the imperial " admiral " having found it more difficult to form a navy than to raise an army, began seriously to think of peace, in order, as he writes, to lead the " armada " against the Turks.

To effect the first of these objects, Wallenstein submitted a memorial to the Emperor, in which he explained the difficulty of carrying on the war without a navy, against enemies, who, like the Danes, were completely masters of the sea. This document alone, if we knew nothing else of its author, would prove him to have been a man of first-rate military talents. He shews, in the clearest manner possible, the great advantage which the Danes derived from their naval supremacy. " They can attack us," he says, " on all points with superior strength. No army can be imagined sufficiently numerous to guard every accessible part of the coast against disembarkations ; and scattered detachments may be cut up, in detail, by an enemy who is inaccessible in his islands, and whose naval operations can neither be followed nor observed by land forces alone."

Here is an officer already explaining, in the seventeenth century, what we could not understand, even in the nineteenth ; the tremendous force, namely, resulting from the combined power of naval and military armaments. Wallenstein could see that victorious fleets lend wings to armies ; augment their numbers in a tenfold degree, and render boundless the sphere of military operations. While armies, on the other hand, give permanent effect to the success of fleets, and gather in, for the benefit of the mutual country, the fruits of naval conquests. It is really difficult to say what might not have been achieved, had such a man appeared in Downing Street during the last war.

The Emperor submitted, as usual, to the views of his general, and authorised him and Tilly to treat with the Danes. There being on all sides, a willingness to bring the war to an end, peace was already concluded at Lubeck in January 1629. By this treaty, the Danes recovered, without reserve or indemnity, all their former possessions; only pledging themselves, not again to interfere in the affairs of the Empire. Considering that the cession of Holstein, together with the payment of several millions, had been demanded from them little more than a year before, the very moderate terms granted at Lubeck, cannot fail to surprise us ; and we are strongly tempted to suspect, that the newly created Duke of Mecklenburg, was willing to make a friend of his nearest and most powerful neighbour, the King of Denmark.

No sooner was this peace concluded, than Wallenstein dispatched Field-Marshal Arnheim, at the head of 10,000 men, to the aid of King Sigismund. The avowed object of the expedition was, to keep up the war in Poland, and to prevent Gustavus Adolphus from landing in Germany. Arnheim achieved little against the Swedes, and not liking his command, retired altogether from the imperial service. The enterprise helped only to give Gustavus an additional cause of complaint against the Emperor, and to hasten the execution of a project which had long been determined upon.

The peace of Lubeck left Wallenstein absolute master in Germany, and without an equal in greatness : his spirit seemed to hover like a storm-charged cloud over the land, crushing to the earth every hope of liberty and successful resistance. Mansfeld and Christian of Brunswick, had disappeared from the scene : Frederick V. had retired into obscurity. Tilly and Pappenheim, his former rivals, now condescended to receive favours, and to solicit pensions and rewards through the medium of his intercession. Even Maximilian of Bavaria, was second in greatness to the all-dreaded Duke of Friedland : Europe held no uncrowned head that was his equal in fame, and no crowned head that surpassed him in power. Standing in so proud a position, and with all the cares of his new Duchy pressing upon him ; it is rather curious and afflicting, to see Wallenstein volunteering, as it is said he did, the service in which we next find him engaged.

Ferdinand, elated with success, had neglected the

opportunity, again afforded him by the peace of Lubeck, for restoring tranquillity to the empire. The barbarity of the imperial soldiers, the rapacity of their generals, had exceeded all bounds. Germany, traversed in every direction by plundering and destroying bands of Condottieri ; occupied by the dreaded and oppressive hosts of Tilly and Wallenstein, lay exhausted, bleeding and panting for repose. Loud and universal was the call for peace : but Ferdinand heard it not : to him the voice of a monk " was the voice of God," and the Church of Rome, or some of those who, by their conduct dishonoured its doctrines, had still further demands on the yielding will of their sceptered slave.

Instead of a general peace, Ferdinand signed the fatal Edict of Restitution, by which the Protestants were called upon to restore all the Catholic Church property they had sequestrated since the religious pacification of 1555 : such sequestration being, according to the Emperor's interpretation, contrary to the spirit of the treaty of Passau. The right of long-established possession was here entirely overlooked ; and Ferdinand forgot, in his zeal for the church, that he was actually setting himself up as a judge, in a case in which he was a party also. It was farther added, that, according to the same treaty, freedom of departure from Catholic countries, was the only privilege which Protestants had a right to claim from Catholic princes.

This decree came like a thunder-burst over Protestant Germany. Two archbishopricks, twelve bishopricks, and a countless number of convents and clerical domains, which the Protestants had confiscated, and applied to their own purposes, were now to be surrendered. Imperial commissioners were appointed to carry the mandate into effect, and, to secure immediate obedience, troops were placed at the disposal of the new officials. Wherever these functionaries appeared, the Protestant service was instantly suspended; the churches deprived of their bells; altars and pulpits pulled down; all Protestant books, bibles and catechisms were seized; and gibbets were erected to terrify those who might be disposed to resist.

All Protestants, who refused to change their religion, were expelled from Augsburg: summary proceedings of the same kind were resorted to in other places. Armed with absolute power, the commissioners soon proceeded from reclaiming the property of the church to seize that of individuals. The estates of all persons who had served under Mansfeld, Baden, Christian of Brunswick; of all who had aided Frederick V, or rendered themselves obnoxious to the Emperor, were seized and confiscated. The surviving parents of those, who had been condemned for former offences, were obliged to resign their property; and children were, in like manner, forced to give up what they had inherited from parents who had been declared guilty. Twenty florins was the largest sum given, more in derision than in pity, to those who were turned out of house and home *.

---

* Raumer's Geschichte Europas seit dem Ende des 15. Jahr hunderts 3. Baud 471.

Universal as were the complaints raised against proceedings so tyrannical, little local, and no general resistance was offered : the hand of violence was still too strong. But t'1e Protestants saw plainly enough, that the destruction of their religion was determined on ; they learned to know, that resolute opposition could alone save them ; a proper spirit was awakened, and all were prepared to rally round the first victorious banner that should be unfurled in their cause.

While the defeated party were thus acquiring the first elements of future strength, dissensions began to appear among the victors, who already differed about the spoil which they had acquired. In few cases were the convents and domains restored to the original orders or possessors : it was declared that the Pope and the Emperor could alone dispose of whatever surplus might remain, after the expenses of the war should be defrayed. The minions of power were, as usual in such cases, the greatest gainers by the robbery : and it is lamentable to find Wallenstein among the distributors, if not among the partakers, of such unworthy booty.

The Duke of Friedland, who now ruled with dictatorial sway over Germany, had been ordered to carry the edict of restitution into effect, in all the countries occupied by his troops. The task, if we believe historians, was executed with unbending rigour: appeals and solicitations were addressed to him in vain, and princes of the empire were made to wait, with the crowd of ordinary petitioners, in the antechambers of the haughty commander. Wallenstein, who always appears to far greater advantage in his own letters than in the accounts which contemporary writers give of him, has left us no authority on which we can contradict the accusations brought against him in regard to these transactions.

The town of Magdeburg, formerly the seat of a Catholic archbishop, had refused to submit to the edict, and to receive imperial troops within its walls. It was immediately surrounded, and it is probable that the recollection of Stralsund, and the payment of a large sum of money, alone saved it from a regular siege. In no other quarter was opposition attempted : in some places, indeed, the imperial agents were slain by the exasperated populace ; but such isolated outbreakings of powerless indignation were soon suppressed. So absolute was Wallenstein at this period, that Tilly applied to him for " a piece of land," meaning the Duchy of Kalenberg, in addition to the 400,000 crowns, which the old Walloon acknowledges to have received through his intercession : and Pappenheim, speaking more distinctly, requests, at once, to be made Duke of Halberstadt.   Wallenstein, as liberal of the property of others as of his own, took summary measures to comply with both requests ; and would probably have carried his point, and made his comrades in arms princes of the empire, at the expense of the House of Brunswick, had not his power been cut short in the manner we are now to relate.

A general Diet had been convoked to meet at Ratisbon early in 1630.   The settlement of all remaining differences, and the establishment of a permanent peace, were the reasons assigned by Ferdi-

nand for calling this assembly together. Besides
these important objects, the Emperor also wished
to have his son, the King of Hungary, elected King
of the Romans, to insure the young monarch's future succession to the imperial throne. The Diet
met ; but no sooner was the election of the King of
Hungary mentioned, than the members burst out
into loud, indignant, and reiterated complaints, of
the cruelty, rapine, and tyranny exercised by the
imperial troops. From every part of Germany, the
voice of the ruined and oppressed called for vengeance ; and memorials, detailing deeds of the most
savage barbarity, poured in, from all quarters, upon
the astonished Emperor *. The fame and power of
the imperial army had been acquired under Wallenstein : its crimes were now to be charged against the
envied and all-dreaded commander, and the call for
his dismissal was loud and universal. This object
alone seemed to have brought the members of the
Diet to Ratisbon, and it actually appeared, as if no
other business could be entered upon, till this important point was carried.

From the nature of his career, Wallenstein could
hardly fail to have many and powerful enemies.
Reports had, at different times, been circulated, that

* Ferdinand's defenders say, that he knew nothing of these excesses. It would speak ill for an Emperor to have been ignorant.
But when one of Dampier's dragoons carried off his Majesty's
favourite falcon, and seriously injured the valuable bird, the mischief was soon known, and a sharp note sent to Wallenstein on the
subject, directing, however, that the offender should not suffer in
life or limb for the crime.

his life was to be attempted ; and a letter addressed to him on the 14th June 1629, by the Chancellor Slavata, contains the following very remarkable passage : " I have been told by several persons of consequence, that Tilly has orders to seize your highness, and to throw you into prison ; or, if that cannot be effected, he is to send you out of the world in a shorter and more summary manner." Wallenstein laughs at this sort of warning, and in his reply says, " I really wonder how you can give ear to such childish tales. The Emperor is a just and grateful sovereign, who rewards faithful services in a different way from what you suppose. Count Tilly, also, is a cavalier of honour, who knows not how to commit murder." Lightly, however, as he treated the matter, it would still appear that he entertained some apprehension of danger, for on the 2d of March 1630, we find his friend, Count Questenberg, sending him an antidote for poison. " This reminds me," says the imperial minister, " to send your highness the counter-poison,—*recept contrà venenum*,— which you required, and which you will receive herewith."

From the first of Wallenstein's elevation, reports had already ascribed to him ambitious and daring plans. There seems to have been something about the man, that awed and repelled minor spirits : his lofty imaginings had no communion with them ; and they believed that his gloomy look and haughty reserve, could indicate only a guilty mind, brooding over dark and dangerous projects. His boundless liberality, brought thousands to his standard : the

large sums which, as Count Prierato tells us, he distributed at the court of Vienna, purchased for him
plenty of advocates, ready to sound his praise as
long as he remained in power : he had many adherents who, trusting to his fortune, willingly followed
him ; but there is no appearance, in the voluminous
correspondence lately brought to light, that he had a
single friend ; while entire nations were his enemies.

At the head of the hostile party stood Maximilian
of Bavaria, the companion of Ferdinand's studies, the
second prince of the empire, whose first step, at Ratisbon, was to take an open and decided part against
Wallenstein.   He was supported by the whole Electoral College ; Catholics and Protestants : all were
unanimous in preferring charges against the man
who, with much to answer for, was chiefly guilty in
having deeply offended the pride of peers, princes
and electors : even men of humble station rarely
forgive the wounds inflicted on their self-love ; men
of high station more rarely still.

The following is an abstract of the registers of
crime handed in, at the Diet, against the imperial
general and his army :

" Wallenstein," it is said, " a man of restless and
ferocious spirit,—*vir inquies et ferox*,—has, without
consent of the states, and contrary to law, obtained
absolute power in every part of the empire.   And he
uses this power, as if he, the mere nobleman, were
the lord and director of princes, and they only his
servants and subordinates.   He raises and quarters
troops at will, levies contributions, and enriches himself and his followers in the most unworthy manner.

Law, right and justice are completely set aside. Magistrates, established authorities, and the states of provinces, are neither noticed nor consulted. And occasional proceedings instituted against delinquents and malefactors, tend but to exasperate, and excite them, and their comrades, to the commission of new crimes.

" In reply to our complaints of extortions, and of the insupportable burdens imposed upon us, we are scornfully told that the Emperor prefers to have his subjects poor to having them rebellious ; as if excess of misery did not, of itself, cause insurrection, and put an end to obedience. When the Duke of Wirtemburg represented that the 8000 men quartered in his country, completely ruined the land, he was informed that they would remain till the Edict of Restitution was carried into effect. When the citizens of Stargard complained of hard usage, the Italian, Torquato-Conti, commanded them to be stripped naked, that they might have sure grounds for complaints. Magistrates who were unable to levy the sums demanded of them, were beat, thrown out of windows, or shut up, without food, in overheated apartments. Not only were the people disarmed, but churches and graves were broken open and ransacked.

" In Pomerania, the entire revenue of the province, hardly enabled the Duke to keep an ordinary table ; while imperial captains and rittmeisters were living luxuriously in quarters, and remitting money out of the country. The soldiers also behave in the most barbarous manner towards the people : they ill-use and dishonour the women, beat and torture the men.

They burn and plunder in every direction ; and by depriving the peasantry of their wholesome food, force them to resort to the use of unnatural and destructive aliments, and to the commission of crimes the most revolting, such as consuming the flesh of children and dead bodies.

" Houses, furniture, and the implements of agriculture, are destroyed out of mere wantonness ; young women have been driven to suicide, to escape dishonour ; and others have died in consequence of the ill-treatment they had experienced. Turks and heathens never conducted themselves as the imperial troops have done; nor could the fiends of hell,"— we translate literally,—" have behaved worse. In this manner, has our unhappy country been used, though there is no enemy near. Religion, pity, mercy, and old German faith, have entirely vanished from the land ; nor is there any appearance that a change of fortune will bring relief to our sufferings. And all these excesses are perpetrated under the command of Wallenstein ; the great captain of the age ; the champion, as he is called, of Christendom ; under Wallenstein, a man who was born, not like your heathen Titus to be the delight of the human race, but to be its disgust and abhorrence,"—in the terrible words of the original,—" *odium ac nausea generis humani.*" Where was a man, so heavily accused in life, to find defenders after death ?

We have seen that the Duke of Friedland strove, with honest zeal, to remedy the disorders here complained of ; and the dreadful severity with which he punished offenders against discipline, is well known.

On one occasion, no fewer than fifteen soldiers, caught in the act of plundering, were ordered to be immediately executed. Officers were often disgraced, dismissed, or cashiered with infamy, and their names affixed to public gibbets ; while others, who had fled from justice, were ordered to be brought back dead or alive.

But at a time when organization and discipline were so imperfect in the imperial, as well as in most other European armies, mere severity could effect little. There was no general chain of responsibility extending through all ranks and gradations, which insured to the commander the punctual execution of his orders in the most distant cantonments, as well as on the most distant points of operation. Such a chain of responsibility can be founded only, on the honour of individuals ; for no commander, however active, upright and vigilant, can possibly watch over the conduct of the thousands placed beneath his rule. He must depend upon others, and when they cease to be faithful, he can only be blamed for employing the unfaithful, and even then only, where better subjects may be obtained. The elements necessary to the formation of well-disciplined armies are not to be found at all times and in all countries. We see Christian states of Europe wanting those elements even at this moment : and, at the period of which we are speaking, they were only taking root in Europe, and had taken feeble root in the Catholic countries.

Those among us who witnessed the campaign in Portugal, and recollect the dreadful cruelties committed by the French army under Massena, when

discipline was already much better understood than
it was in the seventeenth century, will pause before
they condemn Wallenstein on the report of his enemies. The excesses of which, according to Segur,
Napoleon's army was guilty, when marching through
Lithuania in 1812,—the accounts given of the Russians in Champaign, after the campaign of 1814,—the
traditions still extant, of the enormities perpetrated by
the troops of the same nation in East Prussia, during
the seven years' war, all prove how difficult it is to
control masses of men, living by requisition, even
when the war-horse is better curbed ; and when the
reins of discipline are more firmly grasped in the
hands of commanders, than they could have been in
the time of Wallenstein.

The composition of the armies he commanded must
also be considered. They did not consist of well paid
and well organised mercenaries, ruled by strict discipline and military honour; for the avarice and short-
sighted policy of the court of Vienna, generally left
them as destitute of money as of supplies ; and high
professional feeling was little known to the officers.
Still less were they patriots, banded together for the
defence of a native land ; or enthusiastic champions,
called to the field by the resistless voice of religion.
No ; they were adventurers from all countries, wan-
derers on the face of the earth, who had no home
but the camp ; no kindred but their comrades : they
were deserters from all armies ; renegados from all
religions, avowing but a momentary obedience to the
standard which had allured them by the greatest prospect of booty : they were men who fought for plun-

der and for the power of oppressing the afflicted
countries which the fortune of war placed at their
disposal. And it was the employment of such troops ;
the giving to such lawless hordes, the mastery over
provinces and empires, that caused the Thirty years'
War to be so dreadfully fraught with crime and sorrow.

We know from Wallenstein's letters how strenu-
ously he exerted himself to maintain discipline, and
to remedy the evils resulting from the ruinous system
followed; but the task was too great for a single hand;
and he was evidently not very successful, for we shall
find him using artifice to insure compliance with the
most important commands. And when we recollect
the well-authenticated rapacity of so many of his principal officers, and the terrible severity with which he
punished every dereliction from discipline that came
within his reach, we are strongly tempted to believe
that, the very man who, in so many tales of terror,
falsehood and folly, has been represented, as a ruthless and sanguinary barbarian, fell, after all, a victim
to his generous zeal in the cause of discipline and humanity. He tried to prevent plunder and extortion,
and was betrayed to death by those who prospered
by such practices.

There were not wanting persons, about the Emperor, who represented the danger of dismissing
Wallenstein and reducing the army, at the very time
when a new storm was gathering in the north. " It
was," they said, " an act as ungrateful as it was im-
politic, to remove from the command, an officer who
had rendered such eminent services to the House of

Austria.   Where was Wallenstein's equal in reputation, and who could replace a chief, the idol of the soldiers ?" " As the general," they continued, " did not receive from the Emperor the sums necessary for the support of the troops, how were the soldiers to be maintained, unless at the expense of the countries in which the war was carried on ? The complaints of the electors were, in reality, directed much more against the Emperor than against the commander ; but not daring openly to attack the sovereign, they contented themselves with attacking the servant."

The court of Madrid, then very closely connected with the court of Vienna, had, from the first, used all its influence to obtain the removal of Wallenstein from the head of the army.   He was too high, and too domineering, for the courtiers and confessors of Philip III. ; had rendered the Emperor more powerful and independent, than accorded exactly with their wishes ; and as quick to penetrate the views of others, as impenetrable himself, he could hardly fail to be an object of dislike to Spanish statesmen.

France, for different, but more politic reasons, followed in the same course.   Richelieu was at that moment negotiating his secret treaty with Gustavus Adolphus ; and to deprive the imperial troops of the general who had so often led them to victory, was to deprive them of half their strength, and to give the King of Sweden comparatively free hands.   Louis XIII. sent an ambassador to Ratisbon ; ostensibly for the purpose of putting an end to the war which had broken out in Italy, between France and Austria, relative to the Duchy of Mantua.   But in the minister's

train, though in no official capacity, was the celebrated
capuchin friar, Father Joseph; the intimate friend and
nominal confessor of Cardinal Richelieu; who had
instructions to press the dismissal of Wallenstein by
all the means in his power. Nor could an abler and
more artful agent have been selected. " It were
well," he said, speaking to the Emperor on the subject, " to oblige the electors in this trifling matter;
it will help to secure the Roman crown for the King
of Hungary; and when the storm shall have passed
away, Wallenstein will be ready enough to resume
his former station."

Ferdinand yielded, with a heavy heart, it is said,
and protesting before God and man, that he was innocent of the mischief which might result from the
measure. But feeble and unwarlike sovereigns, are
so often jealous of the fame and power acquired by
successful commanders, that we may perhaps be allowed to doubt the sincerity of the regret expressed
by the Emperor on the occasion. In return for this
important concession, Father Joseph counteracted the
imperial plans so skilfully, that the King of Hungary
lost his election; and the victorious Ferdinand, after
sacrificing 30,000 men of his army, and giving up a
general who was alone worth an army, had to leave
Ratisbon without effecting a single object for which
he had called the. Diet together. " A worthless
friar," he said, " has disarmed me with his rosary,
and put six electoral hats into his narrow cowl."

Wallenstein was at Memmingen, at the head of
100,000 men, to whom his will was absolute law,
when his dismissal was determined upon at Ratisbon.

Two noblemen, Counts Werdenberg and Questenberg, with whom he had always been on terms of
friendship, were dispatched to communicate to him,
in the best and most conciliatory manner possible,
the resolution which had been adopted ; and to assure him, at the same time, of the Emperor's continued friendship, favour and protection. The task
was looked upon as one of great delicacy, not altogether free from danger, and doubts seem to have
been entertained, whether the haughty commander
would yield implicit obedience, and descend from his
" high estate," to the powerless rank of a private
individual. " It was singular," men said, " that the
Emperor should obey the Electors ; but it would
be more singular still, should the General obey the
Emperor."

Always well informed of what was passing at court,
the official announcement, of his removal from command, did not take Wallenstein by surprise. He received the deputies with cheerful politeness ; assured
them that the object of their mission was well known
to him, as the stars had already foretold it. Then
producing an astronomical calculation, " You may
observe by the planets," he said, " that the spirit of
Maximilian predominates over the spirit of Ferdinand : I can attach no blame to the Emperor therefore, though I regret that he should have given me
up so easily : but I shall obey."

Whether Wallenstein intended to conceal wounded
pride, by thus ascribing his removal from command
to an authority superior to that of Emperors and
Diets ; or whether policy made him anxious to im-

press on the deputies, that he harboured no ill-will against Ferdinand, and considered him only as an executive agent of higher decrees, is now uncertain. How far he was the dupe of his own art, or tried to make others the dupes of his artifice, can no longer be decided ; but the anecdote is too well attested to be called into question.

The imperial messengers, not knowing, perhaps, what the really great man owes to his character, were surprised at the calmness with which the haughty Duke of Friedland received their unwelcome tidings. They expected to witness some low burst of undignified anger, and were amazed to find themselves sumptuously treated during their stay at head-quarters, and loaded with presents when they took their departure. They were also charged with a letter to the Emperor, in which Wallenstein thanked the sovereign for all his former favours, and only requested that " His Majesty would not lend an ear to the evil reports, that malevolence might spread to his disadvantage."

In none of the letters which he writes at this period, is there the slightest appearance of the hostile or revengeful feeling which he is said to have entertained against the Emperor and the House of Austria. On the contrary, he seems to have devoted his whole attention to the improvement of his domains and principalities. " His parks are to be well stocked with game ; his palaces are to be splendidly furnished, decorated with pictures; and his gardens to be adorned with grottos and fountains." No sooner had his dismissal from the command been determined up-

on, than he writes to Taxis, saying, that he intends
to reach Gitchin, his future residence, about the end
of October. He desires that a store of " good wine
and other necessaries may be laid in, as he proposes to
keep a great establishment." The apartments to be
prepared for his friends and visitors, are to be ele-
gantly furnished ; and hung " with satin, velvet, or
gilt leather tapestry ;" stabling must be provided for
about 800 horses, which these visitors will " bring
along with them."

Having laid down the command of the army, he
left Memmingen on the 3d of October, and set out
for Gitchin, attended by a large party of friends, followers and retainers. Why he retired at this time into
Bohemia, instead of Mecklenburg, is not very intelligible. True it is, that Gustavus Adolphus had landed in Pomerania ; but he had not yet approached the
confines of Mecklenburg, which it might be supposed
could not have been better protected than by its own
warlike Duke. The Diet of Ratisbon had, indeed,
refused to ratify the imperial grant by which the
Duchy was bestowed upon Wallenstein ; but no attempt was made to deprive him of its possession ; and
the Emperor continued, to the last, to style him
Duke of Mecklenburg.

But if he did not personally exercise the functions
of a sovereign, the pomp of a king surrounded him in
his retirement. Six gates conducted to the palace
which he inhabited at Prague, and a hundred houses
were pulled down to enlarge its avenues and approaches. Similar structures were raised on several
of his estates ; and Carve tells us that the palace at

Sagan would have been one of the wonders of the world, had Wallenstein lived to see it finished. Gentlemen of the best families courted the honour of serving him ; and imperial chamberlains resigned office at Vienna to fill the same situation in Wallenstein's establishment. He had sixty pages who were instructed by the best masters in all polite accomplishments : and fifty chosen yeomen guarded his halls and ante-rooms. A hundred dishes were every day placed upon his table : a hundred carriages, and fifty led horses followed him when he travelled, and his court accompanied him in sixty state coaches.

The richness of his liveries, the splendour of his equipages, and the decorations of his halls, were all in keeping with the rest of his state. Six noblemen, and as many knights, were constantly near his person, ready to obey the slightest sign or direction. To keep every noise at a distance, twelve patroles performed their regular circuits round his habitation : his ever active mind required stillness ; and he was as silent himself as the avenues that led to his presence. Dark and reserved, he was more sparing of words than of presents, and the little that he spoke, was uttered in a harsh and unpleasant tone. He seldom laughed ; was a stranger to conviviality ; and the coldness of his temperament rendered him inaccessible to the seduction of the senses. Always occupied in the formation of vast and extensive plans, he shared in none of the empty pleasures with which others cast away the valuable hours of life. A correspondence, extending over all Europe, was conducted principally by himself ; and a great many of

the letters written with his own hand, in order that
he might be as independent as possible of the fidelity
of others.   Princes and sovereigns are among his
correspondents ; and our own King, Charles I, writes
to him in the most friendly terms, and solicits his
intercession in favour of the Palatine Elector, Frederick V, Charles's brother-in-law.   The King of
England styles Wallenstein, " *Illustrissime et cel-
sissime princeps amice et consanguine carissime ;*"
and says, that " he is well aware of Wallenstein's
great and deserved influence with the Emperor, and
how much he is therefore capable of effecting."

In person, Wallenstein was tall and spare : he had
a sallow complexion ; dark hair, and small, but quick,
penetrating dark eyes.   A cold, stern, even repulsive
earnestness, was ever fixed upon his high gloomy
brow ; and nothing but his boundless profusion and
liberality kept the trembling crowd of attendants
around him.

" In this ostentatious retirement," says Schiller,
" Wallenstein awaited quietly, but not inactively, the
hour of glory and the day destined to vengeance.
Seni, an Italian astrologer, had read in the stars, that
the brilliant career of Friedland was not yet ended ;
and it was easy to foresee, without the aid of astrology, that an adversary like Gustavus Adolphus,
would soon render the services of a general like Wallenstein indispensable.   Not one of all his lofty projects had been abandoned : the ingratitude of the
Emperor had, on the contrary, released him from a
galling and oppressive curb.   The dazzling brilliancy
of his retirement, announced the full altitude of his

ambitious projects: and liberal as a monarch, he seemed to look upon his coveted possessions as already within his grasp, and fully at his disposal."

In none of Wallenstein's letters,—in no document which historians have yet produced, is there the slightest indication to show that he entertained the sentiments of hatred towards the Emperor ; or ever formed those projects of vengeance which have been so universally, and, being without proof, so unjustly ascribed to him.   Even Schiller, instead of taking, as a great man should have done, the part of a great man who had been condemned without being convicted, joined the unworthy cry against Wallenstein. The historian of the Thirty years' War, not satisfied with representing him as a " mad," " extravagant," and " blood-thirsty tyrant," describes him also as brooding, in his retirement, over dark and dangerous plans of treason, the existence of which, have never yet been established by the slightest shadow of evidence ; while we shall see the suspected traitor giving Ferdinand the best advice that could possibly have been followed.

Wallenstein was proud, haughty and ambitious : he had been injured, and treated with ingratitude ; and it is unfortunately too congenial to ordinary human nature, to suppose that hatred and plans of revenge would spring up in such a heart in return for such treatment.   There are so few men capable of rising above the feelings of resentment occasioned by wounds inflicted on their self-love, so few really able to burst asunder the chains by which the meaner passions of our nature drag us down to earth ; that we

hasten to condemn as guilty all those who come
within the range of suspicion. We are slow to believe,
that there are minds capable of rising altogether above
injuries, though we cannot deny the existence of such
noble pride.

If, in the present case, for instance, we reason only
from what we know, and put merely a liberal, not
even a partial, construction on what appears obscure,
we shall be forced to confess that the man of whom
we are speaking, the accused, condemned and but-
chered Wallenstein, whose name and memory have,
for two centuries, been loaded with reproach and
obloquy, possessed such a mind, and that he was above
harbouring, even anger, in return for the ingratitude
with which he had been treated. He got no credit
indeed, for such disinterestedness ; and from the moment of his dismissal, designs hostile to the Emperor
and to the House of Austria were universally ascribed
to him.

On the 21st of February 1631, Tilly writes to him,
and " out of friendship and affection," as he says,
" sends him some French newspapers, in which it
is stated that Gustavus Adolphus had, immediately
on landing, dispatched a messenger to the Duke of
Friedland, who had been greatly delighted with the
King's communication, and had given the messenger
a gold chain, in token of his satisfaction." Wallenstein, in return, thanks Tilly for the information ;
·and says that " he is not surprised by the reports circulated at his expense, such having been the world's
good fashion from time immemorial ; and as to the
papers, they are amusing to read, though best an-

swered by being laughed at. The open and defenceless town of Gitchin," he continues, " situated in
the midst of the Austrian dominions, is not a place
wherein to form dangerous projects : and I can assure your Excellency that I should have presented
the Swedish messenger with a very different chain
from the one he is said to have received at my hands."
To prevent these reports, however, from making an
unfavourable impression at court, he forwards the
papers to Questenberg, as containing " idle fooleries,"
and concludes his letter with the Spanish proverb,
" *Piensa il ladron, que todos son de su condition* *."
His aversion to the Swedes we have before noticed :
it was not likely to be diminished by the proclamation
of Gustavus, calling on the people of Mecklenberg
to " arrest or slay all the agents of Wallenstein, as
robbers, and enemies to God and the country."

We now turn with pleasure to the brightest page
of our dark history.

* The rogue believes every man to be of his own stamp.

CHAPTER IV.

WITH the landing of Gustavus Adolphus in Germany, begins the dawn of a new and a better era. Not only is the fortune of war changed almost immediately, the mode of conducting it is changed also, and the voice of humanity is again listened to even amidst the din of arms. Military operations are more concentrated, and bear more directly on the attainments of the objects contended for; so that greater results are produced in the field, while less of suffering is inflicted on the defenceless. For the first time since the decline of the Roman legions, an organised and well-disciplined army appears in Europe; and the noble character of its leader, gives to its actions an impress of greatness which succeeding ages have confirmed rather than effaced.

Gustavus Adolphus, on whom friends and foes conferred, with one accord, the name of " Great," ascended the throne of Sweden when only seventeen years of age. Unlike most other young princes, he began his reign by giving peace to his country, which was involved in heavy and expensive wars with Denmark, Russia and Poland. He made concessions to the Danes, his nearest and most formidable adversaries; availed himself, with wisdom and moderation, of some success achieved against the Russians, and thus gained the friendship of both nations.   Having obtained free hands, he directed his attention to the internal affairs of his kingdom, which he administered with great ability, while he concentrated all its military efforts against his cousin, and most inveterate foe, Sigismond, King of Poland ; who claimed the crown of Sweden, as nearest in descent from Gustavus Vasa ; though excluded from the throne by his attachment to the Catholic religion.   It was during the war occasioned by this disputed succession, a war which had been as often renewed as suspended, that the dangerous progress of the imperial arms, attracted the attention of Gustavus.

The German princes had been successively defeated; their real independence was annihilated, and the King of Denmark, driven from his continental possessions, had been forced to seek shelter within his islands.   The Protestant religion, long threatened, was almost proscribed by the Edict of Restitution ; and Wallenstein, at the head of a powerful army, was besieging Stralsund, and fortifying the other German ports of the Baltic.

This enterprising leader had already assumed the title of imperial admiral on the high seas, and was endeavouring to form a fleet which could only be destined to act against the Scandinavian kingdoms.   To these causes for apprehension, insults had been added. Swedish couriers had been intercepted on their way into Transylvania ; Swedish ships had been plundered in the German ports occupied by the imperial troops.   Wallenstein had haughtily refused to admit Swedish ambassadors to the Congress of Lubec ; and the Emperor continued to withhold from Gustavus, the title of King.

The hostile dispositions of the court of Vienna were thus sufficiently manifested, and Gustavus soon perceived that just policy and the interest of Sweden, would ultimately force him into the German quarrel: his chivalrous feelings and upright Protestant zeal, also urged him to become the champion of an oppressed church and people, who, from all quarters, called to him for aid in their affliction. He stated this so clearly in his farewell address to the senate, that we cannot refrain from quoting the closing words of his admirable and affecting speech. " The object of this enterprise," said the great King, in speaking of his expedition, " is to set bounds to the increasing power of a dangerous empire, before all resistance becomes impossible. Your children will not bless your memory, if, instead of civil and religious freedom, you bequeath to them the superstition of the monks, and the double tyranny of Popes and Emperors. We must prevent the subjugation of the continent, before we are reduced to depend upon a narrow sea, as the only safeguard of our liberty; for it is a mere delusion to suppose, that a mighty empire will be unable to raise fleets, wherewith to attack us, if it is once firmly established along the shores of the ocean." It will be long ere the schoolmaster, who is now abroad, shall give us a more valuable lesson.

Gustavus Adolphus had, as we have seen, sent troops to aid in defending Stralsund, when that place was attacked by the Imperialists. Wallenstein, after the peace of Lubec, had dispatched Arnheim with

an army to aid the Poles.   Hostilities had thus
commenced, though no declaration of war had taken
place ; but it was the continuance of the Polish contest alone, that prevented the King of Sweden from
turning the full force of his arms against the Emperor.
Cardinal Richelieu had the merit of removing this
difficulty.   Charnace, a French minister, appeared
in Poland, and exerted himself so effectually as me-
diator, that a six years' truce, by which the Swedes
retained all their conquests, was established between
the parties.   No actual alliance was yet entered into
between France and Sweden.   Richelieu, the minister of a Catholic King, and himself a high dignitary
of the Church of Rome, could hardly venture, openly
to assist a Protestant prince, about to attack a Catholic sovereign : he contented himself, therefore,
with promising ample subsidies, in case Gustavus
should invade Germany : England made similar promises, and Holland also held out a prospect of support.
   Thus encouraged, urged on above all by his own
gallant spirit, Gustavus embarked his army, and
sailed from Elfsnaben in Sweden, with a fleet of 200
transports, escorted by sixty ships of war.   He landed
near Pene-Münde, in Usedom, on the 24th June
1630 : exactly a hundred years after the presenta-
tion of the Confession of Augsburg.   The King
was the first who leaped on shore ; and his first act
on German ground, was to kneel down and return
thanks to God for the protection, which had been
vouchsafed to his fleet and army, during the passage.
Then turning round, and replying to some remark
made on this act of devotion, " a good Christian,"

he said, " can never be a bad soldier ; and the man who has finished his prayers, has already got over the best half of his day's work." These words were immediately circulated over Germany ; and were not, perhaps, the worst advanced guard that could have preceded the march of the conqueror.

Gustavus Adolphus belongs to the class of men, who appear too rarely on the page of history. Well acquainted with the military institutions of the ancients, he strove, on their model, to render himself independent of the mere power of fortune, which so often decides the fate of battles ; and endowed with a high and inventive genius, he devised a system of tactics, not only superior to the one then in use, but in principle, much superior also, to any which has since been followed. He was the first, so far to do homage to the fatal power of artillery, as to diminish the ranks of the infantry from twelve to six. It was the custom of the period to draw up battalions into large, square, unwieldy masses of mail-clad spearmen, flanked and surrounded by musqueteers, as if to prevent the lances from being used against the enemy. These formations Gustavus broke up entirely : he separated the spearmen from the musqueteers, formed small divisions of each, so as to render them more moveable, and capable of supporting each other, according to the actions of their respective weapons. The divisions were so drawn up, that the musqueteers could file out between the intervals of the spearmen, and again fall back, like the Roman velites, through the same intervals, when the parties came to push of pike. The spears were shortened, from 18 to 14 feet, and the men relieved from the most cumbrous part of their armour. The matchlocks of the infantry, were likewise so much reduced in weight, that the soldiers could dispense with fork or *fourquette*, over which the former heavy pieces had alone been fired.

The system of cavalry tactics was also improved; and the weight of the cavalry appointments lessened: the men were taught to depend more on the sword than on fire-arms, to which the horsemen of the period so generally resorted. Only a single volley, with pistols, was to be fired by the front rank; and was to be immediately followed by a sword-in-hand charge, at full speed. These just views of cavalry tactics, accord ill with the received statements, that Gustavus mixed infantry with his horsemen, in the manner of the ancients. The Romans, who were bad riders and rode without stirrups, knew nothing of cavalry action, and certainly resorted to such practices; but Gustavus, who well understood the nature of cavalry action, as certainly did not. That a mixed formation may, on some particular occasion, or for some particular purpose, have been adopted, is possible: but as a regular order of battle, it is a contradiction of which the French under Napoleon, with their slow and heavy masses of cavalry, might have been guilty, but which could never have entered into the head of the gallant King of Sweden. Horsemen tieing themselves down to the movements of infantry, tie their horses' legs, sacrifice all their speed and impetuosity, and cease to be horsemen; for they are placed on horseback in order to avail them-

selves of the speed and strength of the horses.   Such
a mixed body can neither hurry on from a distance,
nor dash in upon the enemy with the full force of
cavalry : all that cavalry so situated can effect, is to
pursue the enemy, leaving the infantry behind : but
then they also leave the infantry behind when they
are forced to fly ; and in that case, they leave them
to certain destruction.   Gustavus knew how to combine the action of infantry and cavalry, and the
moderns, unable to understand the principle, thought
that he mixed up the arms.

Historians have also asserted, that this great King
followed, in his military operations, the course of
rivers, though a single look at the map, should have
convinced them of the contrary.   Had Gustavus followed the course of rivers, the Elbe must have led
him into Bohemia ; whereas he crossed the Elbe,
the Rhine, and the Danube, and generally marched
on lines diverging as much as possible from the course
of those streams.   Gustavus followed the inspirations
of genius, for which historians looked in vain on their
maps.

Except that both were tall, and that both had high
features, no two men could be more dissimilar in
manners and appearance, than Wallenstein and Gustavus : it might have been said, that nature intended
them to be adversaries.   We have seen what Wallenstein was, and must now attempt to sketch his great
opponent.

In person, the King of Sweden was remarkably
stout and full chested ; he had a ruddy complexion,
blue eyes, light hair, and a pleasing expression of

countenance. In character and disposition, he was
frank, open-hearted and courteous; and though
temperate himself, a friend of conviviality; a good
speaker;—master of several languages, and rather
fond of displaying his oratorial powers. Kind, generous, humane, easy of access, his affability never
failed to gain the hearts of all who approached him ;
his popularity was therefore universal, and even the
enemies of his cause and religion, always avowed the
highest respect and admiration for the man.

Unaffectedly pious, he prayed openly before his
troops ; of fiery courage, he was the first to charge
at their head on the day of battle ; and the boundless
sway which he exercised over the minds of his soldiers, became, when added to his intrepid temper,
the principal cause of his success. It naturally led
to the adoption of vigorous and decisive measures :
and Alexander and Charles XII. excepted, no great
commander seems to have been more fully convinced
than Gustavus, that a bold onset in war, is already
half the battle. But the very qualities, that almost
chained victory to his standard, were ominous of his
fate. He had received thirteen wounds, during his
early campaigns ; and this generous prince, the admiration of his own, and of all succeeding time, died
at last, on battle plain, the death of a private soldier.
He appeared on the dark scene of the Thirty years'
War, as the sun, when it bursts in splendour through
a tempestuous sky ; and even as that sun, gilds with
its parting beams the stormy clouds around ; so did
the lustre of the great King's fame, brighten the
black horizon to the last, and throw far aloft the

rainbow of hope which continued to animate his followers, long after his gallant course was closed for
ever.

The small army with which Gustavus Adolphus
landed in Germany, forms a singular feature in his
history ; for it now appears, from certain documents,
that he brought only 13,000 men along with him.
David Leslie occupied Stralsund and Rügen, with
6000 more, making a total of less than 20,000 men :
a force which the genius of its leader could alone
render equal to the task of assailing the combined
power of Spain, Austria and Catholic Germany.

The Swedish Chancellor Oxenstiern, who, at times,
acted both as general and minister, was indeed, stationed in East-Prussia, with some 8000 men ; but
these were only new-raised troops, intended for the
protection of the lately conquered provinces, and
could not be looked upon as disposable. Sweden
must have been a very thinly peopled country at the
period, for even this small force was, in a great measure, composed of foreigners, principally Germans and
British. In his third campaign, Gustavus had under his command, of British alone, mostly Scotch,
6 generals, 30 colonels, 51 lieutenant-colonels and
10,000 men : a number sufficient to entitle Britain
to a fair proportion of the honour acquired. But
though the soldiers of the Swedish army were natives
of very different countries, they were moulded into
one united body by habits of discipline, and animated by one spirit. From the very first, they acquired the most decided superiority over the Imperialists ; who, completely disorganised by their crimes

and excesses, had degenerated from soldiers into mere robbers.   Forced to fly before the Swedes, the stragglers from these dishonoured bands were slain, without mercy, by the exasperated peasantry whenever they could be set upon with advantage.

Gustavus had studied Quintus Curtius too attentively, not to extend himself, like Alexander, along the coast before he penetrated into the interior of the country.   This accomplished soldier, evidently understood the vast importance of establishing a just basis of operation ; the very first rule of strategy, and one of the many of which the moderns have been so strangely ignorant.   He began by taking Wolgast, then Camin ; he next cleared the island of Wollin, and advanced towards Stetin, where he forced the unwilling Duke of Pomerania, to accept his proffered friendship and alliance.   " Who is not with us," said Gustavus, " is against us."   The Duke had, therefore, nothing left but to yield, and dispatch a courier to Vienna to excuse his conduct on the plea of necessity.   The Emperor, in return, sent orders for his generals to ravage the country ; a task they had not waited for instructions to execute.   While the Imperialists were plundering, Gustavus was conquering ; and as most of the German towns were fortified at the time, the campaign was a succession of sieges, of which, we shall only give a general sketch, to prevent the necessity of describing them in detail.

The approaches were usually made under cover of the suburbs ; and if these were burnt down, the ruins still facilitated the advances.   The Swedish soldiers were quick at the spade and axe, as all good soldiers should be : they soon covered themselves, and then protected their works by palisaded redoubts. In the first campaigns they knew not how to connect the zig-zags by parallels, though they were ultimately the first to fall upon the discovery. In general, the towns were only surrounded by old walls, flanked with towers : these defences were too high to be easily escaladed ; but as they were mostly built of brick, it was not difficult to batter them down.

When a breach was formed, the ditch was either filled up or passed on rafts, as the towers could not throw out a sufficient flanking fire to prevent the progress of such operations. In many cases the gates were burst open with petards, and entered sword-in-hand. The garrisons of places taken in this manner were not always, as a matter of course, put to the sword. The profession of arms began to be a regular trade, the members of which, had a sort of fellow-feeling for each other, and were sometimes willing to show the mercy they might in turn have occasion to solicit. Such fits of humanity were not, however, of every-day occurrence, and depended a good deal on the character and influence of the officers who led the attacks. When a town capitulated, it was usual for the victors to call out to the garrison, as they filed past, " Who will take service ?" and it was not uncommon for the entire party to accept the invitation ; numbers almost invariably did so : nor do we see any acts of severity exercised against them when retaken. Sometimes all the prisoners were forced to enter the ranks of the conquerors, and at Steinau, Wallenstein augmented his army by the whole force which he had captured.

Frederick II. afterwards did the same with the Saxon army that capitulated at Pirna. From these courtesies, the Croats were however excluded : they were always cut down as heathen barbarians. During the Pomeranian campaign, the Swedes also cut down most of the Italians that fell into their hands, owing to the treacherous attempt, made on the King's life, by some Italian officers.

Places of greater strength and more regularly fortified required, of course, to be more regularly attacked. But even the most difficult of these sieges were in a great degree facilitated by the very heavy artillery with which the armies of the period encumbered themselves; for both Swedes and Imperialists dragged twenty-four pounders along with them in the field. The light artillery was, on the other hand, extremely light : the falconet, the lightest, carrying only a two-pound ball. It would now appear that none of the leather ordnance which Gustavus had used during the earlier campaigns, were, as historians assert, brought to Germany. The guns of the Swedish light artillery consisted, besides falconets, of four, six and twelve pounders, constructed upon a new and improved principle, by a Scotch gentleman of the name of Hamilton : these guns continued to be used in the French army down to the year 1780, under the name of *pieces Suedoises*.

The misfortune which about this time, befell a detachment of 700 Scotch soldiers, under the command of Colonel Robert Monroe, deserves to be recorded, as it shews what courage and resolution can effect even in situations that appear hopeless. These brave men, while on their voyage to join the King's army, were shipwrecked near Rügenwalde, and lost every thing except their swords, lances, and about ten wet muskets. Thrown destitute upon an inhospitable coast, in the midst of the enemy's quarters, and distant at least eighty miles, from the nearest Swedish post, their ruin seemed inevitable. But bold men find resources where others see only destruction.

Colonel Monroe, instead of awaiting, on the open beach, the prepared attack of the Imperialists, was before-hand with them. He surprised the town of Rügenwalde, during the night, and afterwards defended it for nine weeks, against all the attempts of the enemy. At the expiration of that time he was relieved by his countryman, Colonel Hepburn ; to distinguish himself again at the blockade of Colberg. This important place having been reduced, almost to extremity, by the Swedes, the imperial general Montecucoli, the same who afterwards acquired so much fame as the opponent and rival of Turenne, was dispatched to its relief at the head of 10,000 men. As soon as the direction of his march became known, Monroe, with some companies of Scottish infantry, took post at Schevelin on the Rega, a small town through which the Imperialists had to pass. Montecucoli surrounded the place and summoned the garrison to surrender. " My instructions contain no mention of capitulation," replied Monroe, and continued the defence. A sharp assault followed. The Scots, unable to defend the town, set it on fire and retired into the castle, which they maintained so reso-

lutely, that Montecucoli was forced to raise the siege
and change the direction of his march. The future
rival of Turenne having lost both time and men, before an old ruinous castle, was unable to relieve Colberg, which surrendered shortly afterwards.

Though winter had arrived, it arrested not the
progress of Gustavus. The Austrians proposed, indeed, a cessation of arms, in order that the troops
might be placed in winter quarters : the King, however, would listen to no arrangement of the kind.
" The Austrians," he said, " may do as they please ;
but the Swedes are soldiers in winter as well as in
summer :" an assertion he fully justified, by some
very gallant actions performed notwithstanding the
rigour of the season. This continued success, at last,
emboldened Richelieu to enter into an open and regular alliance with him. France agreed to pay a subsidy
of 400,000 crowns a year ; and Gustavus promised,
on his part, to maintain an army of 35,000 men in
Germany. Some little difference took place on this
occasion between Gustavus and Charnace. The
French ambassador insisted, that, in the treaty, the
King of France should take precedence of the King
of Sweden, and that his name should always be mentioned first. " Merit alone gives precedence among
Kings," said Gustavus indignantly, and refused to
grant the slightest concession. England contributed
also, at this time, L.108,000 towards the expenses of
the war ; so that the King was enabled to give his
soldiers a handsome gratuity, over and above their
usual pay, which, compared to the starving allowances
granted to modern soldiers, was very considerable.

The landing of the Swedes had excited little or
no apprehension at Vienna. The imperial ministers,
accustomed to success, thought the Emperor invinci-
ble, and treated the invasion lightly : the courtiers
even exercised their wit on the subject, and called
Gustavus, a " King of snow, held together by the
frost of the north, who would soon melt under the
influence of a southern sun." But as these jests did
not arrest the progress of the invaders, it became
necessary, after the dismissal of Wallenstein, to ap-
point a new general-in-chief, in order to unite all
the scattered forces of the Emperor and the League.
Maximilian of Bavaria, and the King of Hungary
were both candidates for this high office ;. the fears
of the court of Vienna excluded the first, and the
jealousy of Maximilian, the second, so that the choice
fell ultimately on Tilly, who exchanged the Bavarian
for the imperial service.

This general, who could boast that he had never
lost one of the six and thirty actions in which he had
commanded, was born in 1559 at Tilly, in the county
of Liege, and was descended from an ancient Walloon
family. He first served in the Netherlands against
the revolted Flemings, and afterwards under the
Emperor Radolph in Hungary, where he rose rapidly
from one station to another. On the conclusion of
the peace in that quarter, the Elector of Bavaria appointed him to the command of the Bavarian army ;
and it was to the skill and ability which Tilly displayed in this capacity, that Maximilian's superiority
in the field was principally due. He was an ancho-
rite in temperance, and though moderate and disin-

terested, when compared to Wallenstein, he was, like
him, accused of being cruel and severe ; and there is
too much reason to fear, that the accusation is not
without foundation.   His fidelity to his sovereign,
and his devotion to his church, were boundless and
unshaken : but the religion of Christ was with him, as
with so many men of the period, a persecuting creed,
rather than a creed commanding charity and universal
benevolence.   Educated by the Jesuits, and trained in
the exterminating wars of the Netherlands,—carried
on at first, by executioners rather than soldiers,—his
intolerant zeal and dark fanaticism, rendered him the
terror of Protestant Germany.   On the other hand,
many traits of generosity are related of him : his
courage was of the highest order, and his word was
always sacred.   His military and political talents
were never disputed ; and he more than once gave
advice, which, if followed, might, perhaps, have restored peace to Germany.

As it was Wallenstein's wish to lead the army
against the Turks, so it was the wish of Tilly to lead
them against the people of Holland.   Both may have
been influenced by the force of early impressions ; or
the first may, in accordance with his character, have
looked for power, spoil and renown, in contending
against the Osmanli, the wealthiest and bravest enemies of Christian Europe ; while the second, in his
high notions of legitimacy, would deem the suppression of heresy and rebellion, the most glorious services that could be rendered to God and his sovereign.   Tilly must ever be considered as one of the
most remarkable men of his age ; but he was not,

like Wallenstein and Gustavus, capable of raising
himself above the age.   His personal appearance
corresponded with his gloomy disposition.   He was
of short stature, very meagre ; had sunk cheeks, a
long nose and pointed chin ; his eyes were large and
dark, and he had a broad, wrinkled forehead.   In
dress he was equally singular : he wore a green silk
coat with slashed sleeves ; a narrow brimmed, high,
conical hat, surmounted by a red ostrich feather, that
fell down over his back.   His image associated itself,
in the minds of beholders, with the idea of the too-
celebrated Duke of Alba ; and his actions were far
indeed from removing the impression his appearance
created.

Driven out of Pomerania, the imperial troops
sought shelter in the Duchy of Brandenburg, where
their excesses were such, that the Elector, who had
no men to defend his country, was forced to issue a
proclamation, ordering his subjects to repel force by
force, and slay every imperial soldier taken in the act
of plundering.   Yet such was the dread still entertained of the Emperor, that the Elector, even in this
extremity, declined forming an alliance with Gustavus, and requested permission to remain neutral, at
the very moment when the Imperialists were in full
possession of his country, and directing all its accessible resources against the Swedes.

From the first moment of his arrival, the Protestant people of Germany, every where received Gustavus with boundless, in many places with extravagant, demonstrations of joy ; but, strange to say,
not one of the oppressed Protestant princes dared to

join him till victory had declared in his favour.
Caution is, no doubt, a commendable quality in sovereigns ; but the enthusiasm displayed by the subjects, on this occasion, will, we suspect, be far more
admired than the wariness of their superiors.

The heavy penalties men have paid for their timi-
dity, and that of their rulers, exceed in amount, perhaps, what they have had to pay for all the other
errors committed by nations or governments. It is
seldom that we see kings or senates avoiding the
timid paths which have led others to destruction, and
boldly following up, through danger if necessary, a
direct and manly line of honourable and profitable
policy. There have been unprincipled and aggressive kings, as well as unprincipled and aggressive
republics ; but few have kept the middle course, and
refrained alike from oppressing the weak, or bend-
ing to the strong. On the contrary, fear makes
them ingenious in self-deception, and they adopt,
from cowardice, unwise, as well as unworthy measures, which sophistry represents as the dictates of
absolute wisdom, and of fearless liberality. History
shews, from first to last, how certain of ruin it is, to
yield a single step, to grasping and powerful ambition, in the vain hope of courting safety by submission. And yet is there hardly an instance recorded
of men having cordially joined, hand in hand, to
meet threatened danger while it could be opposed to
advantage. They have sometimes been driven to
resistance by excess of tyranny, and have occasionally thrown off the yoke of oppression ; but they have
been more frequently crushed : their subjugation be-

ing as often due to their own dissensions, as to the
force of the aggressor.

Grecian armies accompanied the first Persian invaders of Greece ; and it was the want of union
among the states of Greece, which, at a later period,
enabled the Macedonians to subdue the country.
The next page of the same history, shews us the
second Philip, doubting and delaying, till Hannibal
and the Carthagenians had fallen before the power
of the Romans ; and then receiving on the heights
of Cenocephalæ a tardy lesson in political wisdom.
Turn but the page, and we see the Achaians, called
the wise, joining the Romans, whom they feared
and hated, against the Macedonians, whom they
loved and cherished. On the very same page we
see the deserters from the cause of honour and of
patriotism, receiving, in the fields of Leucopetra, the
well-merited reward of their baseness.   It was even
so at the period of which this volume treats.   The
German princes first left the unfortunate Frederick
without support : they next abandoned Christian of
Denmark : nor could the tyranny and oppression of
the court of Vienna drive them into an alliance with
Gustavus, till their lands and subjects had suffered
countless evils, and till victory had rendered the
Swedes masters of the field.

If we have acquired any wisdom from these monitory
examples, it must have come upon us very lately indeed. During an entire generation, Europe was de-
luged with the blood of her bravest sons, owing to the
weakness and want of foresight displayed by timid
rulers and trembling nations ; for in modern times

nations have governed kings, perhaps, as much as kings have governed nations. To pass over the first coalition against republican France, dissolved after a few unsuccessful skirmishes, let us come down to the year 1805, when imperial France, giving laws to the trembling governments of Spain, Italy and Portugal, already threatened the independence of Europe. We first see Prussia, blind to her own danger, looking tamely on, when Austria was humbled in the field of Austerlitz. In the following year Prussia was overthrown at Jena, while Austria remained a tame spectator of the contest: an obligation that Prussia repaid in 1809, when the power of Austria was broken at the battle of Wagram; where a few squadrons would almost have changed the fate of the war. The consequence was, that in 1812 both powers were forced to march, like vassals, in the train of the conqueror, to attack the very country from which they expected aid and relief.

It was not till the hand which directs the storm, had paralysed the mighty in his career, and strewed the frozen plains of Russia with the bones of unconquered armies, that the great in their generation arose in wisdom. When the danger was looked upon as over, and the spoil only to be shared, then were the nations of Europe enlightened to that interest to which they had before been so blind. The same want of foresight and union afterwards showed itself at the Congress of Vienna, when Poland was sacrificed to the ambition of Russia; it was again seen in 1828, when the interest of Europe called loudly and vainly for the defence of Turkey. Future

events must tell, what the world will have to pay for
this last act of false and feeble policy. Let us now
show some of the results brought about by the timid
spirit of which we have been speaking.

While Tilly was collecting the imperial armies and
preparing to advance against Gustavus, the Elector
of Saxony called a meeting of the Protestant princes;
who assembled at Leipzig in February 1631. This
congress is very remarkable, as showing, not what
men can do, but what they are capable of omitting;
for at the very moment when the fate of the Protestant religion and of the yet remaining liberties of Germany were about to be decided in the field, the Protestant princes, and the ambassadors from a number
of free towns, met in very sober conclave, not to adopt
resolute measures, but to draw up humble and respectful memorials. They deliberated when they should
have acted; and instead of raising armies capable of
giving effect to their representations, expended much
learning and eloquence in making clear their grievances, which could only be redressed, as they had
been inflicted,—sword in hand. The consequence
was, that the Emperor declared the meeting unlaw-
ful; refused to comply with its requests, and ordered
the members to disperse. No mention was made of
the King of Sweden at this congress, nor was his
ambassador, Chemnitz the historian, admitted to a
hearing. Fortune soon atoned to Gustavus for the
slight attempted to be put upon him by an assembly
against which the voice of humanity charged the
dreadful catastrophe we shall presently have to relate.

Tilly had advanced into Pomerania at the head of

a powerful army; but finding the King's post at Swedt unassailable, he left a strong force at Frankfurt on the Oder, and then proceeded towards Magdeburg, which had openly declared in favour of the Swedes. All this was strategically correct. On his way, the imperial commander took the small town of New-Brandenburg, which was defended by the Swedish General Kniphausen, with a garrison of 2000, one half of whom were Scotchmen.

Military history is as valuable and instructive, when so related as to give a clear and just view of the events described, as it is useless and unprofitable when it merely tells of results without explaining the causes by which they were produced. Campaign after campain is fought and recorded in this manner, without furnishing a single lesson worth preserving; so that we may generally say of it,

> " What boots the oft-repeated tale of strife,
> The feast of vultures, and the waste of life,"

since the perusal leaves us as ignorant of professional principles at the close of the volume, as we were at the opening. And yet will the capture and defence of the small, and unimportant town of New-Brandenburg present us with two important lessons that should never be overlooked. The place was only surrounded by an old wall, and a moat nearly half filled up, and the artillery consisted of two falconets, or two-pounders, which the garrison had brought along with them. Resistance against a whole army, provided with an efficient battering train, seemed altogether hopeless; but Kniphausen expected to be re-

lieved, and held out. He defended the town successfully for eight days ; on the ninth, three wide
breaches having been opened, he was for the second
time summoned to surrender, and was advised to do
so by the officers of the garrison. In reply, he produced a letter from the King, containing a promise
of relief, with an order to defend the place to the last
extremity. Men and officers submitted without a
murmur : they all, successively, took the sacrament
in the different churches, which, from the commencement of the siege, had been crowded with the towns-
people, imploring grace and protection ; and then repaired to their posts, resolved to perform their duty
to the utmost. After a repetition of fierce assaults,
the place was entered, and the assailants, exasperated
by the loss of more than 2000 men, put the garrison
to the sword. Kniphausen, his wife and daughter,
and about 50 soldiers only escaped. In the old town-
records, from which this statement is taken, and which
give an afflicting account of the cruelty exercised towards the citizens, a Scotch nobleman, called Earl
Lintz, is mentioned as having defended his post, long
after all other resistance had ceased : the strange and
unknown title, gives us an opportunity of relating a
gallant action, which we might not otherwise perhaps have been allowed to bring forward.

This nine days' defence of an old rampart without
artillery, proves how much determined soldiers can
effect behind stone walls ; and is exceedingly valuable
in an age that has seen first-rate fortresses, fully
armed, surrender before any part of the works had
been injured, often indeed at the very first summons.

It must further be mentioned, that an order had been dispatched to Kniphausen, subsequent to the one on which he acted, directing him to evacuate the town on the approach of Tilly, and not to expose the garrison to an unequal contest. This order miscarried, and the neglect caused 2000 brave men to be uselessly sacrificed ; shewing, for the thousandth time, what terrible consequences the slightest errors may produce in the dangerous and difficult business of war. And yet, with this knowledge fully before us, military rank is still sold in the British army : and staff appointments are given, according to the interest of the parties ; though we here see how easily thousands may be sacrificed by a little neglect or inability, on the part of an adjutant or quarter-master-general.

While these operations were in progress, Wallenstein, who had already lost his Duchy of Mecklenburg by the events of the war, conceived a project that evinced great political sagacity ; and would have been worth whole armies to the Emperor, had it been duly followed up. He proposed to gain over to the imperial cause, no less an ally than the King of Denmark ; who, by means of his fleet, was master of the Baltic. This bold plan, if carried into effect, would have raised up a new enemy in the very rear of the Swedish army ; and would not only have threatened their communication with the north of Germany, but with Sweden itself, and must certainly have prevented their advance into the empire. With this clever project, Wallenstein sent his chamberlain, Colonel Brenner, to Vienna, where the suggestion was most gladly received. Ferdinand was as much pleased with the proposal, as with the quarter from whence it came ; for it convinced him, that the deeply-wronged Wallenstein was above allowing personal injuries to influence his conduct, when the cause of his country was concerned. In the joy of his heart, he wrote to Wallenstein with his own hand, before the ministers could dispatch the official answer. He fully approved of the Duke's proposal, requested him to carry on the negotiation with his usual " dexterity," though, at first, in his own name only : and concluded, by expressing himself " delighted to find that his dear friend did not forsake him in the hour of difficulty." Not satisfied with this, he immediately afterwards invited the dismissed general to Vienna, as " he wished to consult him on various important points concerning the war, as well as on other matters of public interest :" he also asked his opinion about a corps of 10,000 men which a Count Palatine had proposed to raise.

Wallenstein never went to Vienna, alleging illness as the cause of declining the invitation ; but it is said that he was afraid of not being treated as Duke of Mecklenburg, though always addressed as such by the Emperor. But, though he did not visit the capital, he entered with great spirit into the Danish negotiation. The favourable terms, so unexpectedly granted to Denmark by the treaty of Lubeck, had established a good understanding between Wallenstein and the King, of which the former now availed himself with considerable ability. He represented how prejudicial to Denmark the rapidly augmenting power of Sweden might become, and recommended that Christian should join the Emperor, the King of Spain and the House of Austria, in time to arrest the progress of this dangerous enemy. Christian IV. lent a willing ear to the proposal.

If we could always follow to their sources the leading events of the world, how much of what is deemed greatness and glory, to say nothing of sorrow and evil, might not be traced to impure springs : how much to the spirit of envy alone, which spreads its poisoning influence through the whole frame of society. In love, in commerce, in all the subordinate pursuits of life, its power is constantly seen ; its far extended sway is exhibited in the countenances of thousands. It shines through the smile of the courtier, and is as little concealed by the assumed sternness of the soldier, as by the vapid and unmeaning coldness affected by the man of fashion. In war, in politics, and in the government of empires, its influence is felt. Where virtue and patriotism have produced one honest reformer, malignant envy has produced a thousand. How often are men of merit arrested in mid career, by the jealousy of their superiors : how often are the most gifted individuals prevented, by the same cause, from serving their country in situations in which their talents might be of the greatest advantage ; while feeble and incapable men are committing, perhaps, irremediable follies. Thrones are not above the reach of the noxious vapour, and even the kings of the earth are liable to the fatal contagion. Christian IV. was a wise and able prince : his reign had, in many respects, been glorious to himself and beneficial to his people : yet was he willing to risk the peace of his country, and sacrifice the interest of his religion ; the very religion for which he had fought with honour, if not success, to the mere workings of that jealousy, which the growing fame of the King of Sweden excited in his breast.

On the receipt of Wallenstein's letter, he sent Colonel Oynhausen to Gitchin, " there to treat confidentially on various matters with the Duke of Mecklenburg and Sagan." Wallenstein immediately communicated to the Duke of Eggenburg the nature of the Danish proposals. Christian, after expressing the greatest affection for the House of Austria in general, and for the Emperor in particular, agreed to join them, on condition of receiving, as a reward for his exertions, the bishoprics of Bremen and Verden. These bishoprics had been taken from the Protestants by the Edict of Restitution ; and Ferdinand's conscience would not allow him to replace them in the hands of heretics ; particularly, since the Pope had conferred them on his second son, the Archduke Leopold. While this point was negotiating, the Swedes took the bishoprics, and settled the point of conscience, so that other compensations had to be proposed. The Emperor suggested, that the Danes should receive part of Wallenstein's Duchy of Mecklenburg, for which the latter was to be repaid in money : the ministers also recommended in their letters, that the King should be " flattered with the prospect " of obtaining other conquered provinces. The treaty was really so far advanced, as only to require the Emperor's signature, but it was never ratified ; though for what cause we do not learn. It required, no doubt, some time to arrange the details, and Wallenstein had probably been appointed to the command of the army, before the diplomatists were ready with their parchments ; and once at the head of a gallant host, the proudest of men might not, perhaps, be willing to share, even with a king, the honours and the conquests he expected to achieve.

It is particularly necessary to notice this Danish negotiation, as the very act which the Emperor had approved and encouraged, was charged " as a secret practice," against Wallenstein in the official statement afterwards published by the court of Vienna. The treasonable correspondence, which, in the same document, he is accused of having carried on with Gustavus Adolphus, is also placed at this period ; at the very period when he was striving to call up a champion, whose first appearance in the lists, must have been ruinous to the interests of the Swedish monarch. It is not easy to acquit the imperial Cabinet of unfair dealing in this transaction ; for they had all the papers relative to this Danish negotiation under their hands, when they drew up their charges against the Duke of Friedland.

CHAPTER V.

Gustavus Adolphus seems not to have suspected this threatening negociation ; for Tilly had no sooner withdrawn from the banks of the Oder, than he broke up his camp and advanced towards Frankfurt. The town was large and ill fortified ; but defended by 8000 men ; an army rather than a garrison. Some taunting insults offered by the Imperialists, and the general spirit of the Swedish troops, occasioned the first investment to be turned into an immediate assault. The place was carried, sword in hand, and between two and three thousand of the garrison cut down ; vast numbers perished in the Oder ; few escaped, as the bridge was blocked up by carts and waggons, and still fewer received quarter. " New-Brandenburg quarter " was the reply given to every man who implored mercy ; and the enraged soldier thought himself justified in imitating the very barbarity which he was condemning in others.

The town having been first plundered by the Imperialists, was again plundered by the Swedes : the usual fate of towns and nations that are morally or physically too feeble to defend themselves. It is afflicting to find our countrymen already fighting against each other on this occasion. The Scottish troops in the Swedish army, took an active part in this assault ; and among the defenders was an Irish regiment, in which served the infamous Walter But- ler, of whom we shall see too much hereafter. This corps is said to have fought with peculiar gallantry ; and it is generally asserted, that the attack would have failed, had the rest of the garrison behaved with equal bravery.

Tilly was already on the march to relieve Frank- furt ; but when he heard of its capture, he turned again, and began the siege of Magdeburg in form. The place was extensive, but not strong ; and the citizens were unfortunately better economists than soldiers. They thought the storm would blow over, as it had done before; or that it would be time enough to take precautionary measures when the enemy were at the gates. The King of Sweden had sent Colonel Falkenberg, an experienced engineer, to assist them ; but no persuasion could induce them to advance money for the purpose of raising troops, though the garrison consisted of only 2000 infantry and 200 cavalry ; a number totally inadequate to the defence of the extensive works. The citizens performed, in- deed, military duty, but they performed it more like civilians than like soldiers. The rich thought them- selves exempted from attendance, provided they sent their servants to the ramparts ; and the middle classes objected to serve along with menials ; so that the number of defenders diminished daily. It was also said that the Imperialists had friends and adherents in the city, and even in the senate.

These insufficient means caused the strong and ex- tensive outworks to be abandoned as soon as they were seriously attacked; and the besieged found themselves reduced to the defence of the inner wall, without being able to maintain even the covered way. The Imperialists quickly availed themselves of the advantages offered, and erected batteries on the crown of the glacis: several breaches were opened; but as the passage of the ditch had not been effected, owing to the fire of the besieged, they were not deemed very accessible, and Tilly had doubts of the result. Pappenheim's impetuosity overcame his scruples, and a general assault was determined upon; but not before the citizens had been lulled into security by the pretended retreat of the besiegers.

On the ninth of May, the fire of the imperial artillery suddenly ceased; the guns were withdrawn from the batteries; an unusual silence prevailed in camp; and every thing indicated that the siege was raised. Count Gualdo, who was present in Tilly's army, informs us, that the imperial adherents in the town, helped to render this opinion general; but we should not believe that any men, having life and fortune depending on the issue, could have been deceived by so gross an artifice, were we not assured of the fact from undoubted authority. A respectable clergyman, who was saved by the avarice of an imperial officer, tells us himself, that he was addressing his congregation, and returning thanks for their general deliverance, at the moment when the enemy were ascending the ramparts.

At seven o'clock, on the morning of the 10th of May, the town was attacked at four different points. As the citizens always retired to their houses at daybreak, the soldiers only were at their posts; and from the small number of the original garrison, and the extensive nature of the works, few could be assembled on vulnerable points; so that no very formidable resistance was offered. Pappenheim * first planted a standard on the rampart: it was hailed with the loud cheers that generally prognosticate success: the other columns which had been arrested in their progress, again rushed on to the attack; and the walls were soon in possession of the assailants. The gallant Falkenberg was killed at the commencement of the attack: a Captain Smith, who tried to rally the unhappy citizens, also fell: the confusion became general, and all attempts to dislodge the enemy failed completely. Those who had first entered burst open two of the gates, and admitted more of the spoil-breathing bands; cannon were pointed along the principal streets, and the ill-fated citizens driven to their houses, there to await their fate.

" They were not," says Schiller, " left long in suspense. A general, endowed with humanity, would vainly have recommended mercy to troops like those which Tilly commanded; but the imperial leader did not even make the attempt; and the soldiers, thus rendered absolute masters of the lives and fortunes of the people of Magdeburg, rushed into the houses, and gave way to every low and vile desire. Suppliant innocence found mercy before many a Ger-

* In writing to Wallenstein, Pappenheim says, that he carried the rampart with the loss of only five men; but suffered severely afterwards; because, from not being supported in time by the other columns, he had to maintain his post against the whole garrison.

man ear : none from Pappenheim's infuriated Walloons.   Scarcely had the scene of blood commenced,
when all the gates were thrown open, and the entire
of the cavalry, followed by the whole swarm of mur-
dering Croats, were let loose upon the unhappy
town.

" And now began a scene of death and crime for
which history has no language, and poetry no pencil.
Not guiltless infancy, not helpless age ; neither
youth, sex, beauty nor station, could disarm the fury
of these ruthless conquerors.   Wives were dishonoured in the arms of their husbands ; daughters at the
feet of their parents; and the defenceless sex had only
the privilege of serving as victims to twofold fury.
No place, however secluded, however sacred, offered
an asylum ; and fifty-three women were found beheaded in one church alone.   Croats took a pleasure
in throwing children into the flames ; Pappenheim's
Walloons in fixing infants with spears to the breasts
of their mothers.

" These horrors continued till smoke and flame
put an end to rage and rapine.   To augment the
confusion, and break the resistance of the defenders,
several houses were set on fire, in the first instance.
A tempest now arose, which spread the conflagration
with fearful rapidity ; so that the whole town was
soon enveloped in flame.   Dreadful was the pressure
through fiery vapour and over dead bodies, through
the midst of flashing swords, falling ruins, and
streams of blood.   The atmosphere glowed, and the
burning heat forced, at last, even these murderers to
seek shelter in their camp.   In less than twelve

hours this great, rich, strong and prosperous city, one of the finest in Germany, was, with the exception of two churches, and a few huts, completely reduced to ashes.   The administrator, Prince Christian William, was, after receiving several wounds, taken prisoner; along with three senators.   Many officers and magistrates found, sword in hand, an enviable death.   About 400 of the richest citizens were saved by the avarice of imperial officers, who expected to extort from them a heavy ransom.   Most of the individuals who displayed, even this sort of humanity, were officers of the League; and the unsparing cruelty of the imperial soldiers, caused them to be looked upon as guardian angels.

" Scarcely had the flames subsided, ere the plundering bands returned, with unquenched voracity, to seek, amid ashes, for additional spoil.   Many were suffocated by smoke and vapour: many found rich booty ; as the citizens had concealed most of their valuables in vaults and cellars.   On the 13th, after the principal streets had been cleared of ruins and corpses, Tilly himself appeared in the town. Horrible was the scene presented to humanity ; the living, crawling out from under the dead, children wandering about and seeking, with loud lamentations, for their lost parents, and infants striving to obtain nourishment from the breasts of their slaughtered mothers.   More than 6000 dead bodies were thrown into the Elbe, before the streets could be cleared : a great many more had been consumed by the flames : the total number of slain amounted to 30,000.

" On the following day the plundering was put an end to ; and all who had till then escaped, were pardoned. About a thousand persons were brought out of the Cathedral, where they had remained for three days and nights without food, in constant fear of death. Tilly assured them of safety, and caused bread to be distributed among them. Mass was celebrated in the same church on the day following, and a solemn *Te Deum* was sung under the discharge of artillery. The imperial general rode through the streets to report, from ocular evidence, that, since the fall of Troy and Jerusalem, no such conquest had been achieved. Nor is the statement much exaggerated, when we consider the wealth, greatness and importance of the city, and the ruthless barbarism which marked its destruction."

Schiller and other historians assert that some German officers, revolted by the enormities committed, applied to Tilly soon after the capture of the town, and requested that he would order a stop to be put to deeds so disgraceful. " Come back in an hour," was his reported answer, " and I shall consider of it ; the soldier must have some reward for his toil." Other accounts say that he quoted the well-known lines of Virgil on the occasion,

> " *Venit summa dies et ineluctabile fatum*
> ——————————*fuit Ilium et ingens*
> *Gloria Parthenopes.*"

It is right to mention these reports; affecting the character of a celebrated man, since history has deemed them worthy of being received as authentic ; but we must still be allowed to express doubts of their accuracy. The indignation of mankind could hardly fail to be aroused by the commission of crimes so dreadful, and the world would, of course, visit on the head of the commander, the misdeeds of the troops, however inadequate to the control of such bands his power might have been. By some, Tilly is said to have shed tears of sorrow and indignation over the fate of the unhappy city *, and to have thrown the blame upon Pappenheim. This however would be no justification; we can easily acquit the general of having willingly sanctioned atrocities more certain to injure than to forward his cause; but we still know enough to condemn him. He survived a massacre which it was his duty to have arrested, sword in hand if necessary, and at peril of his life: he neglected this duty, and his name and fame are for ever tarnished in consequence. Pappenheim seems to have approved of the deed; for in writing to the Elector of Bavaria, he calls it "a punishment justly inflicted by heaven on the town, as a similar punishment was formerly inflicted on Jerusalem,— for the crimes of its people."

Magdeburg's appalling fate spread terror and dismay through Protestant Germany; and placed the merits of the Congress of Leipzig in full and conspicuous view.

The frightful event fell heavily on the spirits of Gustavus. The voice of Europe loudly accused him of pusillanimity for neglecting to strike a blow in

---

* Riscius, 236.   Theatr. Europ. 636.

favour of his allies.   He was obliged to justify himself before the world, and easily did so ; but it was
at the expense of the Electors of Brandenburg and
Saxony, who, instead of aiding him, had thrown
obstacles in his way at the very time when he was
proceeding to aid the beleaguered city.   It is probable, however, that the weakness of his army, though
not stated, was the real cause of the delay.   After
the many garrisons he had left in the conquered fortresses, he could have no large disposable force at
hand ; and we shall see presently, that he was not
equal to meet Tilly in the open field ; and unable
consequently to hazard a battle for the relief of the
besieged.

The imperial general announced the fall of Magdeburg in the tone of a conqueror ; and encouraged
by this new victory, the Court of Vienna, disregarding
the presence of the Swedes, added oppression to oppression, and threatened all the resisting Protestant
towns with similar punishment.   Tilly first marched
into the country of Hesse, there to carry the Edict
of Restitution into full effect ; but was soon recalled
by the movements of the King of Sweden, who had
advanced and taken post at Werben, a position, that
in a strategical point of view, is evidently the finest in
Germany : a good reason, perhaps, why it was never
occupied in modern times.   The imperial general,
unmindful of the adversary to whom he was opposed,
kept his troops so indifferently together, that Gustavus, who was constantly on the watch, surprised
three of his regiments by a night attack, and completely destroyed them.   The art of keeping armies

well together, and well in hand, so as to hover constantly in a threatening attitude over an enemy, ready to strike at the slightest opening, is a species of strategy requiring the highest skill and talent. Gustavus, and above all Frederick and Turenne, understood this difficult part of the science. In modern times Blucher's campaign in Silesia furnishes a proof of such conduct; though modern strategy has, in general, been founded on the power of conscriptions rather than on intelligible professional principles.

The King of Sweden, who had no conscription to supply him with soldiers, was forced to make up, by genius and talent, for inferior numbers. He had no sooner taken post at Werben than he surrounded himself with entrenchments, the remains of which attest, to this day, the skill of the leader in designing, and the exertions of the soldiers in executing such works. It might almost be said of this admirable soldier, that he owed his success in Germany, as much to the spade as to the sword; for he could never be forced to a battle unless when it suited his own purpose; and when not disposed to fight, he was always found too strongly posted to be attacked with success, however inferior might be the number of his troops. This Tilly found to his cost.

Anxious to strike a blow at the Swedes, and desirous of avenging the fate of his three regiments, the imperial commander advanced against the camp, and after a day's cannonade, ventured upon a night attack, which failed completely. The Imperialists were driven back at all points, and pursued far into the plain by the Swedish cavalry, who sallied out through the intervals left between the redoubts. Magdeburg was Tilly's last victory : on his asphodel-covered brows the laurel could spring no more.

From Werben, the imperial general directed his march towards the frontiers of Saxony, where he was ordered to force the Elector, John George, to carry the Edict of Restitution into effect ; to disband the Saxon army, and to admit imperial troops into his dominions. It is due to Tilly to say, that he disapproved of a measure so likely to drive the Elector into the arms of the King of Sweden. Both Pappenheim and himself represented the danger, and always spoke of Gustavus as an adversary already sufficiently formidable. But the Court of Vienna, blinded by former success, thought only of availing themselves of the panic occasioned by the destruction of Magdeburg. The order to Tilly was positive ; he therefore sent it to the Elector, requiring immediate compliance with its mandates ; but John George, indignant at seeing his long subserviency to the House of Austria repaid by such unworthy treatment, refused to submit ; and the imperial army immediately entered the country, laying every thing waste with fire and sword. A hundred villages were burned in the course of a few days ; Leipzig was attacked, and taken ; and the unfortunate electorate would have paid dearly for the resolution of its sovereign, had not the presence of the King of Sweden arrested the progress of destruction. No sooner had the Imperialists entered Saxony than John George hastened to conclude a treaty of alliance with Gustavus Adolphus, who, always ready to take advantage of circumstances, had followed close upon the enemy.

On the day after the conclusion of this treaty, the King crossed the Elbe at Wittenberg, and joined the Saxons at Düben. From thence the combined armies marched towards Leipzig, for the purpose of attacking the Imperialists, who, on their part, advanced as far as Breitenfeldt, to give the new allies the meeting.

Tilly on learning the junction of the Swedes and Saxons, had at first taken up a strong position in front of Leipzig, where he could safely await a reinforcement of 8000 men, which General Altringa was bringing forward; but the eagerness for battle, expressed by Pappenheim, and by most of the younger officers, overcame the veteran's better judgment. Hints were also thrown out that the aged general feared to measure swords with the gallant and highhearted King of Sweden. Tilly was a soldier, and an able one; but he had a soldier's failing, and brooked no taunts directed against what he might deem his honour and military character: his personal courage was undoubted, but he proved on this occasion that he wanted mental courage, a quality equally essential to a commander. He decided on battle, contrary to his own conviction; and the world owes its freedom, perhaps, to his want of resolution; for it is difficult to say what the world's situation would now have been, had the fate of war turned against the allies in the plains of Leipzig.

The battle of Breitenfeldt, which decided the fate of Germany, and of the Protestant religion, was fought on the 7th December 1631. The imperial army was drawn up along the highest ridge of a wide, undulating plain. The troops were formed, contrary to the assertion of Schiller, and those who have followed him, in two lines, having some corps in third line as a reserve. The wings were unsupported ; but as the country was perfectly open, no unseen flank-movement, could be attempted against them, without being readily met by a counter-movement. The principal part of the artillery was dispersed along the front of the infantry. Sixteen heavy guns were posted on the right, most likely on the spot where the monument now stands, and where the ground forms a slight elevation. It was altogether a fair, well-chosen battle-field ; and measured nearly two miles and a half from right to left. The imperial army amounted on this important day to about 35,000 men : of nearly equal strength were the combined forces of the Saxons and the Swedes.

At nine o'clock in the morning, the allies were seen advancing, in two columns, along the plain : the Swedes formed the right, the Saxons the left column. The van of the Swedish army, consisting of three regiments of Scottish infantry, no sooner crossed the Lober, a small streamlet that had to be passed in full view of the Imperialists, than they were immediately assailed by Pappenheim, at the head of a large body of cuirassiers. The Scots availed themselves of the ground which was in their favour ; and being supported by some dragoons, drove back the enemy. Pappenheim set fire to the village of Podelwitz, in order to arrest the progress of the Swedes ; and being reinforced in his turn, fell upon the right

flank of the advancing column. But General Banner
wheeled the leading divisions to the right, and presented a regular front, which the cuirassiers were
unable to break ; while the rest of the army moved up
and formed in the plain under cover of this Cæsarian
line.   Such skilful movements, though easy enough
of execution to modern troops, to those at least who
are capable of moving under fire, were unknown to
the Imperialists, and impracticable with their unwieldy formations ; a circumstance that naturally
made them fight to great disadvantage.

On the present occasion, the repulsed cuirassiers
retired so rapidly to the main position, that the Holstein regiment of infantry, which had been sent to
their aid, was left alone on the plain, where their faulty
system of tactics was immediately made apparent. The
square, and closely-formed mass of spearmen, in the
centre of the musqueteers, could afford no protection
to the latter, who seemed placed round the square only
to render the spears useless.   They were instantly
charged by some Finland cavalry and cut down : the
spearmen thus left defenceless, in their turn were
attacked by two companies of Swedish musqueteers,
and completely routed : their colonel, the Duke of
Holstein, was among the slain.   To the Imperialists,
this was an evil-boding commencement of the action.

The Swedish army, when drawn up for battle, stood
in two lines, having besides some corps of cavalry and
infantry in reserve : there was also, in front of the
second line, a reserve of artillery ; the first we find
mentioned in history. Besides the intervals between
the different brigades, the lines were at a considerable

distance from each other, so that the troops had ample room to move without endangering their order or formation. The cavalry, as in all the armies of the period, were formed on the flanks. The King commanded the right wing, Gustavus Horne the left, General Teufel the centre, and our countryman Colonel Hepburn, the second line. The reserve was under the command of Colonel Hall. The Saxons were on the left of the Swedes, under the command of the Elector and of Field-Marshal Arnheim, the same who formerly served under Wallenstein : in what particular manner these troops were formed we are unable to state.

The cannonade had not lasted long after the armies were in presence, when Tilly fell with great impetuosity on the entire front of the allied line. It was a gallant onset on the main body of the enemy, and resembled in nothing, the partial attacks directed in modern times against hamlets, houses, woods or villages, to which a conventional mode of warfare attaches an unreal value. Genius and the high mental courage resulting from it, strike at once at the main object ; while mediocrity, pretension and bloated vanity, brave only in the waste of brave men's lives, beat about for some piece of good fortune to turn up in their favour : fight battles with skirmishers, leaving armies in reserve, literally to feed the fire, to come, like the wounded Curiatii, successively instead of simultaneously into action, and above all, to protect the fame of some mighty leader, should the Goddess of Chance remain deaf to the prayers of her votaries, notwithstanding the hecatombs of human victims, always so readily offered up at her shrine.

Tilly's gallantry served him but little however, against more skilful and equally brave opponents. The Imperialists made the attack resolutely, but were driven back by the heavy fire of the Swedish infantry. Against the Saxons they were more successful : these newly-raised troops were unable to withstand the fiery onset of the old war-trained bands, the victors in so many fields, and gave way almost immediately. The Elector himself hurried off to Eulenburg, where he arrived in very low spirits, thinking that everything was lost. Two regiments made for a time an honourable stand ; but overwhelmed by numbers, they were, at last, thrown into confusion, and obliged to follow the flight of their comrades.

Arnheim, abandoned by his army, galloped away to the right, to inform the King of what had happened. On this point, where Pappenheim and Gustavus had encountered, the combat had been very severe. But the cuirassiers, clad from head to heel in heavy armour, could not follow up the advantage sometimes gained in their first charge ; nor were they capable of reforming when once disordered by their own success. The Swedes could do both, and were therefore victorious, as men, in other respects equal, always will be over cuirass-encumbered adversaries. The Imperialists were driven from the field notwithstanding the heroic efforts of Pappenheim, who is said to have slain fifteen men with his own hand. It was just when the success of this combat was decided, that the King received, from Arnheim,

the news of the disaster which had befallen the Saxons.
Leaving Banner to pursue the imperial cavalry, he
hurried to the left, to remedy the misfortune of his
allies.   Every thing was already in good train.   Field-
Marshal Horne no sooner saw the flight of the Saxons, than he wheeled up the second line ; and, by
placing their right close to the left of the first line,
formed them *en potence,* and presented a front to the
left, as Banner had before presented one to the right.

And time it was that precaution should be taken ;
for the Swedes had now to contend against double
their numbers, and Tilly saw, and tried right gallantly,
to follow up the advantage he had gained.   He recalled his troops from the pursuit of the vanquished,
brought up his second line, and calling to his men,
" Now, comrades, let us fall upon the left wing of
the Swedes and the empire is ours ;" advanced them
bravely to the charge.   But the tactical skill of his
adversaries more than atoned for their inferiority in
numbers : they were soon formed, and prepared to
receive a better onset than Tilly was able to make.
He only hurled against their line, bodies of men
hastily collected, as fortune brought his unwieldy
masses to his hands ; some returning from the pursuit
of the Saxons ; some arriving from where they had
stood in reserve ; and all, rushing tumultuously on,
without order or concert, were rolled back, with great
slaughter, from each successive attack.

Gustavus seeing that danger was arrested on the
left, made a forward movement with his first line,
charged and took the imperial artillery in his front,
and turned the guns upon the rest of their infantry.

They were soon in confusion.   On the hill, however, where the heavy guns were posted, Tilly made a stand with the reserve, and a severe contest here took place.   Four regiments, who had never fled from a field of battle, and who were determined not to do so now, retired fighting and in good order, after the rest of the army were dispersed.   Reduced to a few hundreds they gained a wood, where nightfall protected them from further pursuit.   Tilly, though wounded, was, with Pappenheim, the last to leave the ground, and had a narrow escape for his life.   A Swedish captain of horse fired a pistol at him, and was trying to dispatch him with the butt end, when a Prince of Lauenburg came to his aid, and shot the Swede through the head.   The imperial army lost about 10,000 men ; 7000 were killed or wounded and 3000 taken : 30 pieces of artillery, 100 standards and all the baggage of the vanquished fell into the hands of the conquerors.   To these losses must be added the fame in arms, and the spell of invincibility which was broken for ever.   The Saxons had 2000 men killed and wounded ; the Swedes 700 only.

Thus ended the most memorable battle recorded in history.   It was not a battle fought, between rival nations, for spoil, power and dominion ; not for the possession of provinces, or the supremacy of empires : it was a battle between the two great divisions of the Christian race ; and fought to determine whether men should be allowed the free agency of thought, or be forced to receive the dictates of self-elected conclaves, on points of vital importance to their worldly and future happiness.   And it is according to the view taken of this question, that the result of the day's action must be determined. As this question shall be answered, so will the battle of Leipzig be termed either glorious and beneficial to men, or destructive to their welfare, and dangerous to their salvation.

Tilly was, of course, much blamed for his conduct on this occasion. No case has, however, been made out against him; and judging only from what we know, and from what his critics have told us, we should say that his arrangements merited every en- comium. His position was a good one ; he was right in trying to impede the advance and formation of the allies; he was right in boldly falling upon them the moment they came fairly within his reach ; and he was right also in turning from the pursuit of the Saxons, in order to break in upon the left wing of the Swedes. His defeat was owing entirely to the tactical superiority of the Swedish troops, and to the skill of their commanders. The promptness with which they first presented a front to Pappenheim on the right, and afterwards to Tilly himself on the left, is deserving of the highest praise, and could not be surpassed by the soldiers of the present day ; quickly and accurately as they are allowed to move. No mo- dern army has, indeed, manœuvred so well in a field of battle as the Swedes manœuvred at Leipzig ; and no Austrian General, of modern times, has behaved with the skill, courage and resolution displayed by Tilly on the same occasion.

The usual accounts of this action describe Gustavus as making a movement to the right, seaman-like, to gain from Tilly the advantage of sun and wind ; and afterwards represent him throwing forward his right wing, *en echelon*, to attack the imperial artillery on the hill. These are either the mere tales of historians, unacquainted with military affairs, or they are the devices of ignorant tacticians anxious to find, in the actions of a great soldier, some support for their impracticable puerilities. Gustavus could not, at the outset of the action, move away to the right without abandoning the Saxons, and presenting his left flank to the enemy : and as to the echelon movement described, it would have brought the right flank of the Swedish troops close to the muzzles of the imperial guns, stationed in their front. The idea of men actually brushing the hostile guns with their right shoulders, and marching away to the left under the fire of those guns, there to attack some other guns, placed upon a distant height, belongs altogether to the transcendental school of modern strategy : the plain good sense of the seventeenth century never soared to such an elevation.

The lustre which this victory shed over the fame of Gustavus, more than doubled his strength, by the moral power which it added to the force of his arms. His friends assumed courage ; those who had before only wished him success, now prepared to aid him ; and his enemies were, in an equal degree, discouraged and depressed. At Vienna the news was not at first believed : no one would credit, " that," as they expressed it, " God Almighty had turned Protestant." But the on-rolling storm soon brought conviction to the most incredulous.

At a council of war, held by the victors immediately after the battle, it was resolved, that the Saxons should invade Bohemia, and the Swedes march towards the Rhine. Gustavus has been much blamed for this plan, and for not marching straight upon Vienna: but the censure seems unjust. An advance on Vienna would have led him, on the approach of winter, to the banks of the Danube, where that river had before arrested the Bohemian insurgents, as well as Bethlem Gabor.

With less than 20,000 men, what could have been effected in the centre of the Austrian monarchy ; all its available resources closing around him, and the forces of Catholic Germany collecting in his rear, and on his right flank ? Arnheim, with the remnants of his fugitive Saxons, could not even have kept the remains of Tilly's army in check. The march on Vienna would therefore have been a mere chance adventure, in the Napoleon style; whereas, by marching into Franconia, and towards the Rhine, the King disarmed the Catholics of those provinces ; rallied the Protestants around him, and not only deprived the House of Austria of all the support it derived from Western Germany ; but raised up a Protestant force, by the aid of which Sweden was enabled to maintain, for sixteen years afterwards, a successful struggle against the combined power of the League and the Emperor. By advancing through Franconia and Bavaria towards Vienna, Gustavus took the Danube and the Austrian defences in reverse ; and had the Saxons performed the easy task allotted them in the execution of this admirable plan, they would already, on the opening of the next campaign, have joined the Swedes under the walls of the imperial capital.

From Leipzig, Gustavus directed his march right into the centre of the empire. He was everywhere received with boundless acclamation by the Protestants : princes, nobles and soldiers flocked to his standard from all quarters. The castle of Wurtzburg was the first important place that attempted to resist. Situated on a hill, on the banks of the Maine, opposite to the town, it is of great strength ; and was taken by one of those bold actions that so often succeed in war, owing to the mere excess of daring, for which they are distinguished.

Not a stone of the works had been injured ; but a Swedish officer, sent with seven men to *reconnoitre* the gate, found the drawbridge down, as the garrison were about to make a sally. On being challenged, he boldly answered, " A Swede," and instantly sprung, sword in hand, upon the bridge. Darkness concealed the small number of the party,—fear magnified it, and the noise of battle soon brought the Scottish infantry and the Swedish regiment of Axel Lilly to the spot. The garrison was strong, and made a resolute defence ; but the fiery impetuosity of the assailants overcame all resistance, and after a short, but sharp contest, the castle was in possession of the Swedes. It was found to contain stores, wine, and treasure to a large amount. Among the slain were twenty monks, who had fought, says Bülow, " not for their religion, but for their wine and their wealth."

An army which the Duke of Lorraine led against

the Swedes, was dispersed at the first sight of the
enemy ; the Duke himself leading the flight.   As he
hurried through a village in Franconia, a peasant gave
his horse a sharp cut with a whip, calling out at the
same time, " Quick, quick, Sir Duke ; those must fly
fast, who fly before the great King of Sweden."

From Wurtzburg, Gustavus descended the Maine.
Hannau was taken by surprise ; Wertheim by storm ;
Frankfurt opened its gates.   At Oppenheim, the
King forced the passage of the Rhine with only a few
boats.   The first troops that crossed were charged
by the Spanish cavalry ; but the Swedish infantry
drove them back, and entrenched themselves so well
and so rapidly, that the Spanish infantry, on advancing, experienced no better success than the cavalry.
Oppenheim was taken by assault, and Mayence, the
capital of Western Germany, after a few days' siege.
Landau, Spiers, Worms, Wiessenburg, Frankcathal,
towns that, in the first revolution war, saved the
independence of France, followed in rapid succession.
It seemed as if no barrier could arrest the progress,—
no fortress withstand the arms of this northern conqueror.

During the few weeks that Gustavus halted at
Mayence, his head-quarters became the seat of active
negotiations.   The Catholic powers of Germany
found that the battle was no longer for empire, but
safety, and sought to shelter themselves under the
wing of France.   Even Richelieu was alarmed by
the success of the Swedes, and trembled at the spirit
he had himself evoked.   He tried to throw obstacles
in the way of the King's farther progress, and to

fetter his hands, by foolish conditions. But Gustavus, who had been untractable enough on the shores of the Baltic, had not learned humility from victory, and as before, the firmness of the soldier easily overcame the feeble arts of the minister. Of all sciences, diplomacy is surely the weakest and most inefficient : it is in fact nothing more than the slave of military success ; depending entirely on the force, ready, in the background, to give weight to protocols. Napoleon and his ministers were great diplomatists after the battle of Wagram, though very poor ones after the battle of Waterloo ; but Attila was always a great diplomatist.

A short breathing-time only, was given to the Swedish army at Mayence ; and early in March the King already appeared before Donauwerth, which was taken as soon as attacked. Here he crossed the Danube, and advanced to the frontiers of Bavaria. To preserve, from invasion, this favoured country, which had so long escaped the evils of war, Tilly took up a strong position behind the river Lech, between Augsburg and Raine. In the choice of this post, the imperial commander displayed great skill, and proved himself far superior to one of his successors. General Mack having the same object in view, took up a position near Ulm ; and leaving thus his right flank exposed, lost his army without striking a single blow.

The depth of the stream, the rapidity of the current and the height of the banks, made the attempt to force a passage, in the face of a well-posted enemy, extremely dangerous. The Swedish council of war wavered : Gustavus alone was resolved. His daring genius made him perceive advantages of position, that were invisible to ordinary observers, and of these he availed himself with skill.

Under the fire of seventy-two pieces of artillery, a bridge was thrown across the river, some infantry passed over, while the cavalry traversed at a ford, which had been discovered a little higher up the stream. Tilly no sooner saw the Swedes forming on the right bank, than he bravely sallied forth to attack them. It was the last of his fields ; a falconet-ball shattered his knee, and fainting from pain, he was carried to the rear. Altringer, the next in command, was also wounded ; and the soldiers, seeing their leaders struck down, gave way and fled.

The Elector of Bavaria, who was present in the action, rallied the troops, and under cover of night led them to Ingolstadt, the defence of which Tilly had recommended with his last breath, and where he died on the following day. This aged commander was regretted by his Sovereign, who placed unbounded confidence in his fidelity ; and by the soldiers, who, it seems, were attached to him. Had he been a strict disciplinarian, this would have redounded to his credit ; but as it was, the attachment of the troops may have resulted as much from the licence allowed them, as from other causes. He left a very moderate fortune, for one who had so long held a high command, in times of almost universal spoliation ; and bequeathed the best part of his wealth to different regiments of his army. He probably felt that the soldiers had done something for the general, and

strove to shew his gratitude accordingly ; and, as the
sentiment was a generous one, it would be pleasant
to relate proofs of its having existed in the breasts of
modern chieftains ; though the opportunity for doing
so has not yet been publicly furnished.   Gustavus
called him the " Old Corporal," owing to his having,
perhaps, some martinet propensities ; but Tilly had
nevertheless qualities which placed him far above the
martinets of a later date.   Many were, no doubt, the
faults of this stern old man ; many were the evil deeds
of which he was guilty ; and heavily and justly have
they been visited on his memory.   But historians, in
drawing his character, should have recollected that
religious adversaries, and deeply aggrieved parties,
were his enemies ; and in loading him with a thousand
crimes, they should not have omitted all mention of
his virtues.   His unshaken fidelity to his sovereign
and to his religion, should have been mentioned with
honour ; his talents, bravery, courtesy ; his disinterestedness, his never-broken word ; as well as his
generosity to the persecuted Bohemians, should all
have been recorded with high and deserved praise.

Gustavus, after taking Augsburg and Landshut,
advanced to Munich : the citizens, afraid that the
fate of Magdeburg was to be avenged on the capital
of their Sovereign, a prince who had brought so many
evils over Protestant Germany, threw themselves at
the feet of the conqueror, and implored mercy : the
King laughed at their fears, and forgave them at once.

The monks and clergy were still more alarmed ;
they had preached up persecution of heretics even to
the last, and never mentioned Gustavus except as

Antichrist, armed with a sword of peculiar construction, the gift of Satan himself. In many parts of the country, their evil counsels had kindled a *guerilla* war, which led to the commission of fearful crimes ; the peasantry slew and tortured the straggling Swedes that fell into their hands, and these excesses were punished again with adequate severity, by the enraged soldiers ; but at Munich, the clergy also were pardoned. The King spoke to them in the most friendly manner ; attended some Catholic ceremony in person, and on one occasion even entered into a theological discussion with the Dominicans : and it may be presumed, that the good fathers took care not to have the best of the argument. The most exemplary discipline was preserved ; religion and property were alike respected ; and Gustavus, after levying a good sum in contributions from the rich, and bringing to light some guns and treasures which the Elector had caused to be buried, very liberally distributed money to the poor.

As the world were in the habit of seeing contributions levied, by all parties, on the rich, the act was not visited with unusual severity on the dreaded conqueror ; but they had never seen victorious foes distributing money to the poor of the vanquished : the King's generosity excited therefore universal admiration ; and gained for him golden opinions, far more valuable, even in a political point of view, than the gold by which they had been purchased.

It was indeed a direct and merciful interposition of Providence, which placed so humane and enlightened a prince at the head of the Protestants, when after

years of adversity, the tide of war turned in their
favour ; for it prevented the long-oppressed nations
from avenging, on Catholic subjects, the many injuries they had sustained from Catholic rulers. Gustavus Adolphus set an example of toleration, very
rare at the period, but which was followed by his
adherents ; for even those were proud to imitate the
conduct of so great a King, who could not always
appreciate the noble sentiments from which it arose.

The tolerant disposition of Wallenstein was also
of infinite benefit to the cause of humanity. He
was the agent of severe measures directed against
the power and possessions of the Protestants ; but
he never oppressed individuals on religious grounds :
he exerted himself, on the contrary, to mitigate, as
far as was in his power, the evils resulting from Ferdinand's persecuting decrees. In one letter only do
we find him touching on the subject of conversion,
and that as concisely as possible. When writing to
his Bohemian agent, from Havelberg, on the 27th
August 1627, he says, " This would perhaps be a
good time for urging the peasantry and citizens to
become Catholics :" not another word is added, nor
is the subject again repeated. On the other hand,
he often recommends that mildness and forbearance
may be observed in carrying on the counter-reformation : " Give the peasantry plenty of time ;"—" do
not press the peasantry and lower orders too hard
about religion ;"—" do not meddle with the peasantry in the mountains ;" are expressions frequently
used in his letters. And on one occasion he directs
that a poor widow, who was about to be deprived of

her estate, because she refused to change her religion, should be allowed to retain her property, " as the Lord would no doubt enlighten her mind, and bring her to a right way of thinking."

To estimate, even this degree of toleration, we must contrast it with the savage barbarity, exercised by commands of the Sovereign in whose dominions Wallenstein's estates and principalities were situated ; and from whom alone the Duke of Friedland held land, power and authority. Two short extracts from a contemporary chronicle, quoted by Forster, at page 358, will be sufficient for our purpose.

Speaking of the year 1623, the writer says, " When in this year, the Protestant clergy were banished, their churches closed, Luther's and Melanchthon's books and pictures burned, twenty ministers of the Gospel were killed along with many others : some of these were cut down, some speared and some stretched out on their books and burned." Opposite the year 1628, we have the following entry : " At the commencement of this year a number of peasants mutinied in the county of Königgrätz, and refused to obey the imperial commissioners. Soldiers were sent against them, when 500 were killed and a number taken prisoners : these were brought to Prague, when they were brand-marked on the shoulders, had their noses cut off, and were then sent home again."

Though scenes of this kind are, for many years, of constant recurrence in various parts of the country, we never find them acted in Wallenstein's principalities. From his own letters, and from a letter of his agent, Taxis, it is evident that he carried on

the counter-reformation with great mildness; with
indifference perhaps, and contented himself with
checking the cruelty of the imperial commissioners,
though never directly infringing the imperial orders.
The letter of Taxis is sufficiently curious to deserve
notice. " If your Highness," says the captain of
the district, " wishes your vassals to become Catholics, you must employ Catholic captains and magistrates ; for the peasants and lower orders cannot,
they say, comprehend why they should change their
religion, while their superiors, who are so much more
learned, remain Protestants." Wallenstein's zeal did
not even carry him to the length of complying with
this recommendation, for he continued to employ
Protestants as well as Catholics even to the last.

How much the world are indebted to Gustavus,
and the Duke of Friedland, for the moderation they
displayed towards religious opponents, has never been
duly appreciated ; though the fearful addition of evil
that would have been inflicted on Europe, had the
two great leaders of the adverse parties, shared in the
fanatic spirit of persecution, for which so many inferior men were distinguished, is almost incalculable.
The example of these princes, who exercised such
boundless sway over the opinions of their age, would
have been followed with fatal zeal ; and the contest,
from being one, carried on between Catholic and Protestant states, would have become a war of extermi-
nation, carried on, for life and death, between all the
individuals professing different religions :—and to the
great men, who gave the directing impulse taken by

their respective parties,—is due the honour of having saved the world from a calamity so frightful.

During the whole of the war, we find government the only persecutors on account of belief ; we find no popular persecutions. Popular indignation was often excited to acts of violence by insults, and by the oppression of agents who carried into effect the tyrannical decrees of persecuting authorities : it was often excited to violence and cruelty against the lawless soldiery of both parties ; and in some districts, as in Jutland and Bavaria, a guerilla war was carried on against the foreign invaders ; but we nowhere find the followers of one religion committing, of their own accord, outrages on the adherents of another. And during the great war for religious freedom, religious hostility seems to have remained almost dormant ; a circumstance highly creditable to the moderation of the German people ; and deserving some attention, perhaps, in this country, where so many efforts are made to excite religious animosities for political purposes.

We must now bring Wallenstein once more upon the stage. A great change had taken place since he retired from public life. The Emperor and the Catholic princes of Germany were then all powerful. Now, the King of Sweden was master from the Baltic to the Rhine, and to the mountains of the Tyrol. The imperial army was no more ; nor could an imperial soldier shew himself in the open field ; and the victorious name of Gustavus alone filled the trumpet of fame. It was under such circumstances, and to oppose such an adversary, that the Duke of Friedland was again to appear on the scene of action.

CHAPTER VI.

WALLENSTEIN was living in the splendid retirement before described, while fortress after fortress
was falling into the hands of the Swedes ; and, while
Gustavus was conquering provinces, his future adversary was building towns, churches and convents ;
raising up a garden in the wilderness, and striving to
domesticate arts, sciences and civilisation, in the least
hospitable parts of Bohemia.   But though removed
from public life, he saw more clearly into public
affairs than the most politic of the imperial ministers ;
and so far from brooding over plans of revenge, as
historians assert, he proposed an alliance with Denmark, which, if followed up, must have been ruinous
to the Swedish cause.   And as he had been the first
to point out a judicious mode of arresting the progress of the enemy, so he was the first from whom
the Emperor sought assistance when every other hope
of relief had failed.

The Saxons had no sooner entered Bohemia, after
the battle of Leipzig, than Ferdinand, who was without soldiers, and who saw his hereditary dominions
open to invasion, applied to Wallenstein for aid and
counsel.   The imperial minister Questenberg, the
same who two years before went to Memmingen, to
deprive the general of his command, now writes, as a

sort of suppliant, on the part of his master.   But
though a courtier and statesman, it must be allowed
that he writes with spirit and frankness.   " *Post
factum errorem agnoscimus*," he says, " we now see
our error plainly enough ; and as the miracles we
anticipated have not come to pass, we would gladly
retrace our steps ; if we only knew how."   And this
is exactly what they want to learn from Wallenstein.

The minister, therefore, asks, whether the Duke
of Mecklenburg, as Wallenstein continues to be styled
by the Emperor and his ministers, is still in correspondence with Arnheim ; and whether he has, in
that case, any objections to hint, as from himself,
" that the Emperor is by no means so much displeased with the Elector of Saxony, but that means
may be found to bring about a reconciliation."
Questenberg is also very facetious, at the expense of
those who principally opposed the Duke at the Diet
of Ratisbon : " Many of the gentlemen," he says,
" who talked so loudly and so boldly on that occasion, are silent enough now."   The man of office
breaks out, however, before the conclusion of this,
otherwise, excellent letter : and Questenberg, a
member of the very cabinet which, at the commencement of the Swedish war, had disbanded one-third of
the army, and allowed a great part of the rest to disband itself for want of pay, now accuses Tilly of not
having had a second army in reserve ; though that
general had constantly represented the danger likely
to result from his insufficient force.

Wallenstein, in reply to Questenberg's letter, expresses his readiness to enter upon the negotiation ;

and the Duke of Eggenberg immediately sends him
some instructions, together with a safe conduct for
General Arnheim, with whom he urges Wallenstein
to hold a personal conference, strongly impressing
upon him, how much more may be effected by a single
interview, than by a long correspondence.   Wallenstein acted on the suggestion, and, after some delay,
—for, as Prague was destitute of troops, Arnheim
secured it before he began to treat,—the Saxon
general met his former commander, at the Castle of
Kaunitz, near Limburg.   Both parties expressed
great anxiety for peace ; but nothing was settled, and
Wallenstein, leaving Count Terzka to continue the
negotiation, departed again on the same day.   But
his voice was still for peace ; and, writing from
Znaim, on the 26th of December, he says, " When
the different countries are laid in ashes, we shall be
forced to make peace ; as the experience of the last
fourteen years has amply shewn."   In the official
statement, published by the Court of Vienna, this
meeting is also brought forward as a charge against
Wallenstein, who is accused of having laid the foundation of his pretended conspiracy, at this very interview, held by order of the imperial minister.

Though this negotiation led to no results, it opened the way for another and a more successful one.
The defeat of Tilly's army, the rapid advance of the
enemy, and the enthusiasm with which the King of
Sweden had been received by the Protestants, soon
made it apparent to the Emperor, that an efficient
military force could alone enable him to treat with
advantage.   But where to find an army when he had

not a single soldier at his disposal;—for the Saxons had occupied Bohemia without meeting the slightest resistance ? Here again Wallenstein was applied to ; not indeed to take the command of the army, for there was none to command ; but to resume his former station, and to bring, as before, an army along with him.

At first he positively refused to accede to the request, alleging illness and severe sufferings from gout. As the danger augmented, however, the requests became more pressing; notwithstanding the efforts of a strong party in the cabinet who always opposed the Duke of Friedland.   This party, who were supported by the influence of the Elector of Bavaria, constantly represented the dangerous character of the man, and recommended, that the King of Hungary, in whom they discovered an absolute treasure of military talents, should be placed at the head of the troops.   The wiser saw, however, that to oppose an inexperienced King of Hungary, to the victorious King of Sweden, was risking too much, in so dangerous a state of affairs ; and the rapid progress of the enemy left the Emperor no choice.   He wrote, with his own hand, to Wallenstein ; and the proud monarch, entreated the discarded general, " not to forsake him in the hour of adversity."   It was impossible, altogether, to resist such solicitations ; and Wallenstein felt disposed to yield, till he found that the King of Hungary was to be joined with him in authority.   At this his pride instantly took fire : " Never," he exclaimed, " will I accept a divided

command, were God himself to be my coadjutor!
No! I must command alone, or not at all."

The point was, of course, conceded ; and the Duke
of Eggenberg, the imperial prime minister, having
gone in person to Znaim, to renew the Emperor's
request, and to hint at the danger which a subject
might incur, by forcing a mighty sovereign to become
an abject petitioner, Wallenstein's real or affected
objection gave way, and he agreed to accept the command for three months ; during which time, he undertook to raise an army of from 40,000 to 50,000
men, which the Emperor might then dispose of at
pleasure.   The title of commander-in-chief he declined, as well as the salary of 100,000 crowns,
offered along with it ; but he strongly urged Eggenberg to press for the payment of 300,000 ducats,
which the King of Spain had promised to contribute towards the armament.   Wallenstein knew that
Spanish payments were always precarious, and slow
at the best.   About this time, the Duchy of Gross-
Glogau was conferred upon him, being the fourth
Duchy he had acquired by grant or purchase.

Never was the magical power of a name made
more apparent than on this occasion.   The Emperor
was totally destitute of troops, and had neither money
nor credit wherewith to raise them ; all who sought
military service, flocked to the standard of the victorious King of Sweden.   The Sovereigns of Spain,
Italy and Austria, the rulers of mighty nations, stood
helpless in the midst of greatness ; dangers seemed
to have paralysed each friendly arm ; not a sword
was drawn in their defence ; but no sooner had fame

announced that Wallenstein was arming, than soldiers flocked from every quarter to his standard.
They well knew the terrible severity of his punishments ; but they also knew how magnificent were
his rewards ; and they trusted, as men naturally do,
to escape the former and to merit the latter.   All
the provinces of the Austrian monarchy, vied with
each other in zeal on this occasion.   More than 300
officers applied for letters of service; some raised companies; others entire regiments ; noblemen and men
of fortune, armed and equipped corps of cavalry and
infantry at their own expense : all were anxious to
acquire renown, and perhaps spoil also, under the
liberal and magnificent Duke of Friedland.   Before
the expiration of the third month, an army of 40,000
men, that seemed to have sprung into life at enchant-
ment's call, stood ready for the field.   They were
commanded by experienced officers, abundantly supplied with stores of every kind : high of heart, and
full of hope, they awaited but the signal for battle,
ready to strike home in a manner worthy the fame
of their extraordinary commander.

Wallenstein had fulfilled his promise : the army
was formed ; but the three months for which he had
taken the command had expired, and he now declared
his intention to retire from the scene, notwithstanding the pressing requests of the Emperor and of
the imperial council.   All historians, and Schiller
among the rest, assert that this was a mere piece of
acting, devised for the purpose of obtaining absolute
and dictatorial power, over this newly raised force ;
which he was well aware could only be wielded and

kept together, by the power which had called it into existence.

Nowhere is there any proof to bear out these statements. Wallenstein pleaded ill health, and want of money, as reasons for wishing to retire into private life. We know, that he suffered severely from gout : his signature, which before was a large, bold flourish, begins to dwindle down to a meagre scrawl ; and the hand which historians describe as grasping at a crown, was scarcely, at the time of the pretended conspiracy, able to hold a pen. That he was in want of money may also be conjectured : the troops had been raised principally at his own expense, and at the expense of the officers who had levied corps and regiments ; for it does not appear that the Emperor contributed any thing towards the armament ; and, of course, the Spanish subsidy never arrived.

The consequence was, that Wallenstein, who had always been a generous landlord and liberal Prince, remitting rents and reducing taxes, began, at this time, to be very harsh towards his tenants and vassals; till he threatened, at last, to strike off the heads of the agents and magistrates, that should fail to collect the arrears due from certain towns and districts. Owing to ill health, the cares of command and the frequent want of money, his temper appears to have completely given way during the last two years of his life, so that his wish for retirement may be easily explained ; but we see no reason why the existence of the army should have depended upon his presence. True it is, that the officers, who had advanced money, had done so more in reliance on the power and for-

tunes of the Duke of Friedland, than on the word of
the Emperor ; but this is no reason for alleging that
they would not have followed another leader, had justice been done them by the Court of Vienna.   Their
wish, to retain as a commander, the only general who
was looked upon as an adversary fit to encounter the
King of Sweden, was natural enough, and can hardly
be made a charge against Wallenstein.

Whatever may have been thought on the subject,
new negotiations had to be entered upon ; and the
Spanish friar, Father Quiroga, the all-influential confessor of the Queen of Hungary, went to Znaim,
nominally for the purpose of explaining something
about the non-arrival of the Spanish subsidy, but, in
reality, to persuade Wallenstein to retain the command.   The monk was received with the stately
courtesy invariably shewn to the visitors of the magnificent Duke of Friedland ; but his mission only drew
from Wallenstein the remark, that " it was strange
to see Kings and Princes employing, in worldly
affairs, men who had altogether renounced the world."

At last the Duke of Eggenberg again made his
appearance at head-quarters, bearing, almost suppli-
cating, letters from the Emperor and the King of
Hungary.   The minister declared that he was authorised to obtain Wallenstein's services at almost any
price ; and as this left him little more, perhaps, than
a choice of dangers ; he was forced to yield.   Moderation had, at no time, formed any part of his character, and the Court of Vienna knew, that they
would have to purchase his services at no very moderate price ; but the conditions which he demanded

exceeded, after all, their most extravagant anticipa-
tions. The following were the terms dictated, rather
than proposed :

" Wallenstein claimed to be made commander-in-
chief, with absolute power, of all the Austrian and
Spanish forces in Germany. Neither the King of
Hungary, nor the Emperor were to appear with the
army ; still less to exercise over it any act of authority. The Emperor was to dispose of no military
appointment, to confer no reward ; nor was any pardon, which he might grant, to be valid without the
sanction of the Duke of Friedland. Whatever might
be conquered and confiscated, was to be appropriated
at the sole will and pleasure of the commander-in-
chief ; without the interference of any other authority.
As a certain reward for his services, Wallenstein demanded one of the hereditary provinces of the House
of Austria ; as an extraordinary reward, one of the
conquered provinces of the empire was to be conferred
upon him. All the Austrian dominions were to be
open for the reception of the army, in case a retreat
should become necessary. On the conclusion of a
peace, he was to be confirmed in the possession of the
Duchy of Mecklenburg ; and timely notice was to
be given him, should it again be thought expedient
to remove him from the command."

In regard to the article of pardon, Wallenstein
added, with his own hand, a note to the effect that,
" His Majesty was always too merciful, and forgiving,"
an assertion, afterwards, rather questionably illustrated at his own expense. He also recommended,
that the King of Hungary should reside at Prague,

on the reconquest of Bohemia, " in order to gain the
affections of the people, and to secure the fidelity of
the army :" a pretty strong proof, that he never
entertained the project so often ascribed to him, of
seizing the crown of that country.

Ferdinand subscribed to these conditions, without
a moment's hesitation; nor does it appear that, though
subsequently brought forward as clear proofs of treasonable intentions, they excited the least murmur at
the time. And the Archbishop of Vienna, writing to
Wallenstein immediately after the conclusion of the
treaty, congratulates him on his noble and heroic resolution, which, the Prelate says, " will redound, not
only to the Duke's own glory, but to the glory and
advantage of the Emperor, and of the whole Catholic
world." The circumstance, indeed, that Wallenstein
was about to encounter a victorious monarch, totally
independent in all his movements, should be borne
in mind, before we ascribe to sinister motives, his very
natural demands for equal and absolute power. A
commander in the field can hardly possess too much
authority; and any interference exercised, from a
distance over an army, by cabinets and ministers, is
sure to prove injurious to the progress of operations :
a truth that no government has more fully and more
frequently experienced, than that of Austria.

Wallenstein's appointment to the supreme command, electrified at once all the imperial armies :
from the shores of the Danube, to the Oder and the
Adriatic, the influence of his genius was instantly felt :
a new spirit was infused into the hearts of the soldiers,
and a new war commenced. The Catholics again

acquired courage, and the Protestants already anticipated, with gloomy apprehension, another turn of
fortune. The town of Nuremberg, which had received
the King of Sweden with boisterous demonstrations
of joy, was the first to send a memorial to the new
general, assuring him, that the senate and citizens
had only yielded to force, but were, in reality, the
Emperor's best, and most devoted subjects. Wallenstein put the memorial into his pocket, and only replied, by inviting the deputies to dinner ; a mode of
proceeding, that deserves the highest praise ; as it
evinced, at once, the general's sagacity, courtesy and
frankness.

We have seen that, by order of the Emperor,
Wallenstein had, even before he assumed the command of the army, entered into negotiations with the
Saxon general Arnheim. These were still continued, as it was from first to last, the Duke of Friedland's object to detach Saxony and Brandenburg,
from the Swedish alliance. This plan was as just
and politic, as his previous plan of a Danish alliance
had been ; for, if it had succeeded, the Swedes would
have been cut off from the north of Germany, and
forced to an immediate retreat out of the central provinces of the empire. The Elector of Saxony was
still, however, too much impressed with the obligation
due to Gustavus Adolphus, to conclude any thing
without his concurrence, and it was Wallenstein's
object to have the King of Sweden excluded from
the treaty, so that nothing was settled.

General Arnheim, who with his Saxons occupied
Bohemia, had allowed the new imperial army to be

assembled, almost under his very guns; unmindful
of the indignant remonstrances of Gustavus, he did
not strike a single blow to impede its formation; and
he justly became the first sufferer by its operations.
On the 4th of May, Wallenstein appeared so unexpectedly before Prague, that it was with some difficulty Arnheim effected his retreat, by sacrificing an
insufficient garrison, which he threw into the place.

No sooner had twenty heavy guns opened from without, against the ramparts, than the Capuchin friars
began, from within, to break down the wall of their
convent, which formed part of the town wall also.
Two breaches were soon effected, and an assault was
given; the first attempt failed; but Wallenstein made
the cavalry dismount, and, sword in hand, drive the
infantry back to the ramparts, which were carried at
the second onset.   The Saxons fled to the castle, and
obtained terms; but the Emperor's Catholic troops
plundered his good Catholic city.   Wallenstein gave
money to every soldier who had been wounded in
the attack: what the monks gained by their share in
the transaction, is not mentioned.   Egra and Leume-
ritz fell as soon as invested; and Bohemia was as
quickly recovered, as it had been lost.   With the
Emperor's letter of thanks to the victor, and his assurances of endless gratitude for these important services, we spare the reader, as they are pretty well
matters of course, and easily supposed.

It was the intention of the new General to follow
up this success by an irruption into Saxony, not only
for the purpose of drawing the King of Sweden away
from the centre of the empire; but for the purpose

also of detaching the Saxons from his alliance; objects as just in a military, as in a political point of view. The Emperor, however, whose dominions were threatened, and the Elector of Bavaria, whose country was in possession of the enemy, brooked not the delay, which this operation might require, and pressed for immediate relief; and Wallenstein, showing that he had power to refuse, yielded to the solicitations of the two Princes. He advanced by stately marches to Egra, where Maximilian joined him with the Bavarian troops, which were to be under Wallenstein's command as long as the two armies acted together.

The frontier town of Egra witnessed the triumph which Friedland celebrated over his proud rival. Not satisfied with seeing before him the Elector of Bavaria, a supplicant for relief, he had obliged the humbled prince to leave his own country without defence, and seek his protector at a distance; thus shewing to the world, how helpless and destitute was the situation of this once haughty opponent. Maximilian submitted: and after a regular deed of reconciliation, in which both parties promised to forget and forgive, had been drawn up and signed, a meeting was agreed on between them.

Maximilian had been Wallenstein's most determined enemy at the Diet of Ratisbon, and had again used every effort to prevent his late re-appointment to the command of the army. Wallenstein, on the other hand, had rendered the Emperor independent of Maximilian, and had, by his power and fame, thrown the proud Elector of Bavaria completely into the shade. All feelings of wounded pride were now, however, to be suppressed; the Princes met and embraced in front of both armies; and exchanged pledges of faith and friendship, at the very time when one heart, at least, was overflowing with hate and rancour. " It was remarked," says the imperial minister, Khevenhüller, who had good access to information, and who could hardly fail to be a judge in such matters, " that the Elector of Bavaria was more perfect in the art of dissimulation than the Duke of Friedland." What the sentiments of the latter were, we know not ; but the former has left more than sufficient proof to justify the historian's assertion.

It is said that Wallenstein, elated at the sight of the numerous and splendid army assembled under his command, allowed his high spirit, pride or gratified vanity, to get the better of his usual reserve ; and that he indulged in some idle and foolish boasts, which were afterwards termed extravagant, because they were not realised. All this, if true, may be called weakness ; but before we are stoically severe on the subject, we must bear in mind the circumstances of the case, and the fortunes of the individual. Wallenstein had, by his own talents, raised himself from humble rank to the high station he occupied ; and which at one time had made him the dictator of princes and the most influential man in Europe. The intrigues of enemies, whom such an elevation could hardly fail to create, had precipitated him from the pinnacle of greatness : his power had excited the fear of the timid, his genius the hatred of the envious ; his faults had furnished the ostensible, his merit the real causes

of his dismissal.   But these attempts to humble him
had failed ; and he was now called from his retirement, as the only person deemed capable of saving his
country and sovereign.   He saw his bitterest enemy
before him, a suppliant for aid and protection : he
found himself at the head of a gallant and war-
breathing army, ready at his first sign to execute any
deed of daring and of gallantry ; and who, so situated,
would not feel his hopes awaken, and his spirit soar,
till carried away, perhaps, beyond the bounds of that
conventional discretion, the wisdom and the idol of
ordinary mediocrity ?

The imperial and Bavarian forces amounted, after
their junction, to about 60,000 men, and formed by
far the most numerous army which had appeared in
Europe since the time of Charles V.   Wallenstein
immediately led them into the Upper Palatinate,
determined, it would seem, to attack the King of
Sweden.   How far Gustavus could have prevented
the junction of the hostile forces, is uncertain : that
he has been blamed by historians, ignorant of such
matters, proves nothing ; but that he could not, after
their union, immediately face them, in the open field,
is perfectly evident ; for he had, at the utmost, only
about 20,000 men at his immediate disposal.   The
advance of the foe rendered a quick resolve necessary, and Gustavus was not the man to despond at
the mere approach of danger.

With just strategical eye, he immediately fixed
upon Nurenberg as the pivot of his future operations.
Situated almost in the centre of Germany, this town
covered his conquests on the Rhine, the Danube and

the Maine ; and left him in perfect communication
with his allies and possessions in the north. To
make up for his temporary inferiority of numbers, he
called in the spade, to aid the lance and musket.
Entrenchments, capable of receiving a large army
were immediately formed : the works completely surrounded the town and suburbs, and extended to a
circumference of at least six miles. The lines were
flanked by bastions and salient fasces, according to
the nature of the ground ; and the numerous outlets
were covered by regular half-moons. The ditch was,
in general, twelve feet broad, and eight deep ; but
from distance to distance there were closed forts and
redoubts of a much stronger construction. The river
Pegnitz, which runs through the town, divided the
camp in two parts, which were connected again by
numerous bridges.

While these works were in progress, the Senate of
Nurenberg, seeing that they were forced to take a
part, did so manfully ; and atoned for their first pusillanimity, by the zeal and ability with which they prepared to meet the pending storm. They collected
stores and provisions of all kinds, and took every possible precaution to ensure the health and comfort of the
thousands about to be assembled around their walls.
The city, with its old fortification, formed the centre
of this vast place of arms, which was completed with
a degree of celerity and stability, that has not been
equalled in Europe since the best times of the Roman
legions. Upwards of 300 pieces of cannon were distributed along the ramparts of the town and camp ;
and before Wallenstein could complete his short march

from the Bohemian frontier, the Swedes stood secure
and unassailable, within their new fortress.

To attack such soldiers so posted was, of course,
out of the question, and Wallenstein, who was urged
to the attempt, said, that " battles enough had been
fought already, and that it was time to try another
method." He resolved, therefore, to subdue by
famine those whom he could not subdue by arms ; and
with great judgment, took up a position about five
miles to the south-west of Nurenberg, so as very much
to narrow, and nearly block up, the channels through
which the King received his supplies.

The imperial camp formed an irregular parallelogram, about four miles in length, and from one
to two in breadth.   It was placed upon a range of
wooded hills on the left bank of the Rednitz, a small,
fordable stream that ran along the front of the works,
and separated the two hostile armies.   The entire
camp was inclosed by a line of entrenchments : strong
redoubts were erected on the most important points,
and treble lines of *abatis* covered all the approaches.
Two hills, the one called, from the ruins of an old
castle, the Alte Feste, the other the Altenberg, form
the highest points of the ground, and were most
strongly guarded and fortified. The steep and rugged
banks of the Rednitz helped to protect the front of
the position ; and ponds and marshes rendered all
access to the right extremely difficult.

From this well-chosen post Wallenstein detached
Croats and light troops to cut off the Swedish supplies, and to harass the Swedish foragers. Gaunt
famine, in its thousand shapes of fear and horror,

was now to do the work of Friedland : it is a melancholy and ignoble ally, no doubt, but the most formidable of all, when skilfully used ; and on this occasion it vanquished even Gustavus.

Wallenstein's plan, led to a constant succession of skirmishes between detached parties of the two armies, in which the Croats proved, at first, very troublesome to the Swedes. The most remarkable of these actions was the surprise of Frienstadt, where the Imperialists had their principal magazine. A large convoy, which had arrived from Austria and Bavaria, was assembled there on its way to the camp before Nurenberg. Gustavus received information of the circumstance, and took immediate measures for attacking the place. A Colonel Hauwaldt, a very distinguished officer in the Swedish army, was detached, with a strong party, so as to arrive by night before the town ; while the King himself covered the movement with another body of troops. Hauwaldt's attack succeeded completely : he petarded the gates, and carried the place, sword in hand : an immense booty was obtained, and whatever could not be brought away was, along with the unfortunate town, given to the flames.

Wallenstein, anxious for the safety of his convoy, had detached Colonel Spar, with about 4000 men, to reinforce the escort. At Burgau these troops fell in with Gustavus and his party. A sharp encounter ensued : the imperial cavalry were soon overthrown ; but the infantry made a determined resistance ; and, it was not till the King himself charged them home, at the head of some squadrons of horse, that they were broken and driven into a swamp, where the greater part were killed or taken. Colonel Spar was among the prisoners : he had concealed himself in the morass ; but was betrayed by his fool : a just punishment, perhaps, for having so strange an attendant, where, as it proved, fool's play was out of the question.

The capture of this convoy, by the Swedes, occasioned great want in Wallenstein's own camp, at the very time when he was endeavouring to subdue his adversary by hunger. The severe loss sustained by Spar's detachment, also cooled the ardour of the Croats,—the hussars of the Thirty years' War,—who had before rendered themselves very useful ; and it was only by a very daring and successful attack on a Swedish detachment, that Colonel Isolan, the commander of these active bands, restored their courage. Wallenstein, who knew how important it was to maintain the confidence of these troops, rewarded the action splendidly. Isolan received 4000 crowns for his share, together with a fine horse, and was, as usual on such occasions, invited to dinner. Wallenstein never appeared at the splendid table which he kept : it was presided over by Count Michna, the commissary-general, who could encourage the boisterous conviviality of the period, which the presence of the stately and reserved Duke of Friedland would only have checked. Before the party separated, Isolan, who was a merry companion and a gambler, had lost at play both horse and money : a page immediately placed 2000 ducats before him. The hussar instantly ran to the apartment of the general, to return thanks for such extreme generosity. Wallenstein, without seeming to notice the subject, only pointed to a report, just received, which announced that a Swedish convoy was on its way from Wurtzburg to Nurenberg. Isolan took the hint, and collecting his men, sallied forth in search of the enemy. He managed so well that he defeated the escort, took 200 prisoners, 3 standards, and 200 waggons loaded with provisions : these last were probably the most welcome trophies which he brought ; for famine was already beginning to show itself in both camps.

Some other instances, illustrative of Wallenstein's character, and manner of gaining on the minds of subordinates, may be mentioned, while we are on the subject. As he knew the value of discipline, though he could not always maintain it, he strove to implant, in the minds of others, the advantage and necessity of paying prompt and implicit obedience to his commands. When forming his new army, at Znaim in Moravia, he issued an order, directing that red sashes only should be worn for the future : a young officer instantly tore from his shoulder, and trampled under foot, a fine, gold embroidered scarf, which he had been in the habit of displaying with some pride. Wallenstein heard of it, and promoted him immediately. Riding out one day, a soldier, taken in the very act of plundering, was brought before him. " Hang up the wretch," said Wallenstein, and was about to pass on : the soldier, who knew that entreaties would be vain, as the decree so pronounced was considered absolute and irrevocable, drew his sword, and calling out, " If I am to die, I shall at

least die guilty," rushed upon the general. He was
instantly disarmed, but pardoned also. " Now let him
go," said Wallenstein ; " he has been sufficiently
frightened." A horseman, who had lost his cuirass,
was disgraced before the whole regiment ; and an
officer, who refused to accept a challenge, dismissed
the service. Another, who drew his sword, and
attempted to avenge, even in the Duke's presence,
an insult offered by a man of rank, was applauded.
A private had been promoted for an act of gallantry ;
but neglected to return thanks. Wallenstein, to
whom the omission was pointed out, declared that he
was flattered by the circumstance, as it proved that
the man was conscious of having only received his
due.

The King of Sweden had summoned to his aid,
all the Swedish and allied troops that were acting in
different parts of Germany, the moment Wallenstein
made his appearance before Nurenberg. And it is
a remarkable circumstance, that this Prince who, two
years before, had landed in Pomerania with only
13,000 men, now saw 60,000 assemble at his first
call in the very centre of Germany ; and that too,
after sufficient garrisons had been left in the numerous fortresses he had captured. From Bavaria and
the frontiers of the Tyrol, from Alsace, from the
banks of the Rhine, the Elbe and the Oder, troops
of all nations flocked in towards Nurenberg. Among
the number were two British regiments, the remains
of Hamilton's corps, who after aiding in the recapture of Magdeburg, now hastened to the aid of their
adopted Sovereign. Oxenstiern assembled all these

reinforcements at Kinzingen, about five marches from Nurenberg, and entered the Swedish camp on the 16th of August with 36,000 men, 60 pieces of artillery and 4000 waggons. The two most formidable armies which had appeared during the war, now stood opposed to each other : the fire-charged clouds of battle had collected from all quarters of Germany, over one point ; and after empires had been ravaged, the long and terrible contest seemed about to be decided in a single field.

Wallenstein has been blamed for having allowed this strong reinforcement to join the King of Sweden; but the censure is unjust. From the moment he had determined to make hunger do the work of arms, and knew his own camp to be impregnable, he was perfectly right in allowing these additional troops to pass unmolested. Directed against the Austrian dominions, or well employed in the rear of Wallenstein's position, the powerful army that Oxenstiern brought to the aid of Gustavus, might have shaken the imperial throne : within the circumference of the Swedish lines, they could add only to the distress already suffered there. And if that distress was great, before the arrival of this reinforcement, it was greatly augmented by the additional numbers which had then to be supplied. The Swedish troops had lived principally on the provisions so wisely collected by the magistrates of Nurenberg, before the arrival of the armies ; but these stores declined exactly in proportion as the number of claimants for food augmented : the surrounding country was completely exhausted, and thousands of the peasantry had sought shelter within the lines, and augmented the scarcity.

Crime and disease, the constant followers of hunger, soon appeared ; and, by breaking asunder the bonds of discipline, added to these evils, all those sure to result from insubordination. Frightful excesses were committed ; and the King of Sweden, besides making severe examples of the offenders, was forced to reprimand the German troops in a speech that, for power and eloquence, has hardly ever been surpassed ; and which is said to have drawn tears from the eyes of the hardened soldiers themselves. The effect ascribed to this address has been doubted ; though unjustly, perhaps; for Gustavus was eloquent, and it is in the nature of multitudes to fly from one extreme to the other : from deeds of cruelty, to repentance, and from shame and sorrow, to the commission of fresh atrocities.

All this suffering, rendered it necessary to employ the army which had been so skilfully, though injudiciously assembled. On the 22d of August, the King erected three strong batteries, along the banks of the Rednitz, from which he cannonaded the Imperialists the whole day ; but, as might have been anticipated, without any result. Wallenstein remained immoveable, within his lines, and only replied to the Swedish guns by a similar fire. Hunger was to do his work for him ; and nothing changed his resolution. Vain were the representations of Maximilian ; as vain the impatience for battle expressed by his army : the entreaties of his friends influenced his

determination as little as the repeated taunts of his
enemies.

The first attempt to dislodge the Duke of Friedland having failed, a more determined effort was to
be made. On the day after this fruitless cannonade,
Gustavus crossed the Rednitz, with his whole army,
near the small town of Fürth ; and took up a new
position, which placed him exactly on the left flank
of the Imperialists. Here he had the hill of the
Alte Feste, the highest and most commanding point
of their camp, nearest to his front; and this he caused
to be attacked with great impetuosity on the morning of the 24th of August. Under the fire of eighty
pieces of artillery, four detachments, each composed
of 500 chosen musqueteers, mostly Scotsmen, as
an old Nurenberg writer of the period informs us,
led the attack : they were followed and supported
by divisions of spearmen, who, on different points,
attempted to force the entrenchments. But their
bravest efforts were unavailing ; no impression could
be made on foes, covered by works which nature and
art alike combined to strengthen ; and after repeated
efforts, renewed with all the gallantry for which these
unconquered troops were distinguished, the assault
was abandoned, and the combat dwindled down to a
mere skirmish, and fire of artillery, which continued
till friendly night cast a mantle of peace over the contending foes.

Nothing was gained by the victors, and little lost
by the vanquished ; for in the melancholy trade of
war, slight is the stress laid upon mere human suffering. In a sally, made on one point, a body of impe-

rial cuirassiers defeated some Swedish infantry, and
made the celebrated General Torstensohn prisoner.
The Cronberg horsemen, who styled themselves
" The Invincibles," were less fortunate : encounter-
ing a party of Finland cavalry, under the gallant Stal-
hansh, they were defeated and forced to fly, leaving
Count Füger, their colonel, mortally wounded on the
field.   It may be presumed that their modestly assumed title was in no way impaired by so untoward an
accident.

Wallenstein, as his duty commanded, was everywhere in the hottest of the fire : he had a horse shot
under him, when in the very act of driving some fugitive soldiers back to their post.   Gustavus exposed
himself with his usual indifference to danger, and a
musket ball tore away part of his boot.   Bernhard
of Weimar, whose horse was also killed, particularly
distinguished himself : he had carried a hill, that at
first promised to lead to some advantage.   Colonel
Hepburn was sent by the King to examine the
ground, and made a favourable report of its commanding position ; but the failure of all the other attacks,
probably deterred Gustavus from following up this
single success.

The advanced musqueteers remained all night on
the ground which they had gained, and the firing
commenced again at daylight ; but the King, mis-
trustful of fortune, which had failed him on this important occasion, and for the first time vanquished,
because he was not victorious, declined to renew the
assault.   Not altogether satisfied, perhaps, with his
conduct as a general, he was determined to perform,

at least, the service of a platoon officer with distinction. Seeing Colonel Munroe, whose duty it was to withdraw the advanced infantry from under the enemy's works, wounded and hardly able to walk, he ordered him to the rear, and seizing the Scotchman's spontoon, brought away the musqueteers in person, closing up the rear, pike in hand, like a captain or lieutenant-colonel. The generous gallantry of the soldier, absolutely disarms the voice of criticism, which, on this occasion, might be disposed to find fault with the kingly commander. The Swedish army retired, unpursued ; and took up a position in front of Fürth, close to the field of battle.

As on the capture of Prague, Wallenstein here also, distributed money among the wounded officers and soldiers. Every colonel received a thousand crowns, every private fifteen crowns, and the wounded of intermediate ranks, sums in proportion. " Such conduct," says a contemporary writer, " encouraged the whole army, and made the soldiers eager for another opportunity to fight." This well-timed liberality alone, shows the man of genius, and places him immeasurably above the generals who have upheld the starvation system of modern times.

The letter in which the imperial commander renders an account of this affair to the Emperor, is rather a curious document. The victor speaks modestly of the action, and in general terms only, but allows that the position was, at one time, nearly carried : on the other hand, he is profuse in praise of the officers and soldiers, and solicits for them marks of favour and distinction. He concludes his letter in the following words : " The King has blunted his horns a good deal in this *impressa ;* and the result has shown, that he can no longer claim the title of *invictissimi,* which must henceforth belong to your Majesty alone." He acknowledges to have lost 400 men and a great many officers ; and estimates at 2000, the loss sustained by the enemy. As these are nearly the exact numbers stated by the Swedes themselves, for the killed and wounded on both sides, it shews that the generals of the seventeenth century had not yet learned to practise that ridiculous system of exaggeration, by which so many commanders of the nineteenth, tried to forge a little fame.

While the armies remained in position, opposed to each other, some courtesies passed between the respective leaders. The Swedish Colonel Dobattle was taken prisoner by the Croats. Wallenstein paid his ransom to the captors, and sent him back free of all expense, desiring him to assure the King that he, Wallenstein, entertained the highest respect and admiration for His Majesty, and looked upon him as the greatest general in the world. He also ransomed another Swedish officer, a Captain Reisel, and released him in a similar manner, saying, that nothing would give him greater pleasure than to bring about a peace between Gustavus and the Emperor. When General Spar was exchanged, the King of Sweden also made some proposals of peace. These Wallenstein forwarded to Vienna : but the imperial ministers seeing that the dreaded conqueror had, for some weeks at least, been arrested in his career of victory, thought that all danger was over, and that they had only to dictate their own terms. The consequence was, that they proposed conditions so extravagant that they were never sent to the Swedish camp.

The town of Nurenberg had made great efforts and sacrifices, in order to support, for eleven weeks, the countless multitudes pressed together upon its territory. At last, however, all resources were exhausted, and a retreat on the part of the Swedes became inevitable. Death had made dreadful ravages among the town's people, and Gustavus had lost by disease and the sword, more than 12,000 soldiers. The surrounding fields had been trampled down ; the villages reduced to ashes, and the peasantry, plundered of all their property, had sought shelter from violence in the recesses of woods and wildernesses. The heat of the season, the want of proper nourishment, and the grave-like exhalations that infected the air, occasioned the most frightful maladies both among men and cattle ; and long after the departure of the armies, the afflicted country continued to suffer from the ruinous effects their presence had occasioned.

The King of Sweden seeing that he could not overcome the constancy of Wallenstein, and that he was only bringing destruction on himself and his allies, by his protracted stay, determined to break up his camp. Having placed a garrison of 5000 men in Nurenberg, under the same Kniphausen who had defended New-Brandenburg against the whole of Tilly's army ; he left his lines on the 8th of September, and with drums beating and colours flying, passed slowly along the front of the imperial entrenchments, and proceeded to Neustadt. Wallenstein, regardless of the bold defiance, remained unmoved upon his hills, and so far from impeding the march of the enemy, ordered his outposts to withdraw on their approach. In his report to the Emperor, he says, " the King made a skilful retreat, and showed clearly enough, how well he understood his business." He assigns as a reason for not obstructing the march of the Swedes, the absence of his cavalry, which he describes as being distributed in distant quarters ; and adds, that he was not disposed to trust to the hazard of a battle, results which he looked upon as already secure. " With the help of God," he continues, " the King's credit is already very much on the decline ; and it will be all over with him as soon as Pappenheim arrives and attacks him on the other flank." If the prediction was verified, it was owing to circumstances on which, as usual in such cases, the prophet could not well have calculated.

It was made a principal charge against Wallenstein, in the official statement afterwards published by the Court of Vienna, that he had neglected to attack the Swedes on this occasion. Judging of these remarkable events, from all the information we can now collect, we are bound to say that his conduct, so far from deserving censure, appears, on the contrary, to merit the very highest praise. To have attacked, tried and experienced soldiers like the Swedes, posted behind works so formidable as those thrown up round Nurenberg, would have been rushing on almost certain defeat. When, with their assembled army, they afterwards defied him to combat on open plain, he was more than justified by circumstances, in declining the challenge, however painful to the feelings of a proud man must have been the taunts to which he exposed himself from friends and foes. But Wallenstein knew his game, and played it resolutely, in defiance of all the efforts made to shake his purpose; and his firmness alone proved him far superior to Tilly at Leipzig.

In numbers and bravery, the two armies may have been nearly equal; but the Swedes had great tactical advantages. They were accustomed to act together; above all, they were accustomed to conquer, and placed the most boundless confidence in themselves, their officers and the Sovereign; and to have risked a field battle against such troops, with a newly raised army, however brave, must have been precarious at all times; but would have been criminal at such a moment. The Swedes, masters of all the fortresses from Colberg on the distant Baltic, to Mayence on the Rhine, were too firmly based to suffer any great loss from a reverse sustained under the walls of Nurenberg. To the imperial party, on the other hand, defeat must have been ruinous. Wallenstein's army was their last stay, and its overthrow would have cost the Emperor his crown, the Elector of Bavaria his dominions, and must have rendered the Protestant religion dominant in Germany: ultimately, perhaps, in Europe. And, as nearly all the chances of battle were in favour of Gustavus, we are not asserting too much, when we say that it was the prudence of the Duke of Friedland, which alone saved the Catholic power from entire destruction. How the great obligation was repaid, we shall soon have occasion to see.

CHAPTER VII.

The long stay which Gustavus made in the camp before Nurenberg, seems the only military error that can be laid, to the charge of this great soldier, during his German campaigns. From the moment that Wallenstein's army was arrested before the Swedish camp, not another soldier should have been brought within its limits ; and the great reinforcement which Oxenstiern led to the King's aid, ought to have marched into Austria and Bavaria, and struck at the heart of the enemy's power.

From Nurenberg the King of Sweden, directed his march to Neustadt, on the Aisch, where he halted and gave his troops some rest. Having afterwards dispatched Bernhard, Duke of Weimar, to Würtsburg, for the defence of the Maine, he returned with the rest of his army into Bavaria, to complete the conquest of that country.

Five days after the King's departure, Wallenstein gave his camp to the flames, and left the banks of the Rednitz. He directed his march on Bamberg, where he separated from Maximilian, who hurried to the defence of his own country. Wallenstein refused him every assistance : it was his object to separate the Saxons from the Swedes, and he now determined to follow up this well-conceived plan with

all the means at his disposal. Having vainly attempted
to reduce the castle of Cobourg, which a Swedish
garrison defended against him, the imperial commander advanced into the very heart of Saxony, and
took Leipzig on the 23d of October.   But, so far
from ordering the country to be plundered and laid
waste, as stated by Schiller and other historians, he
gave strict injunctions to the contrary. We have
before us the letters written to Holk and Gallas on
the subject, and they contain the most positive directions to refrain from all acts of violence. " Let
nothing," he says, " be destroyed or taken from the
peasantry, for we must live during the winter, on
the supplies we can find here." In a postscript is
added : " The Croats must not, under pain of death,
presume to take a single thing from the people."

It is not, however, severity of punishment alone
that insures from troops implicit obedience to the
orders of their superiors. It is only by the perfect
working of the whole military machinery, that obedience is maintained ; and in this essential point, the
armies of the seventeenth century were, as already
stated, extremely deficient. Gustavus Adolphus
was the first who established something like subordination : and he was enabled to effect this difficult
task, owing as much to the moral strength derived
from his character and genius, as from his individual position. Gustavus was not only a King, but a
great King, and his high reputation gave an oracular
force to his orders, that hardly left an opening for dis-
obedience : and not a little of his success was due to
the power which he thus acquired. And yet we learn,

from many of his letters, that he could not always calculate with perfect certainty on the exact fulfilment of his commands.   The Prussian army, under Frederick II, was the first to show an example of perfect military subordination.   The other armies of Europe gradually adopted the Prussian machinery, which worked ill or well, in different countries, according as national character, habits, manners, and the general state of society, were adapted to the military frame-work.   Where power was sufficiently absolute, and well regulated, to enforce equal obedience, from the highest to the lowest ; or where a due sense of honour pervaded all ranks, so as to admit of perfect reliance being placed on the word and faith of the officers entrusted with the most trifling, as well as the most important commands, there, such a system worked well ; but exactly in proportion as these means of control fell short, so did the system of military subordination also fall short of excellence.   Asiatic and South American governments, have never been able to introduce military subordination in their armies, and there are armies in Europe in which subordination is to this day, merely nominal.   In the German armies of the seventeenth century the punishments were extremely severe : death indeed was the most usual; but, as we shall see from Wallenstein's own letters, subordination was very precarious.

The Duke of Friedland, when meditating the invasion of Saxony, had written to Pappenheim, who commanded a separate corps on the Lower Rhine, to march in the same direction, and to join the main army at Leipzig.   Suspecting, however, that some excuse

would be made to evade compliance, he inclosed a
general order, directing the next officer in seniority
to assume the command of the troops, in case Pappenheim should be detained by *illness :* and it was signi-
fied at the same time, that all the officers failing to accompany the army, should forfeit their commissions.
Commands so positive could not well be disregarded,
and Pappenheim appeared accordingly ; but before
setting out on his march, he applied both to the Emperor and to the King of Spain, to have the order
recalled.   It does not appear that the Emperor took
any notice of the application, but the King of Spain
wrote to Wallenstein, saying, that " the capture of
Maestrich had so much augmented the arrogance of
the inflated Hollanders, as to render Pappenheim's return to the Netherlands very desirable." Wallenstein
never allowed the troops to return to the frontiers of
Holland, thinking, perhaps, that as the King of Spain
had kept back the promised subsidy, His Majesty had
forfeited his right to advise the movements of armies,
which he never helped to pay.

Just before Pappenheim's arrival Wallenstein sent
an order to General Altringer, who was still acting
on the Danube, directing him to march immediately
into Saxony, " because," he says, " we hear nothing
of Pappenheim, who will hardly arrive."   This letter he incloses, open, to General Gallass, to be forwarded, and writes to him as follows : " I may acquaint you, however, in confidence, that Pappenheim
has arrived within two marches of us, and will join
me at Leipzig the day after to-morrow ; but as I
well know the Duke of Bavaria, I tell him the re-

verse ; for, were he to know it, he would find means to detain Altringer and his troops." It was no easy matter to carry on systematic operations with such precarious authority, and Wallenstein was more than justified in demanding the ample powers he obtained on assuming the command.

The King of Sweden had reduced Ingolstadt to extremity, when he received the unwelcome intelligence of Wallenstein's irruption into Saxony ; and he was too well acquainted with the character of John George to expose so weak and vain a prince, to the arts and arms of Friedland : for the Elector, though incapable of being himself the head of the Protestant party, was jealous of the fame of Gustavus ; and contemptible as an individual, he was formidable from the power, as well as from the position of his dominions. Gustavus was obliged, therefore, to abandon the brilliant prospects opening in the south, where the road to Vienna was almost clear, and to hurry, with all speed, to the aid of this precarious ally : thus showing how judicious was the plan on which the Duke of Friedland continued to act.

A sufficient force having been left for the protection of his Bavarian conquests, the King proceeded, by forced marches, to Erfurth, where he joined the Duke of Weimar ; from thence the army advanced to Naumburg, which was so rapidly seized, that Wallenstein had not even time to reinforce the detachment which occupied the place. On this, his last march, Gustavus was everywhere received with boundless demonstrations of joy. The people, terrified at the approach of the imperial troops, flocked

from all directions to meet and hail their protectoɪ
and liberator ; they kneeled down before him as he
passed, vied with each other for an opportunity to
kiss, or merely to touch, the hem of his garment, or
the sheath of his sword. " Rise up, rise up," said
Gustavus, more than once, " or God will punish me
for being the cause of this idolatry." These testi-
monies of love, gratitude and admiration, however
foolishly expressed, cast nevertheless a beautiful and
brilliant halo round the closing scene of so great and
glorious a life.

The imperial general, true to his plan of separating
the Saxons from the Swedes, was on his march from
Leipzig to Torgau, where he hoped to destroy the
Saxon army, or to intimidate the Elector, when he
received the unexpected news of the King's arrival
at Naumburg. Another and a more difficult game
had now to be played, and Wallenstein took his part
accordingly. He immediately counter-marched, and
determined to fall, with his whole army, upon the
Swedes, before they could form a junction with the
Saxons. Every appearance of success was in his
favour : his army was estimated at little less than
40,000 men, and the Swedes alone could hardly have
more than 20,000 or 22,000 at hand. The opportunity was therefore not to be lost : it was doubly
dear to Wallenstein ; because his inactivity before
Nurenberg had given rise to a belief that, he feared
to encounter the King of Sweden on level plain.
The army advanced to Weisenfels, and a regular
reconnaissance of the Swedish position at Naumburg
was undertaken. But here, as at Werben and at

Nurenberg, the indefatigable King of Sweden was already so strongly posted and entrenched, as to render hopeless all direct attempts to force his camp.

Wallenstein desired his generals to assemble and consult on the best plan to be pursued : he was not himself present at the meeting, and it is evident that Pappenheim was the person who most strongly influenced the deliberations. A council of war seldom fights ; and on this occasion, all the generals decided against an attack on the Swedish position, which they declared to be too strong to be assailed with any prospect of success. They also expressed the singular opinion that Gustavus intended to make a long stay in his camp, as he had done at Nurenberg. But why the active King of Sweden should have come all the way from Bavaria to shut himself up at Naumburg, they forebore to explain. It was further deemed advisable by this extraordinary assembly, that Pappenheim should hasten to the relief of Cologne, with 2000 Croats, and that the rest of the army should go quietly into winter quarters ; ready to assemble, however, at a moment's notice if necessary. Wallenstein entered into the views of his generals, strange as these now appear, and having placed most of the troops in cantonments, dispatched Pappenheim to the Rhine.

This commander was ordered to dislodge, on his way, a Swedish garrison from Halle, and received for that purpose, six regiments of infantry and six of cavalry ; which were not to accompany the march further than was required for the execution of this

service.   Wallenstein himself took post with some
troops at Lützen, to cover the expedition.

Colonel Diodati, who was quarter-master to the
army, drew up, for the information of the Emperor,
a detailed, and pretty clear account, of all these proceedings.   In this document he states, with great,
and rather singular, candour, that the plan, devised
by the council of war, failed, because " the views of
the King of Sweden did not at all accord with theirs;"
—a circumstance that might, perhaps, have been
anticipated without much deliberation.

Before daylight, on the 5th of November, the
Swedes unexpectedly broke up from Naumburg, and
proceeded towards Pegau.   Their object was evidently to join the Saxons at Dresden, where Arnheim
had arrived with part of his troops : the march on
Grima, as reported by Heart, was totally impracticable.   About ten o'clock in the morning, the King
learned, from intercepted letters, as well as from some
peasants and prisoners, that Pappenheim, with a large
force, had left the army, and that Wallenstein himself was in the plain of Lützen.   The eagle darts
not more promptly, from his tranquil course in mid
air, to seize upon some unexpectedly discovered prey,
than Gustavus turned, on this occasion, to dart
upon the foe, so closely within his grasp.   " Right
shoulders forward " was the order passed along the
column, and the whole army was immediately in full
march for the celebrated field of death and fame.

Three signal guns fired from the castle of Weisenfels announced to Wallenstein the approach of the
Swedes ; and bands of fugitive cavalry soon came

hurrying in to confirm the fearful tidings ; for fearful they were at the moment.   Pappenheim was at a distance ; most of the other troops were distributed in cantonments, and could only arrive successively on the field.   To retreat was impossible ; the Elbe, and a line of hostile fortresses, were behind ; to fall back on Leipzig, was to abandon Pappenheim and the other detached corps to certain destruction ; to follow Pappenheim, was to abandon the only communication with the Austrian states ; to inclose himself in a hostile country, and leave open the junction to all the Saxon and Swedish troops.

In such an hour of fear, courage and promptness of resolution could alone save the imperial army, who were thrown into great confusion by this unexpected advance of the enemy, and Wallenstein was not wanting to his fame.   Though he had hardly 12,000 men at hand, he determined, at all hazards, to make a stand, till the rest of his forces should arrive : the appointed signal guns were fired, and orders sent to all the corps to march immediately upon Lützen.   Pappenheim also was directed to hurry on towards the field with every man and gun he could assemble *.

* *The Duke of Friedland to Field-Marshal Pappenheim.*

" The enemy is marching hitherwards.   Break up instantly with every man and gun, so as to arrive here early in the morning.   And I remain,

A. D. OF M.

" *P. S.*—He is already at the pass and the hollow road."

" I found this letter," says Förster, " in the archives of Vienna : it was covered with the blood of Pappenheim, who had it in his pocket on the day of the battle."

Fortune aided these exertions.   The roads leading
towards Lützen were deep and miry.   The Swedes in
their advance, had to cross the Ripach, a small streamlet with high, clayey banks, that retarded the march.
Isolan defended the passage with Croats and cuirassiers : he was indeed routed with loss ; but even victory occasioned delay.   A thick November fog, so
usual in these low, marshy countries, brought day to
an early close ; and darkness already covered the plain
before the Swedes could profit by the chance that promised so fairly in the morning.   Wallenstein made
good use of the time thus gained.

The plain of Lützen is a perfect level, without tree,
bush or elevation, and offers nowhere any advantage in
point of ground.   But there, as in most of the flat countries of Germany, the roads are separated from the
fields by ditches ; and these Wallenstein turned very
ably to account.   He took post behind the road leading
from Weisenfels to Leipzig ; having the small town
of Lützen on his right : the left was entirely uncovered.   General Holk placed the troops in order of battle as they arrived during the night, and caused the
ditches, that bordered the roads, to be deepened.
The earth of the ditch nearest the Swedes, was thrown
outwards ; and musqueteers placed in the ditch so as
to fire over the excavated earth as over a parapet : the
earth from the inner ditch was thrown inwards, and
another line of musqueteers placed, on the level field
behind it, so as to fire over the parapet, as well as
over the heads of the front line of musqueteers.   This
arrangement was probably more ingenious than judicious ; for, to fire over the heads of soldiers, at such

a distance, and at so small an elevation, tends to make them, at least, very unsteady.

About 200 yards behind this road the army was formed, according to a plan drawn by Wallenstein himself. As we have Förster's copy of it before us, and as the formation differs so totally from the accounts given by historians, we shall here describe it, for the satisfaction of the curious in military antiquities. Unfortunately there is no scale attached to the drawing, so that we can form no certain idea of the extent of front occupied.

The infantry are formed in ten large square battalions, of which six are in first, and four in second line : double the number also represented by historians. Behind the openings left between the larger battalions, smaller bodies of infantry, light troops perhaps, are posted ; so as to make in all, something like four lines, the first three resembling the Roman *quincunx* order of battle. The cavalry are posted on the flanks, six large bodies in column, on each. The entire forms very nearly a parallelogram, the front of which only exceeds the depth by about one-third. On the left, a place is marked for Pappenheim, and a field-work is traced out on the same flank. A battery is marked in front of the centre, where we know that seven guns were stationed. The windmill battery on the right, where, as we also know, seventeen guns were placed, is not marked on the plan. The garden walls round Lützen were loopholed and lined with musqueteers. What was the number of troops collected, is uncertain ; but it is not likely that they exceeded six and twenty or eight and twenty thousand men, even including Pappenheim's cavalry, which, contrary to ordinary statements, arrived in sufficient time to take some rest before the commencement of the action. Göltz commanded the left wing, Holk the right, and Offizius the centre. Wallenstein, as Commander in Chief, very properly assumed no particular post. As he suffered severely from gout, he came to the ground in his carriage, and was carried through the ranks in a sedan chair : it was only when the action began, that he got on horseback. Thus occupied and posted, the imperial army awaited the dawning of the eventful morning.

The Swedes, after the passage of the Ripach, advanced close to Lützen, and having formed their order of battle, remained all night under arms. The troops were drawn up in the same manner as at Leipzig ; the infantry in two lines, with Henderson's Scottish regiment in reserve. There were four brigades in front line, and as many in the second ; but the brigades of the first had twenty companies each, while those of the second had only thirteen companies. The cavalry, which nearly equalled the infantry in strength, was posted on the flanks, also in two lines ; one regiment remained in reserve along with Henderson's infantry. Forty pieces of artillery were distributed along the line : the left reached nearly to the village of Lützen, and the right extended to beyond the Floss-Graben, a shallow canal used for floating timber, and easily passed at all points. The King himself commanded the right wing, Bernhard of Weimar the left, and Kniphausen the second line. In point of numbers, the Swedes, who were probably not

more than 20,000 strong, were inferior to the Imperialists ; but the extended front of their brigades,
the greater pliability of their formations, and the
superior tactical training of the soldiers, gave them,
in all other respects, a decided superiority. The
imperial army might be compared to the alligator,
formidable from its strength and fierceness if attacked in front; but slow, rigid and unwieldly in its
movements : while the Swedish host more resembled
the lion, being active as well as strong ; and as able
to spring directly upon the foe, as to tear, strike and
deal destruction in every direction. Still, the manner in which the armies of the period went to work
in the hour of battle, with their mixed masses of
spearmen and musqueteers, is a difficulty which historians have left unsolved, and which, at this distance
of time, we are not well able to explain. What were
the spearmen doing, exposed, without any power of
reaction, to the shot, when the musqueteers were
engaged ; and what became of the musqueteers when
the battle came to " push of pike ?"

Though these particular points are obscure, we can
very well understand that, in some way or other,
good work might be effected with spears and muskets,
because they are manly and formidable arms. But
what will posterity think of our bayonets ?—Will
they ever believe that such rickety zig-zags were seriously intended to be used in mortal combat ? And
what idea must future generations form of the historians and despatch writers, who have gravely ascribed
victories to the power of such weapons ? What, again,
must be deemed of the military intelligence of an age,

which could tolerate the tactical puerilities founded on the presumed use of a toy, that has been brandished, with bombastic fierceness, for upwards of a century, and has never yet, in fair and manly fight, inflicted a single wound on mortal man ? We must return, however, to a battle fought with different, and more efficient arms.

The morning of the 6th of November broke dark and dimly on the plain of Lützen ; the sun was obscured, and the ground everywhere covered by a thick and impenetrable mist : nature seemed anxious to withhold the light destined to shine on the approaching scene of human destruction. The continued fog enabled the Swedes to advance unmolested, and perhaps unobserved, to within about a thousand yards of the enemy. Here they halted : and while waiting till the haze should clear away, the King commanded prayers to be said in front of every regiment : and afterwards gave out a psalm himself, in which the whole army joined. Service over, he rode along the ranks, and addressed the troops. His speeches have been variously reported, and probably a good deal lengthened. Certain it is that he said to some regiments, " Fight as usual, brave comrades, and you will this day make me the first King in the world." Gustavus, who,—like Alexander, Henry IV, Charles XII, and other generals of what we may call the bold and daring school of tactics,—always attacked at the head of the cavalry, rode very conspicuous horses : on this occasion he was mounted on a white charger of peculiar beauty ; which, according to Gassion, had been thrown in his way by the enemy, in order that it might betray him to their fire, on the day of battle. As at Leipzig, he wore a plain elk-skin coat; a former wound preventing him from wearing armour, the use of which was rapidly declining among officers of rank. Wallenstein also wore a buff coat; but it was laced and embroidered according to the most splendid fashion of the period.

About half-past eleven o'clock the sun began to break, with red and ominous glare through the haze : Lützen was discovered to be in flames : it had been set on fire to prevent the right wing of the Imperialists from being turned ;—and stray shots, from the advanced parties, told that the expectant foes were gradually gaining sight of each other. The ardent courage of Gustavus could no longer be restrained. Placing himself at the head of the regiment of Steinbock, he ordered the army to advance, and exclaiming, " Now Lord Jesus give us aid ; we are going to fight for the honour of thy holy name," led on towards the enemy. The shouts of exulting thousands who, under such a leader, deemed themselves marching to assured victory, replied to the order ; and the gallant display of pennons and standards that waved high above the ranks of ancient war, told that the unconquered host was marching to the onset.

A terrible fire of musquetry and artillery received them as they approached : it checked not the progress of troops who, on level ground, acknowledged no equal foes. The trenches are passed, but a heavy loss is sustained and much confusion occasioned in the ranks of the assailants. The left wing of the imperial cavalry, charged by the Swedish cavalry under the King in person, is thrown and pursued across the plain. Equal success attends the centre : the blue * and yellow brigades, after scattering the troops that lined the road and carrying the seven gun battery, fall with determined resolution on the first line of the imperial infantry. The serried mass of spears bears down all resistance ; Wallenstein's musqueteers perish in the shock of the hostile lances, and his front battalions are broken and forced to fly. The firing continues only near Lützen ; the Swedes, masters of a great part of the field, shout victory, and deem the day already gained.

But on the left they had been less fortunate. Bernhard of Weimar, exposed to a galling fire from the troops posted behind the garden walls and enclosures of the burning village, as well as to the fire of the seventeen gun battery, had been unable to make any impression. Gustavus, informed of the ill success of this wing, hurried to its aid. He reformed the troops, and again prepared to lead them forward. Wallenstein was similarly occupied : riding from rank to rank, and from regiment to regiment, he brought the fugitives to a stand, advanced fresh corps and made a fierce attack on the brigades of the Swedish centre, who, disordered by their own success, were forced back across the road, and obliged to abandon the captured battery. The ever active Gustavus again arrested the progress of the

* The blue brigade was composed of British.—*Hoyer, Geschichte der Kriegskunst.*

Imperialists ; and having, with uncovered head *, returned thanks for the victory he thought already
won, galloped forward, accompanied by a few attendants only, to see how the advantage could best be
followed up.

At this moment a musket ball shattered his left
arm ; and finding himself growing faint from loss of
blood, he requested Francis Albert, Duke of Lauenburg, to lead him out of the battle.   In attempting
to clear the front of their own men, they came too
near a party of the enemy, and the King received
another shot in the back.   " Take care of yourself,
brother," said the unhappy Prince to the Duke of
Lauenburg, " I have got enough," and instantly
fell from his horse.   The foe approached ; the attendants fled ; and even Gustavus, the great, the
generous and the brave was abandoned in his dying
moments.   A page, the son of Baron Lübeling of
Nurenberg, alone remained by the fallen monarch.
This young man leaped from his horse and offered
it to the King ; but Gustavus was too feeble to
mount : he only raised his hands, and the page was
unable to lift him.   A party of Imperialists rode up
and asked, " who was the wounded man ?" Lübeling
replied that he was an officer.   The enemy, not satisfied with the answer, or seeing Swedes advancing,
dispatched the King with several sword and pistol
wounds. Gustavus, in expiring, said, " I was King
of Sweden."   Lübeling remained, mortally wounded, by the side of his master : the storm of battle

* Bernhard of Weimar's letter to Louis XIII.

swept along, and both bodies, stript to the skin, were soon disfigured beneath the hoofs of vaunting enemies.

The King's horse, flying wild, with loosened rein and blood-covered housings, gave the first intimation of what had happened ; and fugitive attendants too soon confirmed the fatal tidings. An equerry named Trueshes, who had seen the King fall, was the first to tell the Duke of Weimar that, Gustavus was either dead, or wounded and in the hands of the enemy. Bernhard hastened to Kniphausen, and whispered the sad news into his ear, asking him, what was to be done ? The General replied, that, as the troops were still in good order, it would be easy to effect a retreat. But of this, the high-hearted Weimar would hear nothing : on the contrary, he expressed his resolution to fight it out to the last ; and to release the King, if a prisoner, or to avenge his death should he have fallen. Calling on the soldiers to follow him, in order to liberate their captive and wounded sovereign, he again reformed the troops and prepared to advance. The colonel of the regiment of Steinback refused to obey : Bernhard cut him down with his own hand ; the rest submitted. Order having been restored, the whole line was again led towards the enemy, who, with great promptness, had taken advantage of his temporary success to restore his battle, and re-occupy his favourable position.

Undismayed by the heavy fire of musquetry from the trenches, the Swedes again cross the road ; they had the death of their great King to avenge ; and who could value life when the noblest had been sacri-

ficed ? Religion, loyalty, patriotism animated the Imperialists : every sentiment that could raise the heart
and nerve the arm of the brave, was in action ; nor
was a sterner combat, than the one which followed,
ever fought by exasperated men.   The gallantry of
the Swedish onset again bears down all resistance :
not only is the windmill battery taken, the large
battery on the right also falls into the hands of the
assailants ; and the imperial guns are turned against
their own battalions.   The left wing is once more
driven from the field, the centre is in disorder ;
powder waggons blow up in rear of the army and render the confusion general : whole regiments already
take to flight : the exulting Swedes shout victory ;
when Pappenheim again tears the blood-stained laurel
from their brows.   This intrepid soldier received the
order to march on Lützen, at the very moment when
his men were engaged in sacking the town of Halle.
He instantly sounded to horse, and leaving directions
for the infantry and artillery to follow, as soon as they
could be assembled, set out at the head of his cavalry,
and hurried, with spur of fire, towards the scene of
action.

The imperial army was beaten, when his heroic
spirit gave them another chance for victory.   Collecting the best of his troops, who had taken little
share in the first part of the action, he threw himself on the fatigued and loosened ranks of the Swedish right wing, and again bore them back.   Wallenstein, profiting by this success, once more brought
the infantry of the centre to the charge.   The fiercest
combat ever known to any of the soldiers present

here took place, and the Swedes, unable to withstand the onset of additional thousands, were forced, with dreadful slaughter, across the trenches, and the twice-captured guns were again retaken. Wallenstein, in the midst of the fire, directed this terrible combat himself : wherever danger was greatest there he was present : all his attendants were struck down by his side ; a cannon shot tore the spur from his heel, and several musket balls lodged in the folds of his buff coat ; but he escaped unharmed. Not so fortunate was Pappenheim, the Telamon of the army, and the most formidable warrior of the House of Austria, and of the Church. Urged on by his fiery impetuosity, he penetrated, at the head of his cavalry,—who readily followed such a leader,—into the very midst of the Swedes, and fell, nobly fighting, in the foremost rank. Two musket balls pierced his scar-covered breast, and fainting from loss of blood, he was carried out of the field. While in the arms of his attendants, a murmur reached his ear that Gustavus was no more. When the report was confirmed to him, a ray of light re-animated, for a moment, his glazing eyes : " Then tell the Duke of Friedland," he said, " that I die happy, since I know that this irreconcileable enemy of my religion, has fallen with me on the same day."

The gleam of victory, which the spirit of Pappenheim had shed over the imperial army, vanished again with the fall of its author. The cavalry which he had so bravely led, fatigued by their long and hurried march, were unable to follow up the advantage they had gained. The rest of the army occupied the ground on which they had fought ; but in broken and mixed-up bands, without officers, without order, and totally incapable, therefore, of any combined effort. The Duke of Weimar profited quickly by the helpless condition of the enemy ; and the superior discipline of the Swedish troops well aided his spirited exertions. The reserves were brought forward, the other troops were formed around them, and as day was closing, the army advanced, for a third time, against the Imperialists.

The resolution itself was enough to insure victory ; for the long and fearful excitement of battle once relaxed, leaves the toil-worn frame nerveless and exhausted ; and the mind itself destitute of the energy and elasticity requisite for any renewal of vigorous exertion. And in war, a bold onset made by a few resolute men, against troops who have maintained, even successfully, a hard day's combat, is pretty sure to turn the scale in favour of the new assailants. And at Lützen, the resistance offered to the third attack of the Swedes, was comparatively feeble : the trenches were passed, the guns captured, and the enemy, whose strength and order were completely gone, was forced at last to leave the long-disputed field.

Under cover of darkness, Wallenstein withdrew his army towards Leipzig, leaving his baggage and artillery in possession of the victors. An hour after nightfall Pappenheim's infantry arrived ; still strong enough to have disputed the ground with the exhausted Swedes: but destitute of orders, and uncertain as to the result of the action, they followed their comrades to Leipzig ; and without having been exposed

to a single shot, shared completely in the defeat of
the army, by falling, like them, into that state of
disorganization, always the surest proof, and worst
consequence of a lost battle.

The number killed outright in both armies, is generally estimated at 9000 men ; but as this would,
according to modern computation, give about 30,000
killed and wounded, we may easily suppose it to be
exaggerated. The loss must, however, have been
very great ; the whole plain, from Lützen to the
Floss-Graben, was covered, as an eye-witness says,
with " heaps of slain ;" and Wallenstein could only
assemble 2000 effective men, on the morning after
the action, when he attempted to bring his lost artillery from the field ; while the Swedes, on their part,
mustered less than 12,000 men at Weisenfels, a few
days afterwards. The imperial army was completely
disorganised, owing to the loss of all its stores and
artillery, and to the fall of its best and ablest officers.

The most lamented of these was Pappenheim, who
died at Leipzig on the day after the action. This
officer, who is still one of the most popular of German heroes, gave at the battle of Prague the first
proofs of that dauntless courage for which he afterwards became so celebrated. At the head of a small
body of cavalry, he overthrew a whole regiment of
the enemy ; and being severely wounded, was left for
dead on the field, till accidentally discovered by those
who were plundering the slain. A few years afterwards he vanquished the insurgents in Upper Austria ; and distinguished himself on all occasions,

during the war, by a spirit of daring enterprise, that rose superior to every toil and every danger.

This heroic gallantry, though it obtained for him the admiration of his subordinates, exposed him, in too many cases, to the envy of his equals and superiors. Forgetful that in war, the dictates of courage are nearly the best that can be followed, these men represented him as a useful soldier, but an incapable commander ; though the result generally proved the reverse. He was long victorious in Lower Saxony : and his romantic expedition to the relief of Maestrich, so emblematic of his character, showed great justness in calculating movements, and failed of success, only in consequence of the mean malevolence of the Spaniards, who did not fire a single shot in aid of the army which had come to their assistance.

At the battle of Leipzig he retarded the defeat of the Imperialists by his exertions, and covered the retreat when the day was lost. It is not true that Tilly ascribed to him the unfortunate result of the action. Both Tilly and Wallenstein were above such practices ; and it redounds to the honour of both, that they strove, on all occasions, to place the merit of their subordinates in a favourable light. Wallenstein deserves particular praise on this account : he was liberal of his recommendations ; but never made family rank, the standard of military merit.

It is further said of Pappenheim, that he was a man of cultivated mind, and had displayed an early taste for learning and the arts, which too soon withered beneath the chilling tempest of war. We know not how the case may have been ; for none of his letters throw any light on the subject : but we cannot agree with those who would make us believe that war tends to harden the heart, to blunt the imagination, or blight genius in the bud. Our opinion is exactly the reverse : there is so much in war to awaken all the better feelings of our nature, that, though it may occasionally harden the bad, it can scarcely fail to improve the good. In civil life the heart is chilled by a daily contact with callous and calculating society, —to say nothing of the vapid affectation of mere fashion, —generous feeling, if called forth, meets with no sympathy : it finds itself in a strange world, and hastens back, ashamed, to the recesses of the heart, where it withers and decays ; if not, as too often happens, turned to rancour and misanthropy by ingratitude and ill usage.

In war, on the contrary, there is so much generous devotion to duty and humanity constantly brought before the eye, that it is impossible not to think well of men. Independently altogether of the gallantry and heroism so frequently displayed, in the hour of battle, by the humblest soldier, there is so much dis-interestedness, so much readiness to aid comrades and friends, even at the hazard of life ; so much willing-ness to make sacrifices for the destitute and forlorn, that no man of fair feeling, can help being impressed with a lofty idea of the excellence which human na-ture is capable of attaining. The iron hand of war shakes off, from men, the trammels of habitual thought that bind down the greater part of the species, to every-day mediocrity : it throws them back, and roughly too, upon their own innate qualities, which are brought rapidly to light and maturity. That, along with the good, many bad qualities are also brought to light, cannot indeed be denied : but the school which leads to perfection, has yet to be discovered.

In returning to the direct thread of our subject, we mention, as a matter of curiosity, that among those who fell at Lützen, was an Abbot of Fulda, who had come to witness the battle. In the request he addressed to Wallenstein, for permission to join the army, this very Christian prelate,—who was killed, not in administering consolation to the dying, but in galloping about the field along with a German Prince,—says, that he is willing to put up with the " fare of the humblest soldier :" and the levelling hand of war kept him to the very letter of his bargain.

Wallenstein abandoned Leipzig, on the day following the battle, and continued his retreat without interruption, till he placed the broken remnants of his army securely in winter quarters, behind the lofty mountains of Bohemia. The victorious Swedes in front, and the unbroken Saxons on his flank, left him evidently no other alternative. He was feebly pursued : the Swedes, uncertain of their position after the fall of their Sovereign, proceeded to Weisenfels, where they mustered at first only 12,000 men. These acknowledged Bernhard Duke of Weimar for their leader ; and it must be confessed, that they could hardly have made a better choice. This Prince, who acted an influential part in the great drama of the times, long after Wallenstein and Gustavus had passed away, was certainly one of the most remarkable men, of that very remarkable period. His skill in

gaining the affections of the soldiers, became the
main-spring of his power : his lofty, gallant and chivalrous bearing, excited their admiration and enthusiasm, and bound them to his fate, as well in adversity as in prosperity.   His method of war consisted
in boldly challenging fortune, under all circumstances ; and no bad method it is, when backed by
a clear head and brave heart. The Duke of Weimar
possessed both, and proceeded, with rare ability, to
raise up a throne, formed of the fragments of conquered provinces, taken from the principal Catholic
states of Germany, and resting on no other foundation than the point of his sword. In daring, promptness and activity ; in deeds of heart and hand, no
general can be placed above him ; and it may be
truly said, that he combined, in his own person, the
Paladin of the olden time, and the skilful strategist
of the modern.

It is impossible to take a final leave of Gustavus
Adolphus, without noticing the reports which have
gradually obtained a footing in history, and which
so generally ascribe his death to treachery, rather
than to the fair chances of battle.   A sovereign, on
whose life such mighty interests depended, could
hardly fall under circumstances, that prevented the
exact details from being immediately known, without giving rise to some of those tales of wonder, in
which the world take such peculiar delight ; and imagination certainly made the most of the death of this
great King.   He was said to have been assassinated ;
and new murderers continued to be discovered, and

new tales of murder to be invented, down even to the middle of the eighteenth century.

It was at first asserted, that Gustavus had fallen by the hands of conspirators, bribed or instigated to the crime, by the Emperor and the Jesuits. The interest which these parties had in wishing for the Swede's death was, indeed, the only proof ever brought forward to substantiate the unjust accusation : but, on the other hand, there was nothing in the character of the supposed culprits, which, of itself, could free them from suspicion. The instigators being thus clearly discovered ; who were the perpetrators of the deed ? Here conjecture was at a loss, for no one received any reward for the murder ; though, as we shall see presently, the Court of Vienna was actually munificent in rewarding assassination. Two of the King's attendants, or persons rather who said that they had accompanied him during the battle, obtained, many years after the action, forgiveness and absolution for having, as they confessed, murdered their royal master. One of these men died at the village of Crailsheim, in Franconia, and the other at Naumburg, in Saxony. The latter gave the clergyman who attended him, a telescope, that he declared to have taken from the murdered King. The Swedish government purchased the glass, which is still preserved at Stockholm ; and as they paid, no doubt, a good price for it, they probably received the tale of wonder into the bargain. Only one of these men pretended to have been instigated by the Catholics to the commission of the crime ; but no particulars are given : the names of the parties are not even mentioned, and both statements rest on the most unsatisfactory evidence possible.

Bernhard, Duke of Weimar, was also accused of having killed the King of Sweden : the accusation arose from some difference which had taken place between the two Princes, shortly before the battle of Lützen. We pass it over as undeserving of notice, and totally inconsistent with Bernhard's frank, loyal and gallant disposition.

The person generally fixed upon as the murderer of Gustavus, is Francis Albert, Duke of Saxon-Lauenburg; and his vacillating character, and strange fortunes appear, after all, to have been the only grounds on which the charge was founded. Francis Albert began his military career in the imperial army, and served, not without some distinction, in the Mantuan campaigns. Thinking himself slighted, he forsook the Austrian cause, and joined the King of Sweden, while that monarch was confronting Wallenstein in the camp before Nurenberg. Oxenstiern is said to have warned Gustavus against him ; but the King disregarded the advice, and allowed the Duke to remain near his person in the character of a volunteer.

When Gustavus soon afterwards fell at Lützen, Francis Albert was the only person near him that escaped unwounded. Not being well received by the Swedish officers after the battle, he went to Dresden, and took service in the Saxon army ; but unable to agree with Count Thurn and Arnheim, he resigned his command ; and endeavoured to obtain service in France. Failing in this, as the French did not wish to offend the Swedes, by employing a person who was obnoxious to them, he attached himself to the fortunes of Wallenstein, and was entrapped by Gordon, the day after the murder at Eger, and sent a prisoner to Vienna.   At the end of a year's confinement he obtained his liberty, and a command in the Austrian army at the same time, by forsaking his religion, and embracing the Catholic faith.

In 1644, he was dispatched with a corps to the relief of Sweidnitz, then closely pressed by the Swedes; but was defeated by the celebrated General Torstensohn, who, calling on his troops to avenge, on the very murderer, the death of the great Gustavus, attacked the advancing Austrians so unexpectedly, and with so much fury, that the whole army was, almost immediately, broken and dispersed.   Francis Albert, a man of distinguished bravery, whatever else he may have been, fought it out to the last, and surrendered only after having been severely wounded.   Torstensohn generously protected him from the rage of the soldiers, who were inclined to deal rather summarily with the supposed assassin of their King.   But his hour was come; his wounds were mortal, and ten days after his capture, he died, in great agony, and " made no sign."   He never, during his life, took any steps to clear himself of the suspicion which attached to his name, though he complained of it bitterly in one of his letters.

His fate, though a strange one, cannot well convict him of murder: historians have therefore thought it right to add corroborating circumstances, the insufficiency of which we can demonstrate, even at this dis-

tance of time. Francis Albert, they say, wore, during
the battle of Lützen, a green scarf which was the imperial cognisance, and thus escaped, when the rest of the
King's attendants were slain. The fact, however, is,
that the green scarf was the Swedish, and the red scarf
the imperial cognisance * ; besides which we all know
that, under a heavy fire, the colour of a scarf would
be little attended to, even if observed. Equally
untrue is the story that this unhappy Duke left the
Swedish army during the battle, and was the first
who brought to Wallenstein the news of the King's
fall. Even during the action, it was reported in the
imperial army that Gustavus was killed, and Wallenstein still knew it by general report only, ten days
afterwards. In his first official letter to the Emperor,
dated from Freyenstein, the 15th November, he
merely says in a postscript, " The King is certainly
dead ; left dead on the field covered with many
wounds." Colonel Diodati, who was the bearer of
Wallenstein's letter, drew up, by order of the Emperor, a written account of the action, and speaks in
the following words of the King's death : " While
the battle was thus fiercely contested, and while it
was yet uncertain on which party fortune would confer the victory, it became known that the King was
lying dead on the field ; officers and soldiers who
knew him very well confirmed this ; but no one
would credit the report."

In opposition to these statements, it is right to
mention the account furnished by another eye-witness

* Hoyer.

of the King's death. Hans of Hazendorff, a private of the Life-guards, who lost a leg at the battle of Lützen, occupied himself, while recovering from his wound, in composing what he calls " Truth and Poetry, on the death of the King of Sweden." In this strange account, the life-guardsman says, that he was one of five persons who accompanied Gustavus, when he rode forward to observe the enemy : two of the attendants were dispatched to tell the Finlanders not to push on so rapidly ; thus leaving only three persons near the King : probably Lübeling, the Duke of Lauenburg, and the author himself. At this moment Hazendorff was wounded and thrown to the ground ; and while in that position, he saw " a great lord " who was of the party,—meaning Francis Albert,—shoot the King through the head, and dispatch him with a sword after he had fallen. This tale has also been received as authority, though bearing, in all its details, the clearest marks of folly and extravagance ; for the author, who, as he says, was fifty yards from the scene, and had just had a leg shot off, not only sees all that passes, but hears all that is said by the dying monarch.

Puffendorff was the first who gave historical circulation to the charge preferred against Francis Albert, by bringing it forward, less as a surmise, than as an established fact. And as the historian had seen persons who were present at Lützen, and had, besides, free access to the Swedish archives, his book was looked upon,—and in many respects justly so,—as deserving every credit. The work was also written in Latin, which was the universal literary lan-

guage of the period, and was thus accessible to all
the literary world ; so that it served as an authentic
source, from whence other writers were contented to
take, without much scrutiny, whatever information
they required respecting the Swedish history of the
time.

The only person present with Gustavus, when he
was killed, was the page Lübeling, whose noble conduct has been already mentioned.   This young man,
who was eighteen years of age, died of his wounds
six days after the battle.   He was perfectly collected before his death ; fully resigned to his fate ; and
related the particulars we have mentioned, in order
that they might be communicated to his father at
Nurenberg.   The entire statement has been published by Murr, in his historical contributions ; and
throws not the slightest suspicion on any one.

Lübeling's statement is fully confirmed by the account of the battle which Bernhard, Duke of Weimar,
sent to Louis XIII, and which is recorded in Siri's
Memoirs.   The document contains not a word about
the supposed murder, and has been too generally
overlooked by historians.

Oxenstiern, in an official letter written eight days
after the battle, says, of the King's death, " I had
long foreseen the misfortune, and often requested his
Majesty not thus to expose himself.   But God had
endowed this Prince with a degree of courage, which
made him disregard all danger : so that we can only
speak of his death as an event that tends to enhance
his fame."

We are bound therefore to acquit the unfortunate

Francis Albert of the crime laid to his charge : there is no evidence against him sufficient even to justify suspicion ; and we are unacquainted with any motive that could urge him to the commission of so foul a deed.   The personal resentment which he is said to have entertained against the King of Sweden rests, in like manner, on a mere device of the enemy ; for it was with the Duke's elder brother, and not with Francis Albert, that the young Gustavus had a boy's quarrel *.   We need, however, be at no loss to account for the death of the great King; where thousands fell in fair and manly fight, the bravest of the brave was but too likely to prove one of the gallant victims.

The body of Gustavus was embalmed at Weisenfels, two days after the battle, and the unhappy monarch was found to have received nine wounds ; four shot and five sabre wounds.

It would be encroaching too much on the province of history to enter into an examination of the ambitious plans which late German writers, Schiller not excepted, have ascribed to the liberator of their country.   The debt of gratitude, due to the King of Sweden, seemed to press a little on the Germans, and the authors of that nation have, in consequence, tried to diminish its weight.   They positively assert that the imperial crown was his aim, and that he intended to establish, by force of arms, and, at the expense of German liberty, an independent power in the empire.   These accusations are distinctly made by Protestant as well as by Catholic writers ; but the

* Lundblat's Swedish Plutarch.

proofs necessary to substantiate the charge are totally
wanting.   That a victorious monarch, in the very
prime of life, whose ambition had been fired by a
splendour of success, unequalled in Europe since the
time of the Romans, would not have gone back
empty-handed to Sweden, after dictating a peace to
the Emperor, is sufficiently probable.   But we have
no right to bring a direct charge against an individual
of the noblest disposition, because ordinary ambition
loses no opportunity to grasp at power and dominion.
We can easily fancy a height of character that shall
rise above these " meaner things," and strive only for
the attainment of glory and renown : and, if we are
just, we must allow that no one, in modern times,
has approached nearer to that model than Gustavus
Adolphus.

If, on the other hand, we are disposed to give the
rein to imagination, we can well suppose that such
a King might, had his life been spared, have raised
up a power in Germany which should have changed
the face of Europe.   Before the onset at Lützen, he
told his soldiers, " Fight as usual, and you will this day
make me the first King in the world :" and such in
truth he would have been, had he lived to see the close
of that fiery combat.` Already master of the north
and of the west of Germany, as well as of a great
part of Bavaria, the road to Vienna was open to him.
He might there have dictated a peace.   His presence
would have rallied round his victorious standard, the
Protestants of Austria, Moravia and Bohemia, while
his tolerant disposition and popular qualities everywhere disarmed his religious adversaries.   The im-

perial sceptre would then have been within his reach, and would, in his warlike hands, have been an ensign of real power. As politic as Charles V. and possessed of the military talents and popular qualities which that Emperor wanted, he might have grasped at universal monarchy with a prospect of success far greater than any of which the Austrian could boast.

The efforts at this universal dominion ascribed to Louis XIV. and Napoleon, belong not to our parallel; for the men were differently situated and of inferior caste. The first succeeded by regular inheritance, to vast power, and his taste for splendour and magnificence gave a brilliancy to his reign which it could never have derived from the mediocrity of his abilities. Napoleon was thrown by the events of the Revolution into the possession of still greater power. A ruthless conscription placed hundreds of thousands of brave and intelligent soldiers at his command, and the victories which he purchased with their blood, dazzled the world, who, in their ready admiration of "imperial sway," willingly overlooked the meanness of his character, and the insignificance of his talents.

CHAPTER VIII.

HAVING followed Wallenstein in his progress, to the zenith of power ; we must now trace his footsteps through the dark and dubious path which led to the close of his career. We have seen him, a friendless soldier ; a wealthy, courted and ambitious noble ; an all-powerful dictator, and a victorious commander, balancing even the fortunes of Gustavus. We must now trace to his end the man of doubt and mystery, the same " whose character, obscured by faction's hatred and applause, still floats, unfixed and station-less, in history." The star that appeared before us, feeble at first, and scarcely noticed, till it burst upon the view a wild and fiery meteor, terrifying by its eccentric course more than it gladdened by its bright-ness, has now to pass away, darkened by murky clouds that veil from the eye the real nature of its parting light.

Immediately after the battle of Lützen, Wallen-stein dispatched the Marquis de Grana to Vienna, to acquaint the Emperor with the particulars of the action. But the Italian, not wishing, perhaps, to be the bearer of indifferent news, was taken ill on the road, so that Colonel Diodati, the quarter-master-general, had to replace him. Owing to this delay,

Ferdinand heard nothing of the battle till thirteen days after it had been fought.

Wallenstein, in the few lines which he wrote, laid no claim to victory, as has been asserted. He was, with all his faults, above these poor practices : he simply referred the Emperor to Colonel Diodati for information, and only mentioned, in a postscript, that the King of Sweden was dead. Ferdinand having heard the colonel's verbal account, directed him to draw up a written statement of the affair ; and it is in this report, which Förster has published, that a victory is claimed for the Imperialists *. The first part of the quarter-master-general's narrative is very good ; and better, perhaps, than some of the modern functionaries of the department would write ; but towards the end there is sad faltering, and the Italian finds it difficult to account for a retreat following so quickly upon a victory : military mystification was then in its infancy. Diodati declares that the retrograde movement was owing to want of provisions ; the battle having been gained, the troops " retired in the night, with the loss of certain pieces of artillery." Ferdinand was willing enough to believe himself victorious, and wrote immediately to Wallenstein, thanking him for the important service he had rendered the state and the cause, and

---

* Tilly's account of the battle of Leipzig is much fairer : he frankly admits having been defeated, and says, that it is " a heavy misfortune, which can only be atoned for by courage and activity." He also sends an officer to Vienna, who draws up, for the Emperor's information, an account of the battle : it is a clear, plain statement ; very different from the generality of modern bulletins.

congratulating him on the death of the " Swede," as he calls Gustavus. The great satisfaction evinced by the Emperor, in offering these congratulations, tends to throw doubt on the story of his having shed tears when he was shewn the blood-stained coat which the King of Sweden had worn at Lützen. Wallenstein spoke more frankly, and more in character, when he said, after the death of Gustavus, " It is well for him and me that he is gone : there was no room in Germany for both our heads."

In all Catholic countries *Te Deum* was sung for the victory of Lützen, and at Madrid, the King of Sweden's death was represented on the stage, in a drama of twenty-four acts, which was repeated for twelve successive nights; and whoever failed to appear was looked upon as an enemy of the House of Austria. Pope Urban VIII. was indeed the only Catholic prince who behaved with Christian feeling on the occasion ; for which he was loudly enough censured by the rest of the Catholic world.

To the Catholic cause, the death of Gustavus was ultimately of more advantage than any which could have been derived from a mere victory in the field ; but it had been balanced by defeat, instead of being crowned by success, and did not immediately lead to any brilliant result. Great therefore was the disappointment of their party : they expected to have been instantly replaced at the height of power from whence they had been precipitated by the victories of the King of Sweden. They now found that they had only escaped destruction, and that the battle for supremacy still remained to be fought : they seemed not to know that the genius of a great man will long survive his fall ; and that ordinary hands may guide the helm, after the master-spirit has once indicated the course that is to be pursued.   Gustavus once removed, they thought that Wallenstein was immediately to carry every thing before him ; and were dissatisfied because the general did not act up to their exaggerated expectations.

The imperial commander had no sooner settled his army in winter quarters behind the mountain ramparts of Bohemia ; than with his usual magnificence he began to reward the officers and soldiers who had distinguished themselves in the battle.   Besides bestowing gold chains and medallions, he gave away, in presents, to individuals and regiments, a hundred thousand crowns, equal perhaps to what a hundred thousand pounds would be in our time ; and an enormous sum certainly, for a private individual to give out of his own funds.   Count Brenner received 12,000 florins ; Colonel Kerhous, 16,000 ; the regiment of Comar, 10,000 ; Colonel Berthold Wallenstein's regiment, 9000, and so on.   The names of all the officers who shared in this bounty are recorded ; but we do not find Piccolomini among the number ; nor does any thing appear to justify the usual report that Wallenstein entertained any friendship for this man. He was rather, we suspect, too good a judge of character to place any confidence in so mean and worthless a person.

Rewards having been distributed to the deserving, the more painful task of punishing the guilty remained to be fulfilled.   And severe as the military

punishments of the period certainly were, those inflicted after the battle of Lützen, were among the
most sanguinary that are recorded*. Twelve officers,
convicted of having misbehaved before the enemy,
were beheaded at Prague, on the 4th of February
1633. Seven others were cashiered with infamy, and
their swords broken, by the public executioner, on
the scaffold. Forty who had absconded, and refused
to stand their trials, were declared dishonoured and
disgraced, and had their names affixed to the gibbet.
As most of these officers were men of high family,—
one was an Italian Count,—and as they were not
even allowed to solicit pardon from the Emperor,
their punishment exposed Wallenstein to severe ani-
madversions. And though he had not acted in the
first heat of the moment, but allowed two months to
pass before he brought them to trial, it was still said
that he only sought to wash out, in the blood of innocent men, the disgrace of his late defeat. Others
maintained that he only wished to show his power and
total independence of the Emperor, by these severities.

Strictly speaking, the punishments were probably
well deserved; but whether men should be punished
with such severity, unless fully and fairly aware of
their duty, and of the consequence of failing in its
performance, is a different question. In the seven-

---

* In 1642, the imperial cavalry regiment of Madloi, which led
the flight at the second battle of Leipzig, was decimated. The
colonel, several of the officers and every tenth man, suffered death
by the sword: the rest were declared infamous in front of the
whole army, and dismissed from the service.

teenth century the rules of duty and of discipline
were too ill defined, and were too frequently deviated
from with impunity, to justify altogether these terrible examples.   Still, it must be allowed that Wallenstein, standing almost alone and unsupported by
a good system or a good staff, for we hardly find a
trace of either, effected wonders by the mere force of
rewards and punishments : he had always a numerous army well in hand ; and it may be doubted whether the Austrians ever fought, either before or afterwards, with more determined resolution, than at
Lützen.

The imperial commander employed the repose
which the winter secured for him, to recruit and re-
organise his army ; and on this occasion we find him,
for once, touching on the subject of tactics.   And it
is curious to see the " creator of mighty armies," as
Wallenstein has been termed, paying in general so
little attention to this important professional subject.
In this respect, at least, he resembles the commanders of the present age, not one of whom has
ever done the slightest thing for the science of tactics, the very foundation on which rests the whole
science of war.   We have had changes of dress in
abundance ; in matters of drill, we have changed from
one puerility to another ; but in regard to tactics we
have not made a single step of progress since the days
of Frederick II.   During the late war some change
took place in the mode of fighting, or rather in the
mode of employing the tactical machines : this arose
principally from the circumstance of unskilful men
being entrusted with the command of large armies ;

but so far from any improvement having been made, the British, who deviated the least from the old method, managed better than those who deviated the most.

Wallenstein's tactical regulations are not numerous: he only gives two orders to the cavalry, but one of these shows that, he well knew wherein consisted the real strength of that arm. In directing the heavy cavalry to be deprived of their carbines, he says, " few of the soldiers know how to use them, and having once given a fire, they think they have only to make a ' caracol,' and turn their back on the enemy :" that is, he wishes to reduce the cavalry to the use of the sword, the only real cavalry weapon. The other order directs all the heavy cavalry to be provided with cuirasses ; " because it was found in the late action that the mail-clad horsemen did their duty, while the others ran away." Of this last order we cannot so entirely approve ; though it may have been less objectionable in the time of Wallenstein than it would be at present. At the period, of which we are writing, artillery was less numerous than it has become since, and fire-arms were less perfect ; so that the weight and inconvenience of the cuirass might be redeemed by advantages, of which it has been deprived by the augmented fire of modern battles, that renders celerity of action so essential. No passive resistance can be opposed to modern arms : their action must be met and destroyed by superior action ; for neither masses nor cuirasses can arrest round shot, grape or musket-balls ; and all the defensive arms and formations, would long since have been consigned to ridicule, but for the pertinacity with which, according to Marshal Saxe, military men adhere to existing practices, however objectionable. Authorities, indeed, will not always perceive that there is a wide difference between disobeying orders and detecting errors : they identify themselves with established regulations, and too often look upon all attempts to point out deficiencies, as little better than direct violations of discipline. Implicit obedience to the rules of the service, and to the orders of their superiors, is the first duty of soldiers ; but men may be obedient without being blind ; though the pride of station is not always disposed to grant even this concession.

To supply the artillery lost at the battle of Lützen, Wallenstein, is said, to have taken down the church bells for the purpose of having them cast into cannon. The assertion rests on no good authority, though it is not likely he would have hesitated much, had there been any necessity for the proceeding. But as his fall has often been quoted as an additional proof of the fate, sooner or latter sure to attend all who quarrel with the Church,—or who formerly, perhaps, quarrelled with the Church of Rome,—it may be as well to say a few words respecting the position in which he stood towards the clergy.

If we suppose the Catholic clergy to have been as ambitious, bigoted, cunning and intriguing, as their opponents assert, we may well suppose that Wallenstein would incur their hatred. Totally free from prejudices ; proud, haughty and overbearing ; en-

dowed with a clear and vigorous understanding ;
gifted with the dreaded

—————————— " power that took
Their thoughts from others at a single look,"

he could not fail of being obnoxious to such a priest-
hood. Always ready to tear aside the slender veil,
beneath which designing and little-minded persons
so constantly strive to conceal the motives of unworthy actions, he stood " in his pride of place," the
natural and declared enemy of the Church of Rome.

If, on the other hand, we give the Roman clergy
credit only for ordinary fair dealing, and forget altogether that they were a class of men who had volun-
tarily dedicated themselves to the instruction of
others, in the ways of virtue and religion,—a pursuit
that could hardly fail to make the mass of the clergy
better than the mass of ordinary laymen ; we can
discover no cause for the bitter hatred which they
are said to have entertained against the lordly Duke
of Friedland. Wallenstein had, at an early age,
become a convert to the Roman Church : he had
fought in its cause, and was its most powerful champion. In his principalities he had endowed churches
and convents ; and at one time favoured the Jesuits,
who, even after his death, boasted of his friendship
as a proof of their merit. He never, in exterior manner, affected to be what is called devout ; but whenever in his letters he touches upon religious subjects,
he always writes in a sincerely Christian spirit.

When directing a convent to be founded, at Stippa
in Moravia, he says, " We must strive to exchange

the worldly for the heavenly, and all that is poor and transitory, for what is great and everlasting." He often writes in the same tone, and is on many occasions very liberal to the church, though he sometimes lectures and reprimands the clergy. The Jesuits also lose favour with him at a later period : they had attempted to enlist, in their order, two young noblemen whom he had entrusted to their charge ; and he declares in a letter, that he would willingly give 100,000 crowns if he could get rid of them again. Some monks at Leippa also come in for a share of censure: he directly accuses them of having spent " on dissolute women and in their usual debaucheries," a sum of 2000 florins which he had given them for the improvement of their convent.

His greatest crime, however, in the eyes of the Church, if he had any such crime, was his spirit of toleration.   Individually, he never persecuted any one on account of religion, and favoured and employed Protestants as readily as the most zealous Catholics. Immediately after the battle of Lützen, he recommended that the Emperor should avail himself of the consternation occasioned among the Protestants by the death of Gustavus—grant universal amnesty, proclaim religious toleration, and proceed, on the strength of such acts, to conclude a general peace. But the noble and exalted views of the soldier, were not calculated for the meridian of the cabinet of Vienna : there the prospect of acquiring spoil and power, overbalanced every other consideration : and sixteen years of sanguinary war were the consequences of this narrow view, while Wallenstein's tolerant spirit was afterwards brought forward as a charge against him.

With his usual ability, Wallenstein had recruited and reformed his army during the winter. It now amounted to 40,000 men, all well equipped ; and on the 5th of May 1633, he left Prague, in order to open his last campaign. An eye-witness thus describes his departure: " The train announced the man who, in power and splendour, vied even with the Emperor himself. The procession consisted of fourteen carriages, each drawn by six horses : twenty cavaliers of rank attended on Wallenstein's own person ; and a hundred and twenty livery servants followed in the suite. All the court attendants were dressed in new scarlet and blue uniforms ; and ten trumpeters sounding their silver gilt trumpets, opened the way. All the baggage waggons were covered with gilt leather ; the greatest order prevailed in the establishment, and every person knew exactly what was his place, and what were his duties. The Duke himself was dressed in a horseman's buff-coat ; and the entire scene resembled more a victor's triumph than the march of a lately baffled commander."

Count Gualdo, who long served under Wallenstein, says, that " in the field, his usual dress was a buff or elk-skin coat, red hose, a red scarf, a scarlet cloak and a grey castor hat adorned with red feathers. He always wore boots and spurs, and never appeared without the order of the Golden-fleece, which the King of Spain had conferred upon him. In the latter years of his life, he suffered greatly from gout, walked with difficulty, and was forced to lean on a

bamboo cane for support. His dislike of noise," which
we have before noticed, " was such, that he could
not bear the barking of dogs, nor the clatter of the
large spurs then in fashion." The story that he once
caused a servant, who approached him with these
large clanging spurs, to be hanged for the offence,
shows what liberties fame took with the reputation
of this dreaded and powerful individual.

" Actions of spirit and enterprise," continues the
Italian, " were sure to meet with his approbation,
even when bordering on extravagance. Wit, promptness and originality were passports to his favour ;
but the qualities he valued most in military men,
were pride, ambition, daring and resolution. He had
a marked aversion to regular court-jesters, as well as
to buffoons of every kind ; but men of genius and
talent were sure of his friendship and protection. He
was a firm friend to the soldiers, and never lost an
opportunity of speaking in their favour.   In rewarding or promoting officers, he was guided solely by the
merit of the candidates, and never influenced by
family connections, or by recommendations from men
of rank, not even by those of the Emperor himself."
We manage things differently here ; for in the English service, no one speaks in favour of the soldiers,
and promotion is sold for money, or given according
to the interest of the parties ; and always as an inevitable consequence of such a system, with the most
perfect disregard of merit.   Gualdo, who, from his
position in the imperial army, could not write very
favourably of Wallenstein, concludes his account of
him, by saying that, " he carried firmness and im-

patience to obstinacy, severity to cruelty, and liberality to extravagance; while he made the highest, the
Emperor not excepted, feel the effects of his unbending pride."

It is to be regretted that the Count does not tell us
how this pride, which has given rise to so many
charges against the Duke of Friedland,—was actually
displayed ; for there are various qualities of pride.
The pride resulting from great actions and great intellect, if perceptible, can only press upon the envious :
whereas the pride of birth, wealth, office, rank and
station, is offensive, and would perhaps be insulting,
were it not for the shade of ridicule which it casts over
the possessor. Thus mellowed, good men pity the
infirmity, and ordinary men forgive it ; because, as
La Rochefoucault says, even the best are too often
pleased with the misfortunes of others. The pride,
again, which, without vulgar condescension,—and so
many men are guilty of showing condescension that
the distinction must be marked,—could be affable
with the humble soldier and high with emperors and
princes, may have been of a nature to deserve praise
rather than the heavy censure, so universally cast upon
Wallenstein. His letters contain no appearance of
offensive pride : a polite and dignified tone pervades
the whole of them : we see nothing of the haughty
and overbearing style, so often affected by little persons in high stations ; and the man who made mo-
narchs and ministers feel the superiority due to talents
and character, when contrasted, even with imperial
power,—always requests where he could command ;
often indeed when the request has to be repeated.

There is still preserved, in the castle of Friedland, a very striking, full length original picture of Wallenstein. The face is like the portrait prefixed to this volume : the Duke is dressed in the buff-coat above mentioned, resembling in cut the surtout of the present day : it is splendidly " frounced and broider'd o'er," fits close to the body, and is buttoned up to the throat. Long boots, fitting the leg, reach above the knee, and join the large trunk hose : a fine point lace collar falls over the breast and shoulders, and point ruffles of the same kind double back over the cuffs of the coat. His gauntlet-fashioned gloves, one of which is on, are, like his scarf, richly embroidered, and he wears one of the long Toledo rapiers, with the large and beautifully worked bar hilts, generally worn by the cavaliers of the period. The entire figure is striking and noble, and the martial and appropriate nature of the dress, contrast favourably with the absurd military costumes which it has since been the fashion to devise.

Before proceeding with our narrative, it may be right at once to state, that every thing which follows, rests, as far as the actions of Wallenstein are directly concerned, on authentic documents, published or inspected by Förster. The German author prints many of these at length; from others he gives extracts : our limits must confine us to the substance only. The Swedish authorities that have been used are nearly as authentic as the German ones ; for it is well known that the work of Chemnitz was written almost under the direction of Oxenstiern, and inspected, previous to publication, by that great statesman himself.

Wallenstein on taking the field directed the greater

part of his force against Silesia, which the Saxons, under Arnheim, had conquered during the Lützen campaign ; and it was expected that the opponent of Gustavus would soon have cleared the province of Arnheim and his troops. But the expectation was disappointed ; for Wallenstein appeared in the field, not to fight, but to conclude an armistice and open negotiations with the Saxons. Förster, who is as often a special pleader as a biographer, accounts for this inactivity, on the grounds of the General's ill health, and of his predilection for the embellishment of his principalities, on which he had expended vast sums. The first excuse, if true, is not a good one, for he might have obtained leave of absence; or he should have resigned the command, if unequal to the duties it imposed : and he might have done so with credit after the death of Gustavus *. The second, is no excuse at all ; for private considerations must never be allowed to influence the public conduct of a public man ; least of all that of a soldier.

Peace was clearly Wallenstein's object ; and, he probably saw, in the then situation of affairs, a better prospect of bringing the war to an end by sparing the Saxons, than by overthrowing them. It is also possible that he wished to establish a balance between the contending parties, which, by the aid of his wealth, reputation and influence with the soldiers, should enable him to give the ultimate decision, and gain

---

* Montecucoli did so after the death of Turenne. " A man," said he, " who has had the honour of commanding against Condé, Mahomet Kuprogli and Turenne, must not risk his reputation in contending against inexperienced and chance-favoured generals."

advantages both for himself and the Emperor. The
Swedes were the most formidable enemies of Austria,
and he knew that the jealousies, existing between
them and the Saxons, had rather increased than diminished since the death of Gustavus.

The Elector of Saxony, who had ill supported the
influence exercised over the Protestants by the King
of Sweden, could still less brook to see that influence
in the hands of Oxenstiern, who acted as legate of the
Swedish crown in Germany. This great statesman,
the greatest, perhaps, that modern times can show,
—because, to profound learning and knowledge of
the world, he added the highest and most brilliant
talents, the noblest integrity of purpose, boundless
activity and unbending firmness,—had been appointed, by the League of Heilbron, to take upon himself
the management of the war. The Protestant states
of the four Upper Circles of the empire composed this
league ; and they invited all their brethren in belief
to join them for the good of the common cause ; but
the Elector of Saxony refused to become one of their
members, though he still carried on the war as an
ally ; and at his suggestion, the Duke of Brandenburg adopted a similar line of policy. This, of
course, put an end to all unity of action among the
Protestants ; and it required not Wallenstein's sagacity to foresee, that opportunities for taking advantage
of their differences would soon offer. We shall find
that he was right in his conjecture : but the short-
sighted policy of the Courts of Munich and Vienna
baffled his honest plans for turning the divisions to
account, and drove him, perhaps, to the formation

of projects, the suspicion of which, still weighs on his memory and darkens his fame.

We have before stated, that rumours, ascribing to Wallenstein the most extravagant and ambitious plans, had been circulated, after his dismissal from the command at the Diet of Ratisbon. The unexpected armistice just mentioned, led to a renewal of these reports. Wallenstein, it was said, had offered to join the Saxons ; the two armies combined were to march against Vienna ; a peace was to be forced upon the Emperor ; the Jesuits were to be driven from the empire ; the Protestants to be placed on the same footing on which they were under Rudolph and Mathias ; the property of the exiled was to be restored ; and Wallenstein himself was to be made King of Bohemia.

All these reports, together with many others, were afterwards collected and published by imperial order and authority, as satisfactory proofs of Wallenstein's guilt ; though many of the idle tales carry their own contradiction along with them. In the first place, the Emperor required not to be forced into a peace, as Wallenstein had authority from him to negotiate one ; and though it is probable, that the Duke of Friedland would willingly have changed his principalities, made up of confiscated property, for a royal crown, we cannot see on what grounds he, a convert from the Protestant faith, could look for the suffrage of the Bohemians ; or how he could expect to maintain himself on the throne of a country which he had so actively aided to oppress. That Wallenstein, as his defenders say, only made these

proposals with a view of deceiving the enemy, seems
equally incredible.   What object could be gained by
such deception ?   And what vigilant enemy would risk
any thing on the mere assertion of one who avowed
himself a traitor ?   Who plays with treason is sure
to be defiled ; and Wallenstein must have known
how dangerous, to life and honour, such an absurd
proceeding would prove under the suspicious government of Ferdinand II.   And, inferior foes, acting
on the defensive, as the allies were acting in Silesia,
would be glad enough to accept a truce, even for its
own sake.   That they afterwards complained of having been injured by its effects, proves nothing ; for
the moment a man is stopped from going forward,
though he may not have been very eager to advance,
he will be sure to assert that, unseasonable interference alone, prevented him from achieving wonders.
And it seems a settled rule with all armies, to blame
delay on the part of their leaders ; though the many
can seldom know the circumstances which render it
necessary or advisable.

But if we cannot well understand the cause of this
inactivity, still less can we understand the following
circumstance.   The Court of Dresden had exerted
itself to bring the negotiation with Wallenstein to a
satisfactory conclusion ; and the imperial commander
had actually signed the preliminary articles, among
which the "junction of the two armies" was included.
When it came, however, to an explanation, Wallenstein said to Francis Albert, Duke of Lauenburg,
who was then in the Saxon service, and conducting
the negotiation on the part of the Saxon Cabinet,

" We must combine our forces, in order to drive the
Swedes out of the empire, for they have no business
here : having once done so, we can, at pleasure, conclude a peace among ourselves."   " This," the Duke
of Lauenburg replied, " would not be acting a very
honest part ; since the Swedes were parties to the
treaty, and had helped the good cause."   The answer
put a stop to the negotiation ; and, as the armistice
was at an end, hostilities were again renewed.   How
a misunderstanding on so vital a point could have
taken place, is altogether incomprehensible ; and we
are forced to recollect, that Francis Albert, of very
suspicious memory, is our sole informant.

The truce had no sooner expired, than Wallenstein
invested Sweidnitz, which he bombarded for some
days ; but heavy rains arrested the progress of the
siege.   And when Arnheim advanced to the relief
of the place, the redoubted Duke of Friedland immediately relinquished the enterprise, and took up a
strong position, from whence he contented himself
with harassing the allies by means of his numerous
light cavalry.   " This," says Förster, " was very
cleverly done ; for it injured the enemy, who loudly
complained of the great loss they sustained."   Such
lamentations must, at times, be received with as much
doubt as pretended victories.   Certain it is, that Wallenstein's conduct led to no important result, and
was therefore unworthy of his fame and reputation ;
for while he was lying inactive on the frontiers of
Bohemia, the Swedes under Bernhard of Weimar
and Field-Marshal Horn, were carrying every thing
before them on the Lower Rhine and the Danube.

The Imperialists were defeated at Oldendorf; Munich, Landsberg and Echsted, were taken; Maximilian was driven from his country, and forced to seek shelter in the Tyrol; while the unfortunate Electorate was ravaged, both by friends and foes.

The rigid and humane system of discipline which the King of Sweden had maintained, vanished with him from the scene of action: even the generous exertions of Horn, who, more than all the other scholars of Gustavus, resembled his great master, were unable to repress the disorders of which the troops were guilty. Acts of cruelty, on one side, naturally led to retaliations on the other, till both parties exhausted invention, to discover new modes of torture, that should exceed in atrocity those last practised by their exasperated enemies. And Wallenstein, while this was passing on the Danube, was skirmishing and negotiating on the frontiers of Silesia. "He would not aid his personal enemy, the Elector of Bavaria," say his advocates: it is an unfortunate defence; for if such a motive influenced his conduct, it redounds not much to his honour.

About this time a congress assembled as Breslau, to negotiate a peace under the mediation of Denmark: but no deputies appeared on the part of Sweden, Brandenburg and the Heilbron League. These parties excused themselves on the plea, of not having received timely notice of the meeting : an excuse, from which we may infer that they were neither very anxious to be present, nor very anxiously wished for by the other powers. The Emperor informed Wallenstein of the approaching congress, and the latter immediately proposed to Arnheim to conclude another truce, which was soon settled between them. This armistice was to extend to all the hereditary dominions of the House of Austria, to Brandenburg and Saxony : it was to continue for four weeks ; and hostilities were not to recommence till three weeks after it should have expired. The other states of the empire were left free to join the treaty, if so disposed ; but no mention was made of the Swedes, who complained loudly of the neglect : though the circumstance throws more suspicion on Arnheim, who was their ally, than on Wallenstein, who was their open enemy. And here we have another of those strange statements that tend so much to obscure Wallenstein's extraordinary history.

Immediately after the conclusion of the second armistice, Arnheim acquaints Wallenstein that he is going to visit Oxenstiern, in order to settle matters about the treaty. To this Wallenstein replies, under date of the 4th September, " I am sorry you are going into the empire, for at this rate the work " (the peace) " will never be brought to a conclusion." Without, however, minding this letter, Arnheim set out for Gelnhausen, where he had an interview with Oxenstiern : and it must be confessed that the proposals which the Saxon general here made to the Chancellor, were sufficiently singular. Arnheim, it seems, told Oxenstiern that Wallenstein had never forgotten the insult put upon him by his first dismissal from the command : that he stood even then in no good favour at Vienna,—that new indignities were preparing for him,—and that the Duke of Feria was to come from Italy, to replace him at the head of the army. For these insults, continued Arnheim, Wallenstein was determined to take vengeance on the House of Austria. He had already secured General Holk and Gallas to his interest, and requested the Chancellor to place six good regiments at his disposal, in return for which, he would give over six of his own. As soon as this exchange should be effected, he would enter Bohemia, restore the old rights and charters of the kingdom, and then march to Vienna and force the Emperor to make peace.

These proposals appeared rather suspicious to the wary Oxenstiern, who thought them too promising to be altogether confided in : he therefore declined the exchange of regiments, said that the Protestant party would not interfere, but would let things take their chance, and concluded by observing, " If this is a jest, it is a bad one, and can tend only to excite mistrust on one side and contempt on the other." He immediately acquainted the Duke of Weimar with what had passed ; and recommended him to be on his guard against the arts of the Duke of Friedland ; but not to throw obstacles in his way should he really declare against the House of Austria.

That the proposals here mentioned were actually made to Oxenstiern, cannot admit of a doubt, since we know, that the Swedish historian Chemnitz had the Chancellor's own authority for the statement ; but what authority Arnheim had for making them is more difficult to comprehend ; as we soon afterwards find him and Wallenstein completely misunderstanding each other.

On Arnheim's return to the army, he had an interview with Wallenstein ; and on the 17th of September, he writes as follows to the Duke of Brandenburg : " The first time I spoke to the Duke of Friedland he promised every thing that was fair ; declared his only object, to be the conclusion of a permanent peace, and desired me to draw out some general plan as to the best mode of proceeding." Further on, Arnheim says, that " the proposal to march, with the combined armies, into the empire, appeared a little suspicious to him, as he did not know what was thereby intended ; till the Duke declared, that no lasting peace could be concluded, before the strangers were expelled from Germany. To effect this he suggested that we should join him, and drive the Swedes out of the country, and then we could make our own peace on our own terms. Hereupon," continues the Saxon general, " I reminded him of his former willingness to enter into an alliance with the Swedes ; but on this he broke off the conversation ; and when I recalled to him what his own proposals had been, he merely replied, that ' he should reserve those to the last.' The end of all must be, that no one will believe him." On the 29th of September, Arnheim sends a second letter to the Duke of Brandenburg, in which he writes, " I declare to God, that I do not know what *finesse* Friedland seeks in this ; but whatever it may be, certain it is, that no safe treaty can be concluded with the man, for there is no steadiness in him."

Now, it must always be recollected, that these strange statements rest altogether on the authority of Arnheim, a man mistrusted by all parties; and of whom Cardinal Richelieu said, that the "Court of Rome had lost, in him, the most perfect Jesuit that ever lived."

Rumours of this friendly intercourse kept up with the enemy, and particularly with Arnheim, began to excite suspicion at Vienna; and the Emperor actually sent Count Schlick, into Silesia, to learn how matters stood. Though the ambassador was very civilly treated by Wallenstein, who well knew the real object of the mission, his report is stated to have been rather unfavourable than otherwise.

Before proceeding, we must here weave another dark thread, into our history.

The congress of Breslau had been dissolved, owing to the murder of Prince Ulrick of Denmark, who was shot by one of Piccolomini's riflemen, while taking a ride, and just after he had passed and saluted that general himself on the road. The King of Denmark naturally complained; and Wallenstein was ordered to institute an inquiry into the affair;— "an order," says Förster, "which could not fail to occasion some ill will between him and Piccolomini." This conclusion is not very evident, nor are the particulars of the investigation given; but the historian thinks, that the murderer acted by order of his superior, and distinctly accuses the "Italian party," meaning the Italian officers in the army, of having, from selfish and avaricious motives, counteracted all Wallenstein's endeavours to bring about a peace. "The war," he says, "enriched them; they wished to spend, in their own country, the wealth acquired

by the plunder of Germany : and as Wallenstein was
the advocate of peace ; they hated him and brought
about his ruin." And it is certain that, the Duke
of Friedland's most active enemies were Italians, and
that all the letters which urged on, and which give
us a clue to the real motives of the catastrophe of
Eger, are written in Italian : Piccolomini was the
most active of the party, and was evidently a worthy
head of such a band.

CHAPTER IX.

FRANCE had taken a deep interest, though no direct share in the German war ; and the alliance entered into with Gustavus Adolphus was, after his death, renewed with the Swedish government. An ambassador was sent to Heilbron ; and besides the Swedish subsidy, France paid large sums to the Protestant states and princes of the empire. Cardinal Richelieu had therefore friends in the country. The gallant Marquis de Feuquires, ambassador at Heilbron, had gone from thence to Dresden, in order to persuade the Electors of Saxony and Brandenburg to join the league of the Upper Circles. At Dresden he learned the conclusion of the first armistice ; and having already heard at Heilbron that Wallenstein was on bad terms with the Court of Vienna, and was actually negotiating with the Saxon government, he determined, at once, to join the intrigue, and to make the most of it for the benefit of his own country.

Diplomacy may have produced some cunning men, but it has produced few men of enlightened wisdom and capacity ; though many able men have served in its ranks : among the ablest, may be reckoned the ambassador of whom we are speaking ; and his best diplomatic qualities were formed in the fields of war. In a despatch, dated the 17th of June, Feuquires says that, " he does not know for what purpose Wallenstein has concluded the truce ; though reports, circulated both at Vienna and in the army, speak of him as intending to forsake the imperial cause." The ambassador soon gets, what he thinks more positive information. There was at this time a Count Kinsky at Dresden, an exiled Bohemian Protestant, who, from having married a sister of the Duchess of Friedland, was nearly connected with Wallenstein ; and from him Feuquires learns that Wallenstein, though highly irritated against the Emperor, wishes to treat only with the King of France, or with the Crown of Sweden.

Richelieu well knowing how valuable such an ally would prove, seized immediately on, what he thought, a fair opportunity for gaining him over : and, as it is easy to be liberal at the expense of others, the ambassador received instructions, " to assure the Duke of Friedland, that the King of France was ready to aid, in placing him, by force of arms, on the throne of Bohemia, and even higher." Richelieu is however cautious ; Father Joseph still more so, and Feuquires is therefore directed to be on his guard, so that Wallenstein may not deceive them all by fair promises. But as Kinsky persevered in the assurance, that Wallenstein was dissatisfied with the Emperor, the Frenchman addressed a memorial to him, which he forwarded by M. de la Borderie. In this curious, and clever paper, the Duke of Friedland is reminded of the " treatment he formerly experienced at the hands of the Emperor ; he is assured that a similar fate again awaits him, as the Spaniards,

who are all-powerful at Vienna, invariably contrive
to ruin those who inspire them with jealousy." The
approaching fall of the House of Austria is predicted,
and the Duke is urged, " not to lose the opportunity
of acquiring, by the aid of such powerful friends, as
the King of France and his allies, the possession of
a crown which he is so well qualified to wear and
adorn."

No direct answer to these proposals was ever received from Wallenstein himself ; but Kinsky carries
on the negotiation ; and Richelieu, fearing that the
Duke might throw himself into the arms of Sweden,
and thus render the Protestant party independent
of France, continues to court his alliance with the
most flattering promises.   Louis XIII. writes to him
with his own hand, in the most friendly terms ; and
on the 16th of July, Feuquires is desired to promise
Wallenstein the Bohemian crown, the aid of two
French armies, and a subsidy of a million of livres
annually, provided he will declare himself against
the Emperor.   But before Feuquires could act upon
these additional instructions, the armistice had come
to an end, and the ambassador writes to Father
Joseph, saying, that " Wallenstein had deceived
them all, and had concluded the truce merely to
strengthen his own army, and to weaken the allies."
And yet we do not find any advantage taken of the
reinforcements so received, or of the weakness thus
occasioned to the enemy.

At a later period Feuquires again writes from
Dresden, saying, that Kinsky had once more called
upon him, to ascertain whether the French govern-

ment still retained their former sentiments on the
subject of the negotiation. In reply to this question,
continues the Marquis, " I told Count Kinsky, that
the Duke of Friedland played far too deep a game
for me ; that his silence regarding the proposals made
to him, indicated too clearly an intention to excite
mistrust between the allies ; and that all his *finessing*
would, in the end, tend only to deprive him of the
aid he might have received from the King of France,
and the Protestant League."

Feuquires is however too good a diplomatist to
break off a negotiation, while a hope of advantage remains ; he therefore promises to obtain for Kinsky
the protection of the French government ; and concludes his letter by observing, that the jealousy entertained against Wallenstein, at Vienna, is so great, as
still to render the defection of the latter more than
probable. Soon after this, Feuquires learns that Wallenstein had offered to unite with the Saxons against
the Swedes ; that the second armistice had terminated, and that hostilities had been renewed. But Kinsky still perseveres in asserting Friedland's sincerity.
This mysterious messenger, who never produces a
single line to authorise his mission, boldly declares
that Wallenstein, exasperated by the ingratitude of
the Emperor,—who seeks only to take his life in return for his many services, is determined to extirpate
the whole of the imperial family, and to send both
Ferdinand and Maximilian, to a place which we shall
not name to ears polite. And so anxious are the
French government to gain this extraordinary man,
that crowns, armies, millions and kingdoms, are to

the very last offered for his acceptance. We shall
see that Wallenstein falls a victim to treason, but we
are unable to discover who is the real traitor.

All attempts to gain the Saxons by negotiations
having failed, and the armistice being at an end,
Wallenstein determined to try what could be effected
by force of arms. The hatred and jealousy existing
between the Swedes and their allies was so great, that
the armies were kept asunder ; and of this division,
the Duke of Friedland determined to take advantage.
The Saxons, under Arnheim, stood at Kauth, while
the Swedes, commanded by Count Thurn, occupied
an intrenched camp at Steinau, on the Oder. The
object was to augment the distance between them ;
and for this purpose, Wallenstein made a feint with
Holk's division, against the county of Meissen, and
broke up, with his whole army, as if intending to follow the same direction. Arnheim hurried away to
defend the Electorate. Wallenstein, concealed by
the Lusatian mountains, allowed the Saxons to get
the start of him, and then turning suddenly to the
right, completely surrounded the unprepared Swedes.

Count Schaffgotch, at the head of 8000 cavalry,
crossed the Oder, at a ford above Steinau, dispersed
the Swedish cavalry that attempted to oppose the passage, and drove in all the outposts stationed on the
right bank of the river ; while the Duke himself,
issuing from the mountains, encircled the works on
the left bank. Count Thurn was instantly summoned
to surrender ; only half an hour was allowed him for
deliberation: and a commander who had suffered himself to be thus surprised was not likely to be very fer-

tile in resources. Thurn was a brave man, but evidently no general. He had 5000 men, with seventeen pieces of artillery under his command, a force that, in most situations, should be able to effect something ; but his intrenchments were not completed : he belonged, it seems, to the class of officers who are never ready, and resistance against 30,000 men, provided with fifty pieces of artillery, was therefore deemed hopeless. The whole corps laid down their arms ; the privates became prisoners of war, and were forced to take service in the ranks of the victors.

By the terms of capitulation, the officers were permitted to depart ; and it was afterwards made a charge against Wallenstein that he had honestly adhered to the conditions. The notorious Count Thurn, the principal instigator of the Bohemian insurrection, was, with other officers, set at liberty by the convention ; having been detained only till it was fully carried into effect ; and the mortification felt, at Vienna, by the escape of this great offender, on whom wounded pride had already determined to inflict signal vengeance, far exceeded the satisfaction derived from the victory gained. " What," said Wallenstein, when taxed with this unexpected clemency, " could I have done with the madman ? It were well if the allies had no better generals : and at the head of the Swedish army he will be of more use to us than in prison." There were persons in and about the Imperial Cabinet who thought differently ; and many believe, that the generosity which saved Count Thurn proved ultimately the cause of Wallenstein's own destruction : honour in the service of dishonour will always suffer for the contrast it occasions; and is a light, certain of being destroyed by the very darkness it unveils.

The victory of Steinau was as rapidly followed up as cleverly achieved. Glogow, Leignitz, Goldberg and Crossen were reduced one after the other. All Silesia was cleared of the enemy; and even Frankfurt on the Oder, and Landsberg, the most important of Gustavus' early conquests, were taken. Wallenstein was now evidently in the right path. The Swedes were about to be cut off from all communication with their own country: and the German Protestants had gained so little wisdom by former disasters and late victories, and were so much divided among themselves, that they could not have maintained the contest without foreign aid. It was impossible to devise a better plan of operation than the one here pursued; and yet no writer has done justice to its merit; all have ascribed it to Wallenstein's hatred of Maximilian, and to his anxiety for the ruin of the Elector's dominions.

The imperial light troops had already penetrated far into Pomerania, and the General himself was on the eve of marching to Dresden, when the fears of the Cabinets of Münich and Vienna again arrested him in his successful career. On the 24th of October, Ratisbon, the last stronghold of Maximilian, and the last bulwark of the Austrian states, had fallen into the hands of the enterprising Duke of Weimar, and messenger after messenger was sent to Wallenstein, requesting that he would march immediately to the south, in order to save Bavaria and protect Austria. Wallenstein, who had the power of refusing,

yielded, though reluctantly, to these solicitations ;
and leaving troops to protect his late conquests, took
his way through Bohemia, towards the Upper Palatinate.

The imperial minister, Count Trautmansdorff,—
universally allowed to have been one of the ablest
and most upright men of his time,—happening, at
this moment, to be on one of his estates near the line
of march, Wallenstein requested an interview with
him ; and specified the town of Pilsen, as the place
most likely to suit both parties.   The minister
came in consequence, and sent the Emperor an
account of the meeting ; and the report is sufficiently
curious to deserve a place here, as it shows the high
estimation in which Wallenstein was held even by
those who were not his friends ; for Trautmansdorff
belonged to the party which opposed the Duke of
Friedland.   The minister writes as follows :

" Having come here to meet the Duke of Mecklenburg and Friedland, I found his Highness far
more excited than I had ever seen him before.   He
had just received letters from Vienna, in which, it
was said, that even high functionaries of state spoke
of him in the most injurious terms.   These persons,
not content with depriving him of all merit, by
ascribing his success to fortune, and his failures to
neglect or incapacity, actually attributed to him the
most sinister projects.   He complained that orders
had been sent, without his knowledge, to Generals
Altringer and Strozzi, and declared that he had
never in his life been so much offended ; and that
he was determined to resign the command of the

army." " I said a few words," continues the minister, " just to pacify him, and give time for his anger
to evaporate. He then spoke on the subject of your
Majesty's affairs, saying, that ' unless peace were concluded, every thing would be lost ; for should your
Majesty gain ten battles, they would lead to nothing ; as the enemy had resources, and could always,
by foreign aid, recover from his losses ; whereas a
single battle lost on your Majesty's part, admitted
of no redemption ;' ' and if,' he exclaimed with an
oath, ' peace is not made, I shall retire, with some
eight or ten persons, to Dantzig, and there await the
result.' "

At this very time the unfortunate Francis Albert
of Lauenburg, whom we constantly find hovering,
vampire-like, over the doomed, arrives with some new
propositions for peace ; but Wallenstein, who suffered
greatly from gout, was unable to receive him. Trautmansdorff mentions the circumstance ; and such is
the confidence he places in the General's talents and
integrity, that he actually advises the Emperor to
intrust him altogether with the negotiation ; or first to
arrange the principal conditions with him, and obtain
his concurrence in them ; should it be thought expedient to carry on the negotiation itself at Vienna.
The report goes on to say, that Wallenstein is determined, next day, to undertake, " in the name of
God, a cavalcade towards Staubingen." He is to
start at the head of a hundred companies of the best
cavalry, all the dragoons and Croats, besides 1600
infantry, and eight pieces of artillery. Cavalry still
formed, in a great measure, the strength of armies ;

and dragoons continued to act on foot as well as on horseback; being, probably, as inefficient in the saddle as out of it. The report declares the recapture of Ratisbon, to be impossible at so late a period of the year, as the attempt could hardly fail to destroy the army. It is equally impossible to avoid taking up winter quarters within the Austrian states : but, on the other hand, Count Strozzi had been sent across the Danube, to the aid of the Elector of Bavaria, with thirty companies of cavalry and dragoons. Traut-mansdorff praises the spirit and confidence of the troops ; and adds, that " the Duke had submitted all the foregoing points to a council of war, by which they had been fully approved."

In a postscript to his long letter, the minister writes : " The Duke has been with me for four hours this afternoon, and has again repeated, in substance, what he said yesterday. In regard to the negotia-tion, he does not wish to interfere with details and minor points ; but hopes your Majesty will consult him on the principal terms, that he may acquire some favour with the empire, for having aided to bring about the desired pacification."

Now this is certainly a testimony honourable alike to Wallenstein's head and heart : and the Emperor himself confirms it, to its full extent ; for in his answer to Trautmansdorff, he declares that he knows nothing of the discourses alluded to, and only requires to have the authors named, that he may call them to account. He denies having given any orders to military commanders without the Duke's knowledge ; and as a proof of his anxiety for peace, sends the pro-

posals brought by the Duke of Lauenburg, to his
" trusty and well-beloved Duke of Mecklenburg," in
order to have his opinion on their contents. This
was only three months before the catastrophe of Eger;
and shows how much skilful malevolence may effect
in a short time.

Wallenstein undertook his " cavalcade," as he
called it, invested Cham, and advanced as far as
Fürth ; but declined an action with the Duke of
Weimar, who crossed the Danube on purpose to give
him the meeting. Having called this enterprising
commander away from his Bavarian conquests, sent
Generals Altringer and Strozzi to the aid of Maximilian, and given the Duke of Feria, time to arrive
with his 10,000 Spaniards, Wallenstein returned into
Bohemia, to protect that country, which the Saxons,
after retaking Frankfurt, had again threatened during
his absence.

On the return of the army, the Emperor sent the
minister of war, Questenberg, to Prague, for the purpose of inducing Wallenstein to place the troops in
quarters, beyond the frontiers of the Austrian dominions. If this should not be found practicable,
Wallenstein was to send to the Emperor, a state of
the distribution, that his Majesty might, according to
ancient custom, arrange with the provincial authorities, for the reception of the soldiers, so as to prevent
the quarters from being made good by violence. " A
mode of proceeding," says Ferdinand in his official
letter of instruction, " by which our high authority
is diminished, and an appearance given to foreign
nations that we possess only divided power in our own

dominions, and have a coadjutor—*corregem*—on the throne." The latter part of the letter, which is dated the 3d December, is in a milder tone ; but for a wise man, the hint here quoted should, perhaps, have been sufficient.

An army, which, during the summer, had acted in Silesia and Brandenburg, which had marched from thence into Franconia, and back again into Bohemia, could hardly, as armies were then supplied and organised, effect much in the depth of winter without first having some rest : and this Wallenstein had represented to the Emperor, a few days before Questenberg's arrival. When the minister therefore came with his instructions, pressing to have the troops removed into distant winter quarters, most of which were still occupied by the enemy, the General submitted the proposal to a council of war, who, it must be confessed, treated the military suggestions of the Cabinet of Vienna rather cavalierly ; declaring that they were totally impracticable, and could only have been drawn up by persons utterly unacquainted with military affairs. Besides this remark on a practice, still very common to cabinets, the officers added distinct complaints of want of pay ; saying that " they had advanced their last farthing in the service, and saw no hope of being either reimbursed or rewarded," and hinted, that, " the army might become disgusted with the treatment which they were made to experience."

Wallenstein sent this paper to the Emperor without remark, requesting only, that his Majesty would give " the necessary orders for the reception of the

troops in their allotted cantonments :" and Ferdinand seeing, perhaps, the justice of the demand,
complied with the requisition. But another cause of
quarrel was in progress. The Emperor, contrary to
the agreement with Wallenstein, had sent repeated
orders to the Baron de Suyes, directing him to cross
the Inn with his corps, and join the Elector of
Bavaria. The Baron, in submission to Wallenstein's
instructions, delayed compliance, and the irritated
Monarch writes to Questenberg, desiring him to get
the necessary orders forwarded to De Suyes, " that
I may not be forced," as he says, " to take different
measures for the maintenance of my imperial authority, and be obliged to make an example fit to serve
as a warning to other officers."

Wallenstein, though he explained the cause of De
Suyes' delay, and sent for that officer " to see what
could be done," still remained blind to these threatening proofs of imperial displeasure ; and seemed not to
know, how " dreadful was the wroth of kings." Was it
lofty consciousness of rectitude that made him slow to
suspect unworthiness in others ? It could not be want
of penetration : for men of high character generally
see at once, as by a very gift conferred on them, into
the darkest recesses of the human heart ; and, as
none saw more quickly than Wallenstein, we should
be at a loss to understand the motives of his conduct,
did we not suppose, that the altered tone of the
Emperor's subsequent letters extinguished suspicion
in his breast. These letters are very frequent, and
very friendly ; and on the 3d of January his Majesty
notifies having sent both money and supplies to the

army. But this appearance of restored confidence
was altogether assumed ; for in the month of December Ferdinand had already determined to deprive
Wallenstein of the command ; and had secretly acquainted Generals Gallas and Altringer with his
resolution.

Wallenstein was, however, slow, or unwilling to
believe in these reports when they reached him ; but
suspecting, at last, that something worse than a second
dismissal might be intended, he determined to be
beforehand with the Emperor, and to resign of his
own accord. He had already, as we have seen, notified this intention to Trautmansdorff, and he now
determined to carry it into effect. For this purpose
he assembled the principal officers of the army at
Pilsen, and declared to them, that the measures of
the Court of Vienna, rendered it impossible for him
to retain the command any longer, with honour to
himself, or with advantage to the service.

The instructions brought by Questenberg had
caused a good deal of discontent ; and the proposed
resignation of the General, on whose word most of
the officers had advanced money, to raise and equip
their regiments, and without whose aid they hardly
ever expected to be repaid, greatly added to the excitement. The officers pressed him to remain at
their head ; and, it is said, that he demanded from
them a promise, pledging themselves to adhere to
him in return. At a banquet given by Count Illo,
at which the temperate and reserved Wallenstein
was not present, but at which the wine circulated
so freely that many of the parties afterwards declared

they did not well know what passed, a petition to this effect, was agreed upon and drawn up. By this document, forty-two officers, among whom was Piccolomini, pledged themselves, " to adhere to Wallenstein to the last drop of their blood, as long as he should continue to command the army, in the service, and for the good of the Emperor." It is not true, as was afterwards stated by the Court of Vienna, that the reserve clause, in favour of the Emperor, was left out in the paper presented for signature, which, by a legerdemain trick, had been substituted for the document originally agreed upon. None of the parties tried, alleged such a circumstance in their defence ; and the proceeding would have been of too unworthy a nature, to have obtained the concurrence of Wallenstein : there was nothing low or mean about him ; his very faults bore some impress of greatness.

On the day after this paper had been signed, the Duke again called the officers together, and told them, that nothing was intended against the Emperor or the Catholic religion, by the compact into which they had entered : it was only formed, he said, for the safety and maintenance of the army, and for the service of the state. Wallenstein and his officers were probably encouraged in this proceeding, by a similar agreement which the Swedish officers had entered into a few weeks before, and by which they had forced Oxenstiern, and the members of the Heilbron League, to grant certain terms which the martial synod demanded. Looked upon with our present ideas of subordination, nothing could be more crimi-

nal than such a combination : but the just principles
of discipline were then unknown ; the early part of
the seventeenth century was the very age of insubordination ; and the combination here mentioned, must
be judged of by the ideas then existing on such subjects, rather than by those which are now entertained.

During the banquet which preceded the signature
of the paper already mentioned, Piccolomini had
made so free with the rapidly circulating wine, that
he drew his sword, and called aloud for a bumper to
the Emperor's health.   No one refused the toast ;
but the two Princes of Toscana, who were with the
army, and who lived on the opposite side of the street,
hearing of this thoughtless proceeding, contrived to
get the intoxicated general removed from the room,
fearing, that he might betray the secret instructions
which, it seems, he had already received respecting
Wallenstein ; respecting the very man to whom he
was just about to pledge fidelity and adherence.
The young Princes themselves were so much alarmed,
that they immediately took horse and set out for
Prague ; from whence they dispatched one Lorenzo
Guicciardini to Vienna, to inform the Emperor of
what had passed.   The Italian was provided with
letters from Piccolomini, and was besides a clever
alarmist.   He had several interviews with Ferdinand, and made some progress in convincing the
Monarch, that Wallenstein was conspiring, to raise
his truncheon of command, even above the imperial
sceptre : " Nothing," he said, " but crushing the
scorpion on the wound, could now avert the dangerous consequences of the mischief already done."

Wallenstein's enemies had before this time been actively at work. Count Ognate, the Spanish ambassador, and all the members of the Spanish and Italian factions, had spread the most sinister reports of the General's intentions ; so that accounts of treason poured in upon the Emperor from every quarter. The Duke of Savoy sent intimation of negotiations carried on with France ; alluding probably to the offers made by Feuquires ; and the Elector of Bavaria, was ready enough with his exertions, to defame the man who had eclipsed the influence and renown of the once all-powerful Maximilian. We perceive the dark web of treachery spinning gradually round its victim ; but we cannot discover the reptiles with whom it originated.

On the 18th of December, just a month after he had sent thirty companies to aid the Elector of Bavaria, the latter already forwarded to Bernhard Richel, the Bavarian ambassador at Vienna, some very strong charges against the imperial commander. Richel was, if possible, to keep them in reserve, and was only to aid others in pressing for Wallenstein's dismissal, if he found the work already in progress. Maximilian himself wished to remain out of sight, " well knowing," as he says, " how Wallenstein would requite him for interfering."

Richel plays his part to admiration ; and on the 30th December informs the Elector, that Wallenstein's removal from the command, is already determined on ; and that secret agents have been dispatched to the principal officers, in order to ascertain their real sentiments. Urged on, however, by the

King of Hungary, and by the infamous Marquis de
Grana, the ambassador, thinking himself well supported, comes forward with his charges, and then
learns that steps will be taken to " remedy the evil."
The great difficulty is, what to do with Wallenstein ;
it being thought as precarious to leave him entirely
at liberty, as to secure his person.

Maximilian no sooner hears of the combination at
Pilsen, than he directs Richel to press on the Emperor the necessity of forming at once, " some heroic
resolution."   But Ferdinand had already got the information from Guicciardini, as well as from other
quarters ; and tells Richel, that measures are in progress for arresting the threatened danger.   " This
business," says the terrified Monarch, " is never out
of my thoughts : it rises with me in the morning, and
goes to bed with me at night, and completely deprives
me of rest."   Richel adds in his letter, that prayers
are offered up in all the churches, for the " successful
termination of the work."   What are the measures
to be adopted, the ambassador is unable to learn, as
the affair is conducted with the greatest secrecy ;
but Eggenberg having said, that " it would be safer
and easier to kill Friedland, than to take him prisoner," the diplomatist, knowing his people, very
coolly concludes, that " this will most likely be the
ultimate remedy."   Eggenberg had further told him,
" that it was Wallenstein's first intention to march on
Vienna, and to attack the Emperor in the capital, had
not God deprived him of his senses, and rendered
him incapable of concealing the project."   And the
infamous Grana writes to say, that the conspiracy is

directed, not only against the Emperor, but against the whole imperial family.

Terrified by so many accounts of treason and conspiracy, Ferdinand, on the 24th of January, sent a secret commission to Gallas and Piccolomini, depriving Wallenstein of the command, and directing officers and soldiers to obey only those two generals. An amnesty, afterwards most shamefully broken, is granted to all who signed the compact of Pilsen, " an affair," in which it is said, " they had gone a little too far." From this amnesty Illo and Terzky are excepted ; and the document concludes, by declaring the Duke of Friedland an outlaw, and commanding him to be taken, " dead or alive." The two generals were to keep these instructions secret, till a safe opportunity for acting should offer, and were to confide them only to those in whom they could most fully rely. On the 13th of February Gallas,—properly Gallasso,—issues in Italian, an order to his countrymen, Piccolomini, De Suyes, Maradas, Collaredo, Carretto, Mohra and Marzini, directing them to receive no orders except from himself and General Altringer : the " *bolletino* " is still to be kept secret for three days, and then to be confided to the most trustworthy officers. To this order, a list of " heretic conspirators," is added : these " heretics " are not all Protestants, but they are all Germans, and are among the most distinguished officers in the army.

The booty, expected to be derived from confiscating the property of the so-called rebels, was probably one of the leading causes of their condemnation. Even before the parties knew that they were accused, a

Count Puscheim received authority from the Emperor, to seize the property of Terzka and Friedland, " now forfeited," as the commission says, " by their flight and rebellion." All military commanders are ordered to aid this functionary, " as the confiscation is intended solely for the good of the army, and will ultimately tend to their profit."

The imaginations of the Italian banditti are absolutely fired by the prospect of the plunder: every one sends information where property is to be found; and every mean beggar, already petitions for a share of the spoil, to be torn from the victims of falsehood and treachery. Among these instigators to robbery and murder, the most conspicuous, by far, is the Marquis of Grana : almost every day brings from this man a tale of terror, accompanied by requests for objects of value which he specifies. It has even been supposed, that the Emperor himself, was willing enough to cancel, by a single blow, not merely a debt of gratitude, but a debt of twenty millions of florins also. His blind fear, his ready credulity, and his haste to condemn, untried, a man of the highest rank and merit, more than expose him to suspicion.

CHAPTER X.

AND how was Wallenstein occupied while the dark
web of treason was weaving around him ? Embodying rebel armies, strengthening himself by foreign
alliances, building strongholds, or corrupting the
soldiers placed under his command ? The reverse was
the case : he was zealously engaged in quartering
the troops for the winter, and in carrying on, with
the full knowledge of the Emperor, the Saxon negotiation.   He was, to the last, in friendly correspondence with Piccolomini and with Ferdinand himself;
and on the 13th of February, the very day on which
Gallasso issues his secret " *Bollettino* " from Pilsen,
the Emperor writes to Wallenstein, WHOM HE HAD
OUTLAWED TWENTY DAYS BEFORE, " confiding the
kingdom of Bohemia to his approved care and protection, should the Swedes," who had assembled in
force near Ratisbon, " advance against the frontier."
   To what extent Wallenstein was apprised of the
measures taken against him, is not very certain ; but he
no sooner heard that an unfavourable construction had
been put upon the meeting at Pilsen, than he again
called the officers together, and signed, along with
them, a joint declaration, expressive of their " entire
devotion to the Emperor, and of their resolution to
shed every drop of their blood in his service."   This

was on the 20th of February. But as every hour now
brought proof, that hostile proceedings, were already
in progress, he dispatched Colonel Mohrwald to
Vienna on the 21st, and General Brenner on the
22d, to assure the Emperor of his perfect readiness
to resign the command, and to appear at any time
and place, to answer whatever charges might be preferred against him. Both messengers were arrested
on the road, the one by Piccolomini, the other by
Diodati ; the latter declaring in his official report of
the circumstance, that the message to the Emperor,
was only a trick devised by Wallenstein to save " *i
suoi ducati.*"

It was not till after the Emperor's proclamation,
which denounced him as an outlaw, had been publicly posted up at Prague, that Wallenstein learned,
or believed, the full extent of his danger. Hearing,
at the same time, that some of the troops had already
refused to obey his orders, and that Piccolomini and
Diodati were marching towards Pilsen, where no preparations had been made for resistance ; he determined to fly to Eger, and to throw himself into the
arms of the allies. Before his departure he sent
Prince Francis Albert to the Duke of Weimar, then
at Ratisbon, to solicit assistance. As the fugitive
General had nothing left, which he could carry over
to the allies, but his name and fame, the aid requested
implied little more than protection for his outlawed
life. And even this was at first denied ; sufficient
proof that no understanding existed between him
and the allied commanders. " If Wallenstein still
lives," says Oxenstiern in a letter to the Duke of

Weimar, " throw no obstacles in the way of his plans : if he is dead, there will be confusion in the imperial army, of which it might be well to take advantage."

When Francis Albert arrived at Ratisbon, the Duke of Weimar positively declined to move on the mere word of the Duke of Friedland : " Who believes not in God," said Bernhard, " will not be believed by man ;" and it was only after the news of Wallenstein's actual departure from Pilsen had been received, that he set out at the head of his army for Eger. But the blow had been already struck, and the Swedes " came but to augment the slaughter."

Wallenstein left Pilsen on the morning of the 22d of February 1634, accompanied by Counts Illo, Terzky, Kinsky, Colonel Butler, and Rittmeister Neumann. As he suffered greatly from gout, he travelled in a sedan chair carried between two horses : and the man, who was to have marched rebellious armies to the gates of Vienna, was only escorted by seven companies of infantry and 200 dragoons. The horsemen were under the orders of Colonel Butler, an Irish Catholic officer, to whose regiment they belonged ; and who sent his chaplain * to tell Piccolo-

---

* This was Carve, the author of the Itinerary, the same who, after Butler's death, was chaplain to Devereux; for all these men had chaplains. Carve was among the number of those who had shared in the bounty of the munificent Duke of Friedland ; and, in a list of donations still preserved, is the following entry : " To Thomas Carve, *Hyberno,* 5 florins on a petition for alms." It is hoped that the comparative smallness of the sum,—for in the same list very large sums are specified as bestowed upon other persons,—

mini that he, Butler, would remain faithful to his
allegiance, and use every effort to thwart the designs
of the rebels. Galass, and the Marquis de Grana,
had, as they inform the Emperor, received similar
assurances ; and the Marquis says of Butler, that "he
is a cavalier on whom His Majesty may place the
most perfect reliance." Of Colonel Gordon, the
commandant of Eger, the Marquis is not so certain,
and fears that " this officer's Calvinistical spirit, will
make a rebel of him." The Italian unfortunately
paid that spirit too high a compliment by his suspicion.

Wallenstein and his escort halted the first night at
Miess, and arrived on the following evening at Eger,
the last Bohemian fortress on the road leading into the
Palatinate. Colonel Gordon, a Scottish Presbyterian,
held the post with the regiment of Terzka, of which
he was Lieutenant-Colonel, and of which another
Scotchman of the name of Leslie, was Major. Neither
of these officers had yet heard of the Emperor's proclamation, and Major Leslie was sent out to meet
Wallenstein, and to conduct him into the fortress.
The fugitive General took up his quarters at the
Mayor's house, in the market-place, and, thinking
himself in perfect safety, communicated to our three
unworthy countrymen, the cause of his being obliged
to fly and seek safety with the allies : he left it to
them to accompany him, or not, as they might think
proper. Gordon and Leslie agreed at first to follow

facilitated, to the worthy chaplain, the task of granting absolution
to the murderers of the donor.

him ; but at a conference which they held during the night with Butler, the latter showed them the Emperor's proclamation and the order which he had received from Piccolomini ; on which they unfortunately came to a very different resolution. What was the exact order produced by Butler, is not known; but from a passage in one of the Marquis de Grana's letters, its purpose may be easily conjectured. That worthy Italian, in recommending Colonel Teufel to the Emperor for a vacant regiment, says, that he was one of the first who offered to " murder the tyrant," *(di ammazzare il tiranno,)* and Ferdinand, "delighted " with the Colonel's " honour and bravery," promises to grant the request. Butler, we may therefore conclude, had direct instructions to kill his General, and had, no doubt, authority also to promise ample rewards to those who should aid in the deed. He found, unfortunately, too many willing accomplices ; and it is painful for a British writer to add, that they belonged mostly to his own country ; the fair fame of which is deeply stained by the infamy of their crime.

Gordon, Leslie and Butler, having pledged themselves to the murder by an oath, which they swore over their drawn swords ; Butler brought seven other officers into the conspiracy : these were, Geraldine, Devereux, Brown, Macdonald, Birch, Pestaluzi and Lerda ; the first five were Irishmen belonging to his own dragoons, and the last two Spaniards, captains in Terzka's regiment. The execution was fixed for the following evening ; and as Illo, Terzka, Kinsky, and Neumann, were to sup with Gordon in the citadel, it was resolved to commence with them ;

as it was well known that Wallenstein never joined such convivial parties.

No sooner had the guests entered the castle on the fatal evening, than the gates were closed, and guards posted so as to prevent all egress. Captain Geraldine was stationed, with twelve dragoons, in an apartment that opened into the supper hall, while Captain Devereux, with six more, stood in the apartment exactly opposite. To prevent noise the soldiers were without fire-arms, and were ordered to use their swords only. Not a shadow of apprehension seemed to cloud the party; the wine circulated briskly as was wont in that bold, jovial and boisterous time, and the guests were in high spirits at the thought of being beyond the reach of their enemies. The easy frankness of the conspirators disarmed suspicion; but the idea of men supping tranquilly with their intended victims, offers a fearful proof of the callousness of which the human heart is capable.

No sooner had the dessert been placed on the table and the servants dismissed, than the signal was given. Geraldine instantly burst in at one door, exclaiming, " *Viva la casa d'Austria*," while Devereux entered at the other, asking, " Who are good Imperialists ?" Butler, Gordon and Leslie sprung from their seats, drew their swords, and called out, " *Vivat Ferdinandus;*" on which the dragoons rushed, at once, upon the designed victims, as bloodhounds rush upon their prey. Kinsky was the first who fell ; Illo was stabbed through the back in attempting to reach his sword, which hung suspended against the wall : Terzka alone contrived to get his sword, and throw-

ing himself into a corner, resisted with the fierceness of a lion at bay. He reproached Gordon and
Butler with their baseness, challenged them to single
combat, killed two dragoons outright, disarmed Devereux and mortally wounded Captain Lerda, before
he sunk beneath the blows of the assassin band.
Neumann had fallen, wounded, under the table, and
in the confusion escaped out of the hall ; but not
knowing the countersign, was cut down by the castle
guard.

   The first act of the tragedy thus concluded, the
principal conspirators proceeded to hold another
council.   Long habits of submission and obedience,
—the fame, greatness and power of their victorious
chieftain,—and the deference with which his subordinates had invariably looked up to Wallenstein,
as to a being of almost superior nature, awed for a
moment even murderers, whose hands were yet drip-
ping with the blood of noble and innocent men.
Their council was of short duration.   Gordon raised
a feeble voice in the cause of humanity ; and though
he hinted that those might rejoice in the murder,
who would yet punish the murderers, his scruples
were overruled by Butler, who better knew the parties he had to deal with.   It was not very clear,
indeed, that the Duke could be arrested : but it was
evident that he would not prove an acceptable captive at Vienna.   As a fugitive outlaw, he was no
longer dangerous to the House of Austria ; but his
escape might be dangerous to those who should con-
nive at it, and would certainly bring them no reward : his death was the most agreeable service that

could be rendered to the Emperor ; and avarice, therefore, sealed his doom.

Two shots having been fired at one of Terzka's servants, who had escaped from the citadel, Leslie made the soldiers of the main-guard renew their oath of fidelity to the House of Austria, admitted a hundred more dragoons into town, and caused them to patrole the streets, and maintain the most perfect stillness. Towards midnight, Butler, followed by Devereux and six dragoons, proceeded to Wallenstein's quarters ; and as it was not unusual, for officers of rank, to call upon the General at late hours, the guard allowed them to enter. Devereux, with his party, ascended the stairs, while Butler remained below to wait the result.

It is said that Wallenstein had, only a few minutes before, dismissed, for the night, an Italian astrologer of the name of Senni, who was then attached to his household, and who declared that the stars still boded impending danger, which Wallenstein himself, either could not, or would not see. He had just retired to bed, and the servant who had undressed him, was descending the stair when he met Devereux and his party, and desired them to make less noise, " as the Duke was going to sleep ;" " but this is a time for noise," shouted Devereux, as he pressed on. Finding the door of the bed-chamber locked, he burst it open with his foot, and entered, followed by the soldiers. Wallenstein was standing at the window : startled by the screams of the ladies Terzka and Kinsky, who lodged in the house opposite, and who had just learned the murder of their

husbands, he had opened the casement, and was asking the sentinel what was the matter, at the moment
Devereux broke into the room. The sight of his
long-honoured and long-obeyed commander, arrested not the hand of this bold and ruthless assassin :
" Thou must die," he exclaimed ; and Wallenstein,
true to his pride of character, disdained to parley, even
for life, with a slave and a stabber. Dignified to the
last, he threw open his arms to the blow, and sunk
without a word or groan, beneath the first thrust of
the traitor's halberd, the blade of which went right
through his breast. Thus fell a man who, as Gualdo
says, " was one of the greatest commanders, most
generous princes and most enlightened ministers of
his own, or of any preceding time :" and thus ended
the work, for the successful termination of which, the
Emperor had caused prayers to be offered up in all
the churches of the capital.

The body was immediately rolled in a carpet,
and carried to the citadel, where it was deposited
along with the others. They were all, next morning, placed in hastily constructed shells, and conveyed
to the castle of Miess. Piccolomini ordered, indeed,
that they should be sent to Prague, for the purpose
of " being exposed," as he tells his worthy colleague
Grana, " in the most disgraceful situations." But
even Ferdinand retained sufficient sense of decency
to prevent such an unworthy proceeding : he directed
that the body of Friedland should be given up to his
friends, and that the others should all, with the
exception of Neumann, be interred in consecrated
ground. The last was, on account of his " slanderous

tongue," to be buried beneath the gibbet. Wallenstein's remains were deposited in the vault of a Carthusian convent, which he had himself built near Gitchen. When, in 1639, the Swedes penetrated into that part of the country, the celebrated General Banner caused the coffin to be opened, and took out the skull and right arm, which he sent to Stockholm.

No sooner was the death-blow struck, than Butler sent an account of it to Gallass, and, with hands stained in Terzka's blood, already begged for Terzka's regiment. Major Leslie carried the report to Vienna. The Emperor, though unable to find the right word for the proceeding at Eger,—having, with his own hand, twice altered the draught of the original answer to Gallass, and effaced the words " killed " and " slain," before he fixed on the term " cut down," —well knew how to reward the service he dared not describe ; and could be liberal, at a moment when he had so rich a legacy at his disposal. Leslie was made Imperial Chamberlain, Captain of the Body Guard, and Colonel of a regiment : he was raised to the dignity of Count, and presented with the lordship of Neustadt in Bohemia ; an estate valued at 200,000 florins.

The moment Butler heard of the Emperor's generosity, he also hurried to Vienna, and, as it proved, had ample cause to be satisfied with his journey. Ferdinand gave him a public reception, shook hands with him, and made the Archbishop of Vienna suspend a gold chain round his neck. Like Leslie, he received a regiment, and the gold key of Chamberlain ; was raised to the dignity of Count, and obtained all

Terzka's Bohemian estates. The estates of Kinsky fell to Gordon's share; and Devereux, who, with his own hand, had slain the Duke of Friedland, was rewarded with a gold chain, and with several confiscated domains. Every private soldier who aided in the murder received 500 crowns. Captain Geraldine got 2000, and the other officers 1000 each. Assassination has seldom been so richly rewarded as on this occasion, and the Emperor, having estates to the value of nearly fifty millions of florins at his disposal, was as liberal to the original instigators of the murder, as to the murderers themselves.

It is needless to go over the list of imperial donations; but there is some pleasure in recording, that the most worthless of the band of conspirators, were those who profited least by the treason. Piccolomini was, at first, entirely passed over, because he had appropriated to himself Wallenstein's plate, and all the moveable property found at Eger, which the menial murderers had, strangely enough, spared: he resigned his commission in consequence, but was afterwards pacified with the estate of Nashod. The meanness of the Marquis de Grana seems, however, to have shocked even Ferdinand. This Italian, whose excess of baseness sets all power of description at defiance, had, in the first scramble for booty, seized the horses, equipages and other valuables belonging to the unfortunate Count Schaffgotsh, who was arrested and afterwards executed as one of the conspirators. The Emperor, who only retained for himself the two valuable Duchies of Sagan and Glogau, reprimanded the rapacious Marquis, and entirely passed him over

when distributing the spoil, which his Italian inge-
nuity had so ably helped to drive into the imperial net.
The estate of Neuschloss was assigned to the Duchess
of Friedland, as a dowager-portion; and Wallenstein's
only child, a daughter, called Maria Elizabeth, was
afterwards married to a Count Kaunitz.

To prove, that the so-called " prompt execution of
Eger " was not a mere act of murder, and that Wallenstein had been sacrificed to justice and not to vengeance, it became necessary to show that some dangerous and extensive conspiracy, calling for so unusual and sanguinary a measure, had really existed.
And, as a plot of this nature could hardly have been
confined to the five persons slain, a number of officers
and men of rank, were arrested and tried as Wallenstein's accomplices. None of these trials tended to
throw the least light on the subject; and with the
exception of Count Schaffgotsh, all the prisoners
were by degrees set at liberty. The last-mentioned
officer, one of the most distinguished in the army,
was alone executed; because, as his sentence declared,
there were " strong grounds for believing that he was
an accomplice in Friedland's treason." He was twice
put to the torture, once before, and what is still more
horrible to relate, once after his condemnation; but
made no confession of any kind; and so little was
proved against him, that the Emperor ordered the
proceedings to be kept secret.

The Marquis de Grana had promised that Wallenstein's papers, which had been secured at Eger, would
disclose the whole of the " diabolical " conspiracy;
but when examined, they were found not to contain

a single line that could throw even a shadow of suspicion on the Duke.   Grana, who was always ready
to justify one falsehood by another, then declared that
Terzka had destroyed six hundred letters the evening
before his execution.

The Court of Vienna, finding that public opinion
was not altogether in their favour, and that many,
even among the Catholic party, termed,—as Khevenhüller allows, " the prompt and noble execution of
Eger, a wicked and infamous murder ;" thought it
advisable to publish, what they called, an official and
authentic account of the conspiracy.   To this was
added the statement of Seschina Ratchin, an exiled
Bohemian Protestant, who, hearing that the Austrian
Government were in want of evidence to justify the
transaction of Eger, came forward and offered, on
condition of having his estates restored, to disclose
Wallenstein's negotiation with Gustavus Adolphus ;
which he declared to have been carried on through
his agency.   The Imperial Cabinet agreed to the
proposal, and Ratchin published his statement ; the
poorest compound of folly, with which it was ever
attempted to impose upon ignorance and credulity.
The author is a person totally destitute of ordinary
talent, who, in pretending to repeat the words, and
disclose the intentions of men of the highest genius,
betrays his falsehood, by making them speak and act
like men of his own mean stamp and capacity ;   an
error, which, on a small scale, we constantly see committed in ordinary society.

The official account published by the Court of
Vienna, is termed, " A particular and detailed ac-

count of the abominable conspiracy of Friedland and
his adherents, showing what were really their wicked
objects and intentions. The entire compiled, from
authentic sources, original documents, private letters,
and the willing confessions of accused accomplices.
Collected and printed in accordance with the special
commands of the Emperor, by Albert Curtius." This
statement, which in point of ability is not much superior to Ratchin's Narrative, is far more discreditable ;
for it contains many charges and assertions which, as
Förster proves, the compilers well knew, from official
documents before them, to be totally destitute of
foundation. As far as the charges are of a treasonable
nature, they are totally unsupported by proof, and
rest solely on the assertion of those who, by their own
showing, were fully capable of falsehood, and had,
besides, a case to make out : " the authentic sources,
original documents and willing confessions," are totally wanting. The principal charges preferred may
be summed up as follows :
     " That after his first dismissal from the command,
Wallenstein entered into negotiations with Gustavus
Adolphus, for the purpose of obtaining Swedish troops
to aid in the conquest of Bohemia and Moravia.
After the battle of Leipzig, he induced the Saxons to
occupy Prague, and granted them too favourable
conditions when he subsequently drove them out of
the kingdom. He purposely left Bavaria exposed to
the inroads of the enemy ; did not avail himself of
his superiority to destroy the King of Sweden at
Nurenberg ; and retired, without cause, into Bohemia, after the victory of Lützen." It is farther add-

ed, that " he liberated Count Thurn, contrary to all
right and justice ; paid no attention to the orders of
the Emperor ; and not only employed Protestants in
his army, but allowed them free exercise of religion
on his estates.   Urged on," it is said, " by ambition
and astrological superstition, he conceived the wild
and wicked project of dividing the Austrian dominions among his generals, and of becoming himself,
after changing the entire face of Europe, the head of
a new imperial dynasty."

We have seen meaner hands accomplish something
like this "wild project," and obtain an imperial bride
in reward for his success.   Times, however, and circumstances also were different, and Wallenstein's
enemies declared, that " his crimes deserved death,
and that the faithful servants of the Emperor dared
not, under the great danger then pending, risk the
safety of the empire and the Catholic religion, by
giving way to false pity, or by tarrying for the ordinary formalities of justice."

All these charges are easily answered.   We have
seen that Wallenstein, so far from entering into negotiations with Gustavus Adolphus, was from the first,
the enemy of that Prince ; and ridiculed the idea of
having had any communication with him after his
landing in Germany.   And though we might refuse
to receive his own testimony in this case, his assertion is so fully confirmed by the silence of Chemnitz,
as to place doubt entirely out of the question.   The
historian does not say a word about negotiations having taken place between Gustavus and the Duke of
Friedland ; and as he wrote, not merely under the

inspection, but almost under the dictation of Oxenstiern, it is impossible that he could have been ignorant of the fact, had any communications passed between them.

This is saying nothing of the character of the individuals, who however dissimilar in other respects,
were so far alike, that neither of them could act
secondary parts.   The proud, stately and imperious
Duke of Friedland, could never become the follower
of a young Scandinavian monarch ; and the fiery
genius of Gustavus, brooked hardly an equality even
with kings.   Besides, we have seen that Wallenstein
was actually carrying on a negotiation with Denmark,
highly dangerous to the interest of the Swedes, at
the very time he is accused of having intended to
join them.

That he did not bring the Saxons to Prague, is
equally evident : they took that very natural direction by the decision of a council of war, held at Halle,
on the day after the battle of Leipzig, and before
Wallenstein could have known the result of the action.

His conduct, and pretended inactivity at Nurenberg, and again after the battle of Lützen, are military questions, of which he was a better judge than
the imperial ministers could be ; and, as already
shown, he seems, on both occasions, to have acted in a
manner deserving the highest praise.   Count Thurn
was liberated in conformity with the terms of a regular capitulation, which could not be violated without a direct breach of faith and honour.   That Wallenstein carried religious toleration far beyond the
spirit of his age, may be safely granted ; but of the

astrological superstition here mentioned, we find no evidence whatever.

How far he amused himself with astrology, or with what faith he consulted the stars, it is impossible to say : on two occasions only do we find the subject alluded to : once, when he applied for the horoscope of Gustavus Adolphus ; and again, when he pointed out to the imperial messengers, who notified to him his dismissal from the command of the army, the domineering influence exercised by the star of Maximilian, over the star of Ferdinand ; an influence that might have been discovered without the aid of the planets. In his letters, Wallenstein is the reverse of a vague and dreaming astrologer : he is clear and direct : we always find him calculating the march of events with great ability, and never depending, like so many of his feeble imitators, on his fortunes or his star. Whatever his faults may have been, he was evidently, if we judge him by the letters he writes, —by the orders and directions he gives,—a clear and high-minded man, endowed with an observant and vigorous understanding, always bold, open and direct in his proceedings.

But the writers who have handed his actions and character down to us, were the reverse of all this ; or, they were intimidated by the power of his enemies. Unable, or not daring, to represent him as a great man, they endeavoured to reduce him to the level of their own conceptions ; and failed even in this attempt ; for the giant-shadow projects at every point, beyond the frame within which they would repress it. But it projects as an imperfect portraiture

only : the greatness of the outline remains ; while
the true lineaments of character, are injured and obscured, by the efforts of ignorance and malevolence.
The official statements, published by the Court of
Vienna, which guided so many historians, and Schiller
among the rest, make Wallenstein speak and act like
one removed, a few degrees only, above mental infirmity ; and as the world were not likely to believe this
of the intellectual Duke of Friedland, it became
necessary to represent him, as influenced in his conduct, and hurried along the path of folly, by astrology and superstition.

This extraordinary man was denied even the usual
appeal to posterity ; for, as all parties were hostile to
him, none would furnish the unbiassed evidence on
which posterity can alone form an impartial judgment.
He had been the open and most formidable enemy
of the Protestants, and could expect little favour at
their hands. The Catholics, who condemned and
slew him as a traitor, were not likely to be more
friendly ; if they slew him justly, their hatred was
just ; if unjustly,—it was probably greater ; because
men too generally end by hating those whom they
begin by injuring.

In this respect, the fortunes of Napoleon, contrast
singularly with those of the Duke of Friedland ; and,
owing to very different reasons, posterity will find it
as difficult to form a just estimate of the one, as of
the other.

Wallenstein incurred the hatred of the two parties
into which the Christian world of his day was divided ;
and as these were, in so far religious parties, that

religious differences had occasioned the breach between them,—they added, to their other causes of
hostility against the Duke of Friedland, all the bitterness for which religious animosities are supposed
to be distinguished.

Napoleon, as General, Consul and Emperor,
fought, successively, against the different powers of
Europe; and the victories he achieved over one nation, proved frequently very agreeable to those who
were neutral for the moment, and in no immediate
expectation of being defeated in their turn ; so that
when he became the enemy of all, he had already
acquired a reputation which few ventured to arraign.
Liberality, too, was the fashion of the age ; and it was
deemed as liberal to praise the talents of an adversary,
as illiberal to question them. Napoleon was also,
from his position, the enemy of established governments ; the ally and idol therefore of all, who, without fixed principles, and at a period of universal
excitement, were eager for change : and this, by a
strange inconsistency, rendered the pretended advocates of liberty and popular rights, the upholders of a
military despot, whose only known sentiment was a
deadly hatred of freedom and of liberal institutions.
A proof, perhaps, that men hated the powers above
them, more than they loved the freedom of which
they spoke.

At a time, when the pen was already in every
hand, the absolute ruler of mighty empires, the dis-
penser of crowns, duchies, titles, pensions and decorations, was sure to be lauded in strains far surpass-
ing, in loudness and extent of circulation, any which

the seventeenth century could send forth in the odd
volumes that issued, in slow succession, from its tardy
presses. In Catholic countries, none dared defend
the fame of the Duke of Friedland ; in Protestant
countries few were interested in doing so : but
nations, empires and individuals, are interested in
upholding the fame of Napoleon. Those who humbled themselves to the very dust before him, must
maintain his claim to greatness, to save themselves
from disgrace and ridicule : those whom he vanquished, must follow a similar course, to lessen the shame
of their defeats: and those who conquered him,—and
all claim a share in the honour,—are, of course, willing enough to represent him as a giant, in order to
enhance the merit of their victories. And, if posterity judge of Napoleon, by the histories, yet written
of him and his time, they will believe this poor, weak
and vain toy of fortune, to have been a man of the
highest genius and intellect ; even as the last two
centuries believed Wallenstein to have been a super-
stitious astrologer, — a sanguinary tyrant,—and a
traitor to his sovereign and his country.

In regard to the military orders issued by the Emperor, as Wallenstein had full power, by the terms
on which he resumed the command, to resist them,—
it is more than probable that he acted wisely in sometimes availing himself of the privilege.

The charge of treason brought against him, has
never been substantiated by a shadow of proof ; and
wanting that proof, we are, in justice, bound to acquit
the accused, however inexplicable some parts of his
conduct may appear. The constant negotiations

carried on during the first months of the Silesian campaign,—the total absence of all military energy and enterprise, — more than injured Wallenstein's reputation as a soldier. It was thought strange, that the adversary of Gustavus, should allow himself to be arrested by Arnheim and the Saxons: and the reports, so universally circulated, of his intention to fall off from the Emperor, naturally augmented the suspicions thus excited.

Arnheim's extraordinary communication to Oxenstiern,—the statements contained in the letters of the Saxon general,—as well as those contained in the letters of Prince Francis Albert,—Kinsky's mysterious correspondence with Feuquires, are all unexplained circumstances, detrimental to the fair fame of the Duke of Friedland ; but they do not constitute proofs of treason ; for we do not know that any of these persons had authority to make the proposals in question, or had grounds for the statements contained in their letters : not a single line of Wallenstein's own writing has ever been produced against him.

From the general tenor of his letters, we know, that he was a decided enemy of Sweden ; and Richelieu's Memoirs inform us, that he entertained feelings equally hostile towards France.　May we not, therefore, suppose, that he was honestly striving to unite the different powers of Germany, in order to clear the empire of foreign influence and foreign armies ; so that a peace might be concluded between the Catholics and Protestants, without being first purchased from strangers, at the enormous price which they ultimately exacted for their interference in the war ?

Such a plan was worthy of the genius and patriotism of Friedland, and accords far more with his known words and actions, than any that has yet been ascribed to him.

There are probably many men who would be ready to strike for crowns and sceptres, if the brilliant baubles could be gained by direct and open violence ; but who would scorn to connect themselves with the bravos, stabbers, gamblers, trading patriots, intriguers, adventurers and other mean tools that treason employs in working out its dark and unworthy projects.   Pride alone will keep men of high character virtuous, and the Duke of Friedland was the proudest of the proud : whether he would have seized a crown, by open force, we cannot say ; but we may safely assert, that he never could have been a conspirator.   It is now evident, that Wallenstein fell a victim to some dark plot, the thread of which has not yet been discovered, though its machinations are amply attested by the letters of the Italian faction, and by those of the Elector of Bavaria.   Maximilian, Piccolomini, Diodati, Grana, Galasso, and others, worked skilfully on the jealous fears of the Emperor, and hurried him into measures, of which he so far repented as to declare, some years afterwards, that Wallenstein was less guilty than his enemies had represented.

The combination of Pilsen was, no doubt, reprehensible, and would now be criminal ; but it was less so at a period when the just principles of subordination were almost unknown ; and the Court of Vienna, so far from looking upon the transaction as a serious

offence, thought it advisable to give a false account
of the proceeding, when they brought it forward as a
treasonable charge. It is said, in the imperial statement, that the paper signed by the officers, had been
fraudulently substituted for the one which contained
the resolutions actually agreed upon, and that the
clause, contained in the first,—suppressed paper,—
by which the officers bound themselves to remain
faithful to the Emperor, had been purposely omitted
in the second paper, to which the signatures were
obtained. These imperial assertions bear falsehood on
their very face: no man would think himself bound
by a signature out of which he had been defrauded;
nor did any of the officers tried, allege, in their defence, that so mean a deception had been practised
upon them.

But allowing that precedent, and the opinions of the
time, palliated, in some degree, this military combination, it must still be a question whether Wallenstein
really intended to resign the command of the army
when he called the officers together: whether the most
ambitious of men was willing to descend from dictatorial power, to the retirement of private life, at the
very moment when France was tendering crowns,
armies and millions for his acceptance. History is
bound to acquit the Duke of Friedland of treason; for
all the power and influence of the Court of Vienna,
failed to make out a case against him. From beyond
the grave the mighty spirit of the man, still overawed
his enemies, and confounded their counsels : it was
in vain that bribes and tortures were employed to
prove him guilty; these criminal efforts only re-

coiled upon their authors, and laid bare to the world
the full infamy of their conduct. But the guilt of
one party, cannot establish the innocence of another ;
and strongly as this presumptive evidence tells in
Wallenstein's favour, the suspicions caused by his
eccentric conduct still remain.   What were the plans
engendered in that lofty and aspiring mind,—what
the hopes cherished in that ambitious and not ignoble
heart,—are questions never likely to be answered !—
Oxenstiern declared, even in the last years of his life,
that he never could comprehend the object Wallenstein really had in view : and as the ablest and best
informed man of the time failed to unravel the secret,
it will be in vain that we attempt to fathom a mystery, over which the gloom of two centuries has now
been gathered.

If we, too often, see the best and most generous
qualities of our nature, crushed beneath the chilling
influence of adversity, so we expect on the other hand,
to find them called forth and cherished by the genial
sunshine of power and prosperity.   We naturally feel
disposed to combine the idea of high qualities with
high station ; and the want of noble and generous
feeling, which in the humbler ranks of life, is but an
absence of virtue, augments to criminality, in proportion as we ascend in the scale of society ; and we can
only fancy such deficiency to exist upon a throne,
when the crowned occupant is composed of the mean-
est materials of which human nature is ever put together.   Ferdinand II. was such an occupant of a throne.
In the hour of danger, and when pressed by the victorious arms of the Swedes, he conferred almost

dictatorial power on the man from whose aid he alone
expected safety. But no sooner was the first peril
over, than the imagination of the terrified sovereign,
magnified into treason and rebellion, the exercise of
the power which he had before delegated. In his base
and unkingly fear,—to acquit him even of envy and
avarice,—he condemned without a trial or hearing ;
and not only handed over the man, who had twice
saved the monarchy, to the halberds of hired assassins,
but rendered himself an active party to the crime by
the treachery of his conduct. In order to deceive his
intended victim, and to render the blow more certain, he remained in constant and confidential correspondence with Wallenstein, for twenty days after
the betrayed General had been outlawed as a rebel.
True it is, that he afterwards caused three thousand
masses to be said for the souls of the slain : and courtiers and confessors may, by such means, have silenced
the feeble voice of the royal conscience. But the
voice of history will not be so silenced ; and the name
of Ferdinand II. will be handed down to latest posterity, as the name of a sovereign in whose callous
heart, not even imperial sway could raise one spark
of noble fire ; who, while crawling in the dust before
images and reliques, remained deaf to the duties of
Christianity ; and repaid the greatest services ever
rendered to a prince, by one of the foulest deeds of
treason and of murder recorded in the dark annals of
human crime.

TERMINATION OF THE WAR.

HAVING gone through the principal events that distinguished the first part of the Thirty years' War, it
will not, perhaps, be unacceptable to the reader, if we
close our history with a brief sketch of the last half
of the long and desolating conflict.

With Wallenstein and Gustavus, all unity of action, and greatness of object, disappeared from the
scene of strife. Sieges were carried on, and battles
fought, in every part of Germany; but they no longer
formed connecting-links in well-combined plans of
military operation; and were little better than isolated
acts of useless destruction. Brilliant valour, and
talents of the highest order, were frequently displayed
in the field ; but the state of weakness and exhaus-
tion, to which the nations were rapidly sinking down,
soon tended to render profitless, the most extensive
victories.

Want of union among the Protestants, prevented
them from deriving all the benefit, which they had
at first anticipated, from Wallenstein's death. The
King of Hungary assumed the command of the army,
and by the aid of money, which was plentifully distributed, the soldiers were, without difficulty, kept in
obedience ; not the slightest attempt was any where
made, to resist the Emperor's orders. On the other

hand, Bernhard of Weimar, and Field-Marshal Horn, were masters of Bavaria. In July 1634, they gained a complete victory at Landshut, over General Altringer, who was slain in the action. This man, who had taken an active share in the Italian conspiracy against Wallenstein, fell, as a traitor should fall; for wounded in the field, he was trampled to death by his fugitive troops. Though Gallass and Piccolomini, the principal partners in his guilt, did not meet so early and striking a punishment; they lived but to see that victory had, for ever, abandoned their dishonoured crests : disgrace and discomfiture settled on their standards, and we have only to mention them, in this brief sketch, as fugitives from almost every field in which they ventured to face brave and open foes.

The Swedes, who had so long been victorious, were, in their turn, destined to taste the bitterness of defeat. Fifteen thousand Spaniards, under the Cardinal Infant, son of Philip III, entered Germany, and in conjunction with the imperial army, under the King of Hungary, laid siege to Nördlingen. Field-Marshal Horn, and Bernhard of Weimar, hurried to the relief of the place. Owing to the superiority of the enemy, who was besides strongly intrenched, the Swedish commanders had no intention to hazard a battle, before the arrival of the Rhin-graff Count Otho, with another division of the army, which was already close at hand ; but the impetuosity of the Duke of Weimar lost every thing. Horn had succeeded in carrying a hill, called the Amsberg, a strong point, which placed him in communication with the town, and almost secured the victory.

Bernhard, thinking that so favourable an opening should not be neglected, hurried on to the attack of another post. It was taken and retaken ; both armies were gradually, and without method, drawn into the combat, which, after eight hours' duration, ended in the complete defeat of the Swedes. Horn was made prisoner ; and Bernhard escaped on a borrowed horse. Cratz, the third in command, and one of the most eccentric men of genius of a period so fertile in such men, refused to leave the field. It was a principle with him, that a soldier should never fly from a field of battle ; and though he had deserted from the Imperialists, owing to a quarrel with Wallenstein, and well knew the fate that awaited him if taken, he continued to walk quietly up and down the ground, after the action was over : he remained long unnoticed in the confusion, till recognised and secured by some of the Croats, who had formerly served under him. He afterwards suffered as a deserter ; but Schiller, who, in the first edition of the Thirty years' War, calls him a cowardly old man, does him great injustice ; for he was as much distinguished by bravery, as by talents.

The defeat of Nördlingen, almost ruined the Swedish cause in Germany ; the spell of invincibility was gone, and the effects of the panic far surpassed those which the sword had produced. Strong fortresses were abandoned, before the enemy came in sight ; provinces were evacuated, and armies, that had been deemed almost unconquerable, deserted their chiefs, and broke into bands of lawless robbers, who pillaged their way in every direction. Bavaria, Suabia and

Franconia were lost; and it was only behind the Rhine, that the scattered fugitives could again be brought into something like order.

The battle of Nördlingen, caused to Oxenstiern the second sleepless night which he had experienced in his life; and it certainly required all his ability, to stem the torrent of misfortune, which followed the disastrous event. The Emperor refused to grant the Swedes, any other terms of peace, than permission to retire from the empire. The Elector of Saxony, forgetful of what was due to his religion, and forgetful of all that Sweden had done for his country, concluded, at Prague, a separate peace with the Emperor; and soon afterwards joined the Imperialists against his former allies. The fortunes of the Protestants, would have sunk beneath this additional blow, had not France come to their aid. Richelieu had before only nourished the war by means of subsidies, and had, at one time, become nearly as jealous of the Swedes as of the Austrians; but no sooner was their power broken, than the crafty priest took an active share in the contest.

The French were not, at first, very successful in the field : their army was completely defeated at Düttlingen by John de Werth; but their movements obtained breathing time for the Swedes, who turned it to admirable account. General Banner again rendered their arms triumphant in the north : after some minor victories, he defeated the combined Saxon and imperial armies, in the great and decisive battle of Witstoch, fought on the 4th of October 1636. Under this commander, we again find British names in their proper places. At Witstoch, a Colonel Leslie commanded the centre of the army, and Colonel King the infantry of right wing ; while Colonel Ruthven, at the head of a separate corps, had, shortly before, gained a decisive victory at Dömitz.

The battle of Witstoch threw Saxony and Bohemia open to the victorious army ; which, like a stream of destroying lava, poured itself over both countries. First, the Saxons had to pay for the ingratitude of their Sovereign towards Sweden, and a heavy penalty it proved ; for the generous and humane discipline which Gustavus had maintained, no longer existed, and the whole Electorate, was placed at the mercy of the enraged soldiery. From Saxony, the torrent of desolation rolled on, into Bohemia. " The unhappy kingdom," says Carnova in his history of the country, " resembled a sea of fire : from the hills, you saw, ascending in every direction, flames that were consuming the dwellings of peaceful inhabitants, the temples of religion, and the monuments of antiquity ; while cliffs and mountains re-echoed with the lamentations of ruined and houseless fugitives." The recollection of these terrible visitations, that resembled more the inroads of the Huns, than the expeditions of Christian armies, is preserved, to this day, among the Saxon and Bohemian peasantry, in a song, called the " Song of the Swedes."

On the Rhine also, the Protestant arms proved successful. Bernhard of Weimar had ably atoned for his former rashness ; and with an army, raised principally by means of French subsidies, captured the important fortress of Breisach, after successively

defeating three armies that advanced to its relief.
So great was the fame of this chivalrous Prince, that
France and Sweden were both beginning to be jealous
of his growing power when he died, not without suspicions of having been poisoned, on the 18th July,
1639, in the thirty-fifth year of his age.

Two years afterwards, the Swedes lost, in Banner,
their third great general; for a great general he was,
notwithstanding his many personal faults. Eighty
thousand men are said to have fallen in the various
battles which he fought during his short command;
and 600 flags and standards, captured and sent to
Stockholm, attested the splendour of his victories.
But the conquerors were too much enfeebled, to profit
by their success. Sweden thinly peopled,—poor in
money,—and exhausted by so many Polish and German campaigns, was no longer equal to any great
continued effort; and Germany could not, after
having been, for more than twenty years, ravaged
alike by friends and foes, furnish the means of supporting vigorous and systematic military operations.
After all Banner's victories, the Swedes were again
on the eve of being driven out of the empire, when
the voice of the nation and the army, forced Len-
nard Torstensohn to rise from a bed of sickness, in
order to place himself at the head of the troops.

This celebrated person had, like Horn and Banner, been trained to war in the school of Gustavus
Adolphus; and, like the other great generals of that
school, was distinguished for letters as well as arms.
All these men were models of commanders; and were
as superior to the mere martinet soldiers of the suc-

ceeding century, as to the revolutionary bravoes who, in our own age, rose to notoriety, by aid of the ruthless conscriptions, which placed a boundless supply of human *materiel*, constantly at their disposal. The Swedish generals have left proofs, that they looked deeply into the means and object of their profession, —that they knew how to combine movements, and to calculate the power of arms. These men never cast the reins of command blindly to fortune ; they effected great things with, comparatively, small means, and remained victorious, in every fair field, in which they were engaged. As leaders of armies, they have not been surpassed in modern war ; and it may fairly be doubted, whether Torstensohn has yet been equalled.

Banner sullied his high military fame, by excess and intemperance ; but Torstensohn, though inferior to Horn in active humanity,—for it was said of Horn, that he knew how to disarm even war of its terrors, —surpassed Banner in moderation of conduct, as much as he surpassed both, by the splendour of his success. His actions border almost on the incredible ; and his operations seemed to have wings, at the very time, when he was himself, chained to a couch of sickness by lameness and suffering. From the shores of the Baltic, he penetrated into the very heart of the Austrian dominions. Near Leipzig, he entirely defeated the imperial and Saxon armies, with which the Archduke Leópold, and Piccolomini, attempted to arrest his progress. Having then captured Olmütz, and reduced all Moravia, he suddenly left the province, traversed Germany by marches that completely concealed the object of his expedition,

and appeared unexpectedly in Holstein and Jutland ;
and overran both duchies before the astonished Danes
were in any degree prepared for resistance.

The hope of profiting, by the state of feebleness
to which Sweden was reduced, had again awakened
the ambition of Christian IV. ; promises on the part
of the Emperor, were not wanting ; and the Protestant King of Denmark, was about to join the Catholic League, when the ability of Oxenstiern discovered the intrigue, and enabled the Swedes to crush
this new enemy, before he could become formidable.
On one side, the victorous invasion of Schönen, by
Field-Marshal Horn, and on the other, the occupation of Jutland and Holstein, soon forced the Danes
to sue for peace ; and in 1645, the treaty of Bremsebroe, already put an end to this short-lived war.

The Emperor tried, indeed, to aid his new ally ;
and sent Gallass with an army in pursuit of Torstensohn.   But the Italian was a more skilful con-
triver of conspiracies, than commander of armies.
Unable to join the Danes before their defeat near
Kiel, and not daring alone to face the Swedes, he
shut himself up in an intrenched camp near Bernburg.
Here Torstensohn cut off his communication ; and
the Austrians, reduced to extremity by famine, tried
to effect a retreat ; but their cavalry were overtaken
and defeated at Jutterbock, and the infantry obliged
to lay down their arms near Magdeburg.   Gallass
returned almost alone, from this inglorious expedition; adding to the fame, of having aided in the murder of his former commander, that of having completely ruined the army intrusted to his own leading.

The peace of Bremsebroe, again gave Torstensohn free hands against the Austrians; and, as Olmütz had been besieged during his absence, this indefatigable commander, who, as well as Bajazet, deserved the name of *Ilderim*, or " The Lightning," hurried from the very shores of the Belt to its relief. In Saxony, he forced the Elector to conclude a final truce with Sweden : and on his march through Bohemia, defeated, at Jankowitz, the last army which the Emperor was able to bring into the field. Ferdinand III. who, in 1637, had succeeded his father on the imperial throne, was with the army, though he took no share in the battle. Trusting to a superiority of numbers, and urged on, it is said, by a dream in which he had received from the Virgin a promise of victory ; he overruled the advice of the brave and experienced General Hatzfeld, and forced him to meet the Swedes. But instead of joining manfully in the combat, he remained in a church, at a distance from the scene, and within hearing of the very guns that, in his cause, and by his orders, were dealing frightful death, and more frightful mutilation around, contented himself with praying to various saints for the success of his arms.

The sound of distant artillery, when every shot tolls, perhaps, the knell of parting man, falls with a strange, wild, heart-chilling effect upon the ear. Presence in the fray changes, of course, this sensation, according to the character of the individual ; but far beyond sight and range,—when the feelings and imagination of the listener are alone engaged,— the mere sound is awful in the extreme. Each hollow and successive roar strikes heavily upon the heart, and for the instant, checks its very action, but only to make it throb with redoubled violence, during every brief interval of appalling silence. The very aspect of men, is unearthly at such a moment : the still, motionless, intense anxiety which marks every attitude and countenance, is absolutely painful to behold; and almost resembles the fancied effect of magic. But the spell is soon broken ; the material particles of human composition resume their sway ; and the death-bearing thunder is listened to with a degree of indifference, that, to say the very least, shows completely how men are, or how readily they become, the children of mere habit.

Ferdinand, unmoved by the melancholy sound, which told that thousands were falling for his sake, remained piously on his knees till the battle was lost ; and then hurried to Vienna with the best speed in his power. The army which he abandoned, was almost entirely destroyed ; and General Hatzfeld himself, with a great part of the infantry, were taken prisoners. In the accounts of this battle, is mentioned the last of the British officers who acted so brilliant a part during the Thirty years' War. The remnants of the British regiments who had been so distinguished under Gustavus, had mostly fallen at Nördlingen ; but many of their officers still held commands in different corps ; and at Jankowitz, Colonel Robert Douglas, a Scottish officer, commanded the left wing of Torstensohn's army, and led the charge of cavalry,— celebrated in military history as the first *charge en muraille,* ever executed against a formed body of in-

fantry,—which, on this occasion, decided the fate of
the day. Profiting by his splendid success, Torstensohn subdued all Bohemia, relieved Olmütz, advanced to the very bridge of Vienna ; and captured the
fort by which it was defended. The tide of war had,
at last, rolled back into its original channel, and the
imperial capital was awakened out of its long repose,
by the sound of Swedish artillery, fired from the very
spot, whence, seven and twenty years before, the Bohemian insurgents had first pointed their vengeful
guns.

  But the Danube, and its fortified islands, which
had formerly arrested the progress of Count Thurn,
and of Bethlem Gabor, now arrested, in like manner,
the progress of Torstensohn.   The means for an immediate passage of the river were wanting ; and the
resources of Sweden, and of the Protestant party
generally, were far too much exhausted to admit of
their giving effect to such distant and continued operations.   From France no support was to be expected.
The French arms had been unsuccessful ; Condé had
been defeated at Freyberg, and Turenne at Mergen-
theim. And Ragotzky, Prince of Transylvania, acting the same part which Bethlem Gabor had acted
at the commencement of the war, made peace, and
forsook the Swedes, as soon as he had plundered the
country under the protection of their army.   These
adverse circumstances, and his inability to reduce
Brün, which was ably defended by a gallant Frenchman, Louis de Suchés, obliged Torstensohn to retire
into Silesia, leaving, as usual, the strongholds which
he had taken, to fall successively into the hands of

the pursuing enemy. In the following year, 1646, ill health forced this extraordinary man,—of whom it was said that he saw with the eyes of Argus, and fought with the arm of Briareus,—to resign the command : he died five years afterwards, at Stockholm. Gustavus Wrangel succeeded him at the head of the army.

In conjunction with Turenne, this commander had already subdued Bavaria, even to the shores of the Izar ; while General Königsmark, with another Swedish army, had taken Prague by surprise, when their further progress was arrested by the news that peace had been signed on the 24th October 1648.

Ever since the year 1643, negotiations had been going on at Münster and Osnabrück. At Osnabrück, between the Emperor and Catholics on one side, and the Swedes and Protestants on the other :— at Münster again, between France and the German empire. But at the very time when Europe was suffering in all her states, and when Germany was bleeding at every pore ; ministers and diplomatists contrived to delay, for five years, the conclusion of the good work. Instead of adopting, at once, the wise and Christian proposal of Pope Urban VIII, and commencing by a general armistice, the operations in the.field were, at the instigation of France, allowed to continue ; so that the demands of the parties, rose and fell exactly in proportion to the success of their arms. Nine months elapsed before the ambassadors were assembled ; it then took sixteen months more, blood flowing all the time, before these men of etiquette could arrange about titles,

precedence and ceremonies.   When at last the giant
work was completed, for a giant work it certainly was,
to reconcile so many jarring and conflicting interests,
it still required two years of doubt and uncertainty
before the conditions were fulfilled on all sides ; the
restored fortresses and provinces evacuated, the in-
demnities paid and the troops disbanded.

The peace of Münster gave Europe the form which
it retained, with slight variations, down to the breaking out of the French Revolution.   Religious freedom was granted to the Protestants, and they retained all the church property which they had acquired
previous to the year 1624.   Sweden obtained the
duchy of Pomerania and the island of Rugen, the
towns of Rostock and Wismar, the bishoprics of Bremen and Verden, and 5,000,000 of crowns.   France,
which had done least, got the largest share of the
spoil : it obtained, besides, the whole of Alsace, the
recognition of the important, and formerly captured
towns, of Metz, Toul, Pigneral and Verdün.   Switzerland and the Netherlands were declared independent of Germany ; which thus lost its two principal
bulwarks towards the west.

But whatever may have been the merits of the
peace of Münster, abstractedly considered, it was certainly the greatest blessing, which, by any sacrifice,
could then have been purchased for Germany.—
Thirty years of war, carried on, not with the surplus
population and resources of the country, but with its
very capital and substance, had brought the empire
to the verge of ruin and barbarism ; and the pictures
of desolation handed down to us by writers and

chroniclers of the period, are absolutely frightful to contemplate.

Of all the commanders who appeared during the war, Gustavus Adolphus was alone able to preserve, in his army, a strict and humane system of discipline. In most armies, the mercenary soldiers, irregularly paid and worse supplied, were obliged to tear, by force, from the citizens and peasants, the means of subsistence. The country people resisted, wherever they were strongest ; acts of violence followed ; the peasantry slew, and in Catholic countries, tortured straggling soldiers, and attacked even small detached parties. The military avenged their comrades ; neglecting too often to distinguish between the innocent and the guilty ; till ruin and devastation, tracked at last, the progress of every march.

The war was carried on without plan or system. Expeditions were undertaken, apparently with no other view than to desolate hostile provinces ; and in the end, provisions and winter quarters, formed the principal objects of the summer campaigns. Want, sickness, distress, and the total absence of discipline, by which these evils were fearfully augmented, when not created, destroyed far more troops than the sword; and entire armies were swept away, before they had even seen an enemy. Soldiers left the ranks singly, or in bands, as it suited them, and generally took to plundering : in 1642, the whole of Marshal Guebriant's army, dispersed itself and broke into robber hordes, that committed the most fearful depredations.

The enormities charged against the French troops of the period, are equal to those charged even against the Croats: but it must be recollected that Guebriant's army was, in fact, the remains of the army which had been raised by the Duke of Weimar; and was composed of adventurers from all countries. It must also be observed, that the French soldiers, of the early part of the seventeenth century, were in a great proportion vagrants and vagabonds, taken up, as bad subjects by the police, and sent to the army, either because troops were wanted, or because the individuals pressed, could give no satisfactory account of themselves. These men resembled in nothing the French soldiers of Louis XIV. and his successors; still less did they resemble the soldiers of the empire, and least of all, the soldiers of the republic. The imperial and republican soldiers were the best men that France could produce: it was their gallantry and intelligence which made the reputation of their leaders; and atoned, on countless occasions, for the ignorance and incapacity of their crowned and laurelled chief. Sometimes these gallant soldiers did even more, and made up, by humanity and good conduct, for a system of war introduced by unprincipled governments and commanders, and naturally fraught, with every species of crime and disorder.

Whether arts, sciences, learning and civilisation, lost or gained by the Thirty years' War, is a question not very easily decided; though historians mostly assert, that Europe was thrown back for a century by its ruinous consequences. In many parts of Germany learning was, no doubt, retarded; in others it was altogether swept away, along with the whole of the population. An entire generation, who would

not, in general, prove the best citizens, also grew up,
amid scenes of strife, licentiousness and the uncertainty of the-morrow. But the amount of knowledge
existing, could not be destroyed; and thousands of
learned, able, and industrious Germans, emigrated,
and carried along with them, into other and less enlightened countries, the arts and knowledge for
which their own was already distinguished. The
Danes, Swedes, Poles, and Scots, who fought in Germany, there came in contact with a state of civilisation, superior to what existed in their own countries :
and along with much unworthy spoil, some fair and
honourable booty, would, at least, be carried home
by the military adventurers. As good sometimes
results from evil, the unworthy plunder may at times
have produced beneficial effects. The Swedes, in
imitation of Maximilian, who had sent the Heidel-
berg library to Rome, sent libraries, paintings, sta-
tues and works of art to Sweden, where, owing to the
scarcity of such treasures, they could hardly fail to
create some taste for learning, literature and refine-
ment.

It was to the pressure and hardness of the times,
however, that Europe owed the progress which it
made : the iron time, forced upon men an excess of
mental exertion, that produced far nobler fruit, than
any likely to have arisen during the calm reign of
ordinary peace. And the young Germany which
grew up, from beneath the ruins of the Thirty years'
War, was already many generations in advance of
the Germany that witnessed the first outbreaking of
the great Bohemian volcano.

But whatever advantages Europe may have gained by the contest, Germany purchased its share of the benefit, at a fearful price. Law, justice, equity,—in many places all the decencies of life,—had entirely vanished from a land, in which force alone, wielded the arbitrary sceptre of command. The country is said to have lost twelve millions of inhabitants by the contest ; and the population, which amounted to sixteen millions, when the troubles first broke out, counted hardly more than four millions when the war closed. Though this statement may, perhaps, be exaggerated, it seems pretty well ascertained, that the population of the Duchy of Wirtenberg, was reduced, from half a million to 48,000 : that of Bohemia, had already been reduced from three millions to 890,000 before the death of Ferdinand II. : Saxony and Brunswick suffered in the same proportion.

In the Electorate of Hesse, seventeen towns, forty-seven castles, and three hundred villages had been burned to the ground. In the Duchy of Wirtenberg, eight towns, forty-five villages, thirty-six thousand houses had been laid in ashes, and seventy thousand hearth fires completely extinguished : seven churches and four hundred and forty-four houses had been burned at Eichsted. Many towns that had escaped destruction, were almost depopulated : three hundred houses stood empty at Nordheim ; more than two hundred had been pulled down at Göttingen, merely to serve for fuel. The wealthy city of Augsburg, which contained 80,000 inhabitants before the war, had only 18,000 left when it closed : this town, like many others, has never recovered its former prosperity. No less than thirty thousand villages and hamlets are said to have been destroyed : —in many others, the population had entirely died out, and the unburied corpses, of the last victims of violence or disease, were left exposed about the streets or fields, to be mangled and torn to pieces by birds and beasts of prey.

In the last campaign of the war, the French and Swedes, burned no less than a hundred villages in Bavaria alone ; and the skulls of St Cosmas and St Damianus, had to be sent from Bremen to Münich, in order to console Maximilian for the ruin he had brought over his beautiful country.   But, even these pitiable relics failed to allay the fears of the unhappy Elector : the share which he had taken in bringing about this desolating contest, pressed heavily on the latter years of his life.   In vain he prayed and fasted : in vain he scourged himself with frightful severity : the dreaded future was constantly before his sight, and the once valiant soldier and ambitious prince, died at last, a trembling and despairing bigot.

The crimes and cruelties of which the troops were frequently guilty, would appear almost incredible, were they not attested in a manner to render doubt altogether impossible.   But independent of private accounts, we have various reports from the authorities of towns, villages and provinces, complaining of the atrocities committed by the lawless soldiery.   Peaceful peasants were hunted, for mere sport, like the beasts of the forest ; citizens were nailed up against doors and walls, and fired at like targets : while horsemen and Croats tried their skill in striking off the heads of young children at a blow. Ears and noses were cut off, eyes were scooped out, and the most horrible tortures contrived to extract money from the sufferers, or to make them disclose where property was concealed. Women were exposed to every species of indignity; they were collected in bands, and driven, like slaves, into the camps of the ruffian soldiery; and men had to fly from their homes, to escape witnessing the dishonour, to which their wives and daughters were subjected.

Houses and villages were burned, out of mere wantonness, and the wretched inhabitants, too often, forced into the flames, to be consumed along with their dwellings. Amid these scenes of horror, intemperance, dissipation and profligacy, were carried to the highest pitch. Intoxication frequently prevented the Austrian General Göltz from giving out the countersign; and General Banner was, on one occasion, so drunk for four days together, that he could not receive the French ambassador, Beauregard, who had an important message to deliver. "Such was the state of triumphant crime," says a writer of the period, " that many driven to despair, denied even the existence of a Deity; declaring, that if there were a God in heaven, he would not fail to destroy, with thunder and lightning, a world of such sin and wickedness."

The peasants, expelled from their homes, enlisted with the oppressors, in order to inflict upon others the sufferings which they had themselves been made to endure. The fields were allowed to run waste, and the absence of industry on one side, added to destruction on the other, soon produced famine, which, as usual, brought infectious and pestilential diseases in its train. In 1635, there were not hands enough left at Schweidnitz to bury the dead ; and the town of Ohlau had lost its last citizen. Want augmented crime, even where an increase was thought impossible. In many places hunger had overcome all repugnance to human flesh, and the tales of cannibalism handed down to us, are of far too horrible a nature to be here repeated.

The cup of human suffering was full, even to overflowing, and the very aspect of the land, was undergoing a rapid change. Forests sprung up, during the contest, and covered entire districts, which had been in full cultivation before the war ; and wolves, and other beasts of prey, took possession of the deserted haunts of men. This was particularly the case in Brunswick, Brandenburg, and Pomerania, where heaps of ashes, in the midst of wildernesses, served, long afterwards, to mark the spots where peace and civilisation had once flourished. In many parts of the country, the ruins of castles, and stately edifices, still attest the fury with which the war was carried on; and on such spots, tradition generally points out the surrounding forests, as occupying the sites of fertile fields, from whence the lordly owners of the mansions, derived food and subsistence, for themselves and their numerous retainers.

Not all the memorable events of our time,—neither the oppression exercised by foreign armies,—nor the shock of contending myriads, that so often encountered on the German soil, have yet been able to eradi-

cate from among the German peasantry, the traditions of what their fathers, and their fatherland suffered, during the long contest for religious freedom.
Legends and traditions still record, in most parts of
the country, the wild events of that disastrous period.
But tradition, though constant in her affections, is
capricious in bestowing them ; and it is often difficult
to account, for her singular fancies.

At Stralsund, and along the shores of the Baltic,
Wallenstein still holds possession of the ground ; and
Tilly, and Pappenheim, are but too fatally remembered at Magdeburg. Near Britenfeldt, the country
people have raised a monument to the " Great
King," as Gustavus is called in Germany ; and, 'ill
within these five or six years, they usually assembled
there, on the anniversary of the battle, to return
thanks for the victory, which liberated their country,
and gave freedom to their religion. Along the
Rhine, and the Maine, the Swedes appear to less
advantage ; and are rarely mentioned, except in
connection with deeds of violence and plunder. At
Hanau, we meet our stern countryman, Ramsay,
who, after the battle of Nördlingen, successfully
defended that town, for nine months, against the
Imperialists. At Würtsburg, Gustavus shares tradition's tale with Frederick Barbarossa, the most
illustrious of the Swabian Emperors ; and, at Nurenberg, he shines in full glory by the side of Albert
Dürer, the painter. But on the adjoining hills, where
Wallenstein held his camp, an ancient knight,—the
original possessor of the ruin that crowns the principal
eminence,—has resumed his rightful sway, and com-

pletely expelled the redoubted Duke of Friedland from his domain : and the leader of mighty armies, has there yielded to the adventurous owner of a robber castle. In the Upper Palatinate, Wallenstein re-appears in all his terrors ; and at Eger, he forms, of course, the subject of every tale. At Lützen, again, where Gustavus died, and Wallenstein fought — where Napoleon achieved one of his last triumphs— all have given way to the fame of some nameless warriors, who, near the same field, gained a battle over the Hungarians and Slavonians, in the thirteenth century. And the spot,—marked only by a rude stone, surrounded with a few trees,—where fell the " foremost man " of all this modern world, is merely pointed to, as a place, " where somebody was killed."

THE END.